# PERICLES OF ATHENS

## AND THE

# BIRTH OF DEMOCRACY

## DONALD KAGAN

The Free Press
A Division of Macmillan, Inc.
866 Third Avenue, New York, N.Y. 10022

Collier Macmillan Canada, Inc.
1200 Eglinton Avenue East
Suite 200
Don Mills, Ontario M3C 3N1

Printed in the United States of America

printing number
1   2   3   4   5   6   7   8   9   10

Library of Congress Cataloging-in-Publication Data

Kagan, Donald.
    Pericles of Athens and the birth of democracy / Donald Kagan.
        p.   cm.
    Includes bibliographical references and index.
    ISBN 0-68-486395-2
    1. Pericles, 499-429 B.C.   2. Athens (Greece)—Politics and
government.   3. Democracy—History.   4. Statesmen—Greece—Athens
—Biography.   5. Orators—Greece—Athens—Biography.   I. Title.
DF228.P4K34—1991
938'.504'092—dc20
    [B]                                                      90–43197
                                                                CIP

*For Myrna,*

*who has taught so many so well.*

# CONTENTS

# MAPS

# PREFACE

o tell the story of an individual's life and to treat him as a powerful force that significantly shaped not only his own times but centuries to come is not fashionable. Still less is it common to attribute to him heroic qualities, as this book does. But I hope that the reader will agree that the evidence justifies the attempt and supports the conclusions.

The biography of a man who lived in the fifth century B.C. presents problems of a special kind. Pericles left no letters, memoirs, or any writing whatsoever. Of his many speeches, accounts of three in direct speech and another in indirect are provided by the contemporary historian Thucydides, and a few lines are quoted by other ancient authors. Contemporary evidence of his actions come only from Thucydides' history of the Peloponnesian War and from satirical references in the plays of Aristophanes and other comic poets. A few useful anecdotes and other bits of information are preserved by later writers in antiquity.

The most reliable source of information is Thucydides' history, but he austerely limits his treatment to the Peloponnesian War and to military, political, and diplomatic questions. Pericles is brought to the narrative only in the third year before his death, and only the public man is dealt with. The comic poets and the anecdotes treat both public and private life and go well back into his career, but they are scattered and isolated references and are hard to use judiciously. More than one scholar has gone badly astray by treating ancient jokes as serious evidence, while others have failed to use valuable clues that can be derived from the comedies and stories.

The fullest ancient account of the career of Pericles comes from a biography, one of a large collection of the lives of illustrious Greeks and Romans written in his native Greek by Plutarch of Chaeronea toward the end of the first century A.D. Plutarch was a moralist rather than a historian, and he lived five centuries later than his subject, but his *Life of Pericles* has great value. Plutarch had an excellent library containing many works now lost to us, some written by contemporaries of Pericles and by men of the next generation. He read the inscriptions of ancient documents and saw paintings, sculptures, and buildings that no longer exist. When used with care, his work is an outstanding source of authentic information.

Yet however carefully combed, these sources do not provide a very clear image of Pericles' internal life, and I have attempted to speculate about that only on the rare occasions when his behavior provides a clue. For the rest, this is necessarily an account of his life from the outside except in one very important respect: It tries to understand the *mind* of Pericles as opposed to his psyche. For this purpose, his actions, the stories told about him, and especially his own speeches provide considerable evidence. They offer a consistent picture of Pericles' ideas, especially his political, social, and ethical vision. If we must do without some aspect of the man, history appears to have left us the more important.

A few remarks about method and style are in order. How to use the speeches reported by Thucydides has long been a vexing question. I treat them as honest attempts to produce a reasonably accurate account of what the speaker said on each occasion, though I do not doubt that Thucydides had other purposes in mind as well. The speeches of Pericles, moreover, are the most likely to have been reported accurately, because Thucydides was surely present at all of them and because they were so memorable that any misrepresentation was likely to be widely recognized. I argue for my view of the speeches throughout my four-volume history of the Peloponnesian War and in an article called "The Speeches in Thucydides and the Mytilene Debate" (*Yale Classical Studies* 24 [1975]: 71–94).

I have discussed many of the questions treated here in the first two volumes of my history, *The Outbreak of the Peloponnesian War* and the *Archidamian War*. The ancient evidence is cited and argued there, as are the views of modern scholars; each volume also contains a bibliography. I have relied on and adapted to my current purpose parts of those volumes, for on most points I have neither changed my opinions nor found a better way to organize and express them.

Some readers may find the tone of this volume far too confident, especially since I have annotated only direct quotations. Almost every important aspect of the life of Pericles is debatable and has been much debated, but it is more likely to annoy than to help the reader to be repeatedly warned of the uncertainties inherent in the study of ancient Greece. Let this passage serve as a single general notice that I have presented my own interpretations of events and intentions, and that they are open to argument.

One feature that requires special explanations is my practice of attributing many actions of the Athenian people to Pericles, as if he could make decisions for the entire people. He was not, in fact, free to do so; almost every action came as a result of a direct vote in the Athenian assembly and freely expressed the will of the Athenian people. My reason for attributing such actions to Pericles when I do results from my belief that, on those occasions, Pericles had effective political control and could see bills he approved of through the assembly and stop those he did not like. That, too, is an interpretation, but I think the evidence supports it. Readers, however, should understand that when I say of a public action that Pericles did thus and so, that is an elision for "the assembly, guided by Pericles," reached that decision.

Finally, I must explain and defend my use of what has been called "counterfactual history." Some readers may be troubled by my practice of comparing what happened with what might have happened had individuals or groups of people made different decisions and taken different actions. I believe that anyone who tries to write history rather than merely to chronicle events must consider what might have happened; the only question is how explicitly he reveals what he is doing. Historians interpret what they recount, which is to say they judge it. They cannot say that an action was wise or foolish without also saying or implying that it was better or worse than some other action that might have been chosen—that, after all, is "counterfactual history." All true historians engage in the practice, with greater or less self-consciousness. Thucydides, perhaps the greatest of historians, does this on many occasions, as when he makes a judgment of Pericles' strategy in the Peloponnesian War: "Such abundant grounds had Pericles at that time for his forecast that *Athens might quite easily have triumphed* in this war over the Peloponnesians alone." (2.65.13; emphasis added)

I think there are important advantages in being so explicit: A clear statement puts the reader on notice that the assertion in question is a judgment, an interpretation rather than a fact. It also helps to avoid the excessive power of the fait accompli, making clear that what really occurred was not the inevitable outcome of superhuman forces or of equally determined and equally mysterious forces within the historical actors. Instead, what happened was the result of decisions made by human beings acting in a world they do not fully control. It suggests that both the decisions and their outcomes could well have been different. I continue this practice in examining the life of Pericles.

I have not tried to be consistent in printing Greek words and names. Consistency would require spelling familiar Greek names in unfamiliar ways, and I have preferred to keep, e.g., Pericles, Cimon and Alcibiades instead of Perikles, Kimon, and Alkibiades. On the other hand, I have transliterated less well known names and words that are not names in a way that more closely resembles the Greek pronunciation.

I was led to write this book by taking part in teaching a course in Yale College called "Periclean Athens." My colleagues have included C. John Herington, Jerome J. Pollitt, Heinrich von Staden, Richard Garner, and Sarah Morris. I have learned much from all of them and been inspired by them to think more broadly and deeply about Pericles and the Athens of his time. John Herington, Jerome Pollitt, and Heinrich von Staden have read parts of this in manuscript and have helped me to avoid some errors. I am indebted also to Judith Glick Barringer who helped me in my research in the field of art and archaeology. My son Fred has read parts of the work and given useful advice. I am especially grateful to my son Bob, who has read the entire manuscript, made many useful suggestions, and given me valu-able advice from the perspective of a professional in the world of politics and international relations. My editor Adam Bellow has made many thoughtful and interesting suggestions that have helped me greatly. They have all made this a better book than it would have been, and none of them is responsible for the mistakes that remain. I am grateful to Yale University for granting me leave to work on this book. Finally, my deepest gratitude goes to my wife, who has taught the wonders of Periclean Athens to many children and to whom this effort is dedicated.

*Hamden, Connecticut*                                        *June 1990*

# INTRODUCTION

In the decade before 500 B.C., the Athenians established the world's first democratic constitution. This new kind of government was carried to its classical form by the reforms of Pericles a half-century later, and it was in the Athens shaped by Pericles that the greatest achievements of the Greeks took place. While the rest of the world continued to be characterized by monarchical, rigidly hierarchical, command societies, democracy in Athens was carried as far as it would go before modern times, perhaps further than at any other place and time. Although limited to adult males of native parentage, Athenian citizenship granted full and active participation in every decision of the state without regard to wealth or class. The Athenians excluded women, children, resident aliens, and slaves from

1 □

political life, but the principle of equality within the political community that they invented was the seed of the modern idea of universal egalitarianism that flowered during the French Enlightenment.

The experience of the world's first democracy is likely to provoke more interest in the next few years than at any time since the eighteenth century, when it became the center of political controversy in connection with the American and French revolutions. Then, monarchists found arguments against popular government in the history of the ancient Greeks, and friends of democracy were forced, in response, to reinterpret that history. The recent rejections of despotic Communist regimes all over Eastern Europe and the widespread demand for its replacement by some form of democracy have led many observers to think that the victory liberal democracy has won is permanent. Most of the nations seeking democratic governments, however, have little or no experience with such a polity, and few people understand how difficult a system it is to create and maintain. Meanwhile, the modern champions of democracy seem unable to provide the intellectual and spiritual support it needs because they have lost sight of its first principles.

Although in our time democracy is taken for granted, it is in fact one of the rarest, most delicate and fragile flowers in the jungle of human experience. It existed for only two centuries in Athens and less than that in a small number of Greek states. When it reappeared in the Western world more than two millennia later, it was broader but shallower. The French and American revolutions extended citizenship more generously than in Greece, ultimately excluding only children from political participation. But modern democracies are also more remote and indirect, less "political" in the ancient understanding of the term.

Only in ancient Athens and in the United States so far has democracy lasted for as much as two hundred years. Monarchy and different forms of depotism, on the other hand, have gone on for millennia. A dynasty or tyranny or clique may be deposed, but it is invariably replaced by another or by a chaotic anarchy that ends in the establishment of some kind of command society. Optimists may believe that democracy is the inevitable and final form of human society, but the historical record shows that up to now it has been the rare exception.

An understanding of that reality should give pause to any who may think that democracy is the natural polity of mankind and that its establishment and success are assured once despotic or "reactionary" rule has been removed. An examination of the few successful democracies in history suggests that they need to meet three conditions if they are to flourish. The first is to have a set of good institutions; the second is to have a body of citizens who possess a good understanding of the principles of democracy, or who at least have developed a character consistent with the democratic way of life; the third is to have a high quality of leadership, at least at critical moments. At times, the third qualification is the most important and can compensate for weaknesses in the other two.

Pericles was not the founder or inventor of democracy, but he came to its leadership only a half-century after its invention, when it was still fragile. He certainly played the chief role in transforming it from a limited democracy where the common people still deferred to their aristocratic betters to a fully confident popular government in which the mass of the people were fully sovereign in fact as well as theory. Thus, aside from its value as a study in political greatness, Pericles' career offers instruction in how a new and fragile democracy can be brought to maturity.

Few eras in human history can compare with the greatness achieved by Athens under the leadership of Pericles in the fifth century B.C. With a population of some 250,000, Periclean Athens produced works of literature, sculpture, and architecture that stand as models, inspirations, and wonders to this day. It witnessed the birth of historical writing, which one of its citizens brought at once to an unsurpassed level of sophistication. It was the home of scientific speculation of an intensity and originality rarely, if ever, equalled, and it was a hotbed of political speculation, controversy, and participation unmatched at least until our own time.

Voltaire designated Periclean Athens as one of only four societies that enjoyed periods of comparable greatness: "four happy ages when the arts were brought to perfection and which, marking an era of the greatness of the human mind, are an example to posterity."[1] The other three were the Rome of Caesar and Augustus, Italy during the fifteenth-century Renaissance, and France under Louis XIV. We might wish to add England in the age of Elizabeth I, but no other era before this century seems to be in a class with those five.

If we are to understand the Greeks' experience we must recognize that it was a freakish exception to that of the overwhelming number of human beings and societies that came before and after. Earlier civilizations—like those of Egypt, Mesopotamia, Palestine-Syria, India, and China—and those that came later in South and

Meso-America resemble one another in basic ways, even as they sharply and fundamentally differ from the Greeks. They had complex, highly developed societies, usually built around urban centers dominated by kings and a caste of priests. Most developed difficult systems of writing that only a small class of professional scribes could master. They had strong, centralized, monarchical systems of government ruling relatively vast areas with the aid of large, tightly organized bureaucracies. They had hierarchical social systems, professional standing armies, and a regular system of taxation to support it all. To one degree or another, they tended toward cultural uniformity and stability.

Hellenic civilization sharply departed from this pattern. Emerging not long before 1000 B.C. from the collapse of the Mycenaean culture, a civilization influenced by Egypt and the Near East, it was born in a world of poverty and of almost primitive culture. Cities were swept away and replaced by small farm villages. Trade was all but ended, and communication not only between the Greeks and other peoples but even among the Greeks themselves was sharply curtailed. The art of writing was lost for more than three centuries. The matrix of Hellenic civilization was a dark age in which a small number of poor, isolated, illiterate people were ignored by the rest of the world and left alone to develop their own society.

During the three centuries from about 1050 to 750 B.C., the Greeks set the foundations for their great achievements. Neighboring families, clans, and tribes joined together for protection against outside enemies and to maintain peace among themselves. The unit they developed for their new way of life was the polis, the Greek city-state. There were hundreds of them, and each evoked a kind of loyalty and attachment from its citizens that made the idea of dissolving one's own polis and merging it into some larger unit unthinkable. The result was a dynamic, many-faceted, competitive, sometimes chaotic world in which the achievement of excellence and victory had the highest value. This agonal, or competitive quality, marked Greek life throughout the history of the polis and has played an unusually prominent role in Western civilization. It also brought forth extraordinary achievements in literature and art, where competition, sometimes formal and organized, spurred on poets and artists, just as in political life the same ethos encouraged individual participation and freedom.

Kings had been swept away along with the Mycenaean world, so the poleis were republics. Since the Greeks were so poor, the differences in wealth among them were relatively small. Distinctions of class were less marked and important than in the civilizations of the East. The introduction of a new mode of fighting some time after 700, when the predominance of cavalry gave way to warfare between serried masses (phalanxes) of heavy infantrymen (hoplites), had a further leavening effect. It removed the chief responsibility for the defense of the state from the few wealthy men, who alone could afford to keep horses, and turned it over to the average farmer, who had wealth enough to buy the body armor that allowed him to hold his own in the hoplite phalanx. At the same time, the shift in military organization emphasized a common effort by most of the people. Greek armies were made up of unpaid citizen-soldiers who returned to their farms after a campaign. As independent defenders of the common safety and interest, they demanded a role in the most important political decisions; in this way, political control came to be shared by a relatively large portion of the people, and participation in political life was highly valued.

Such states needed no bureaucracy, for there were no vast state holdings that needed management and oversight, and not much economic surplus to support a bureaucratic class. Most states imposed no regular taxation. There was no separate caste of priests and little concern with life after death. In this varied, dynamic, secular, and remarkably free context there arose for the first time a speculative natural philosophy based on observation and reason, the root of modern natural science and of philosophy.

It may seem unlikely that the career of the leader of a tiny state on the border of the Aegean Sea that lost its independence and importance more than two thousand years ago can illuminate and inform our understanding of politics in the modern world. Yet many who devote their lives to the study of politics, diplomacy, and warfare in our own time believe that the contemplation of the experience of Pericles and his contemporaries has practical value. Thucydides' history of the Peloponnesian War, our most important source for the career of Pericles and for the Athens of his time, is more influential now than at any time since it was written. Today's political scientists derive their theories of international relations from his work.[2] International congresses of historians and political scientists continue to meet to discuss the Athenians and the Spartans and the meaning of their conflict for our world.[3] No university course in international relations or in the history of warfare is likely to ignore that war. The subject is a staple at the military academies and the Kennedy School of Government at Harvard. When promising officers are told that they have been given the coveted assignment to the Naval War College in Newport, Rhode Island, a key step in the career of flag officers, they are at the same time given a copy of Thucydides on the Peloponnesian War, the first topic in the course entitled "Strategy and Policy."

Pericles was one of those extraordinary people who placed his own stamp on his time and shaped the course of history. He was the leading citizen of a great democracy that had a keen sense of its own special role in history and of the special excellence of its constitution and way of life. It had a booming economy producing wealth and prosperity previously unknown, a combined military and naval power made possible only by such wealth, and international responsibilities that stretched its resources to the limit but could not safely be ignored. It was a democracy confronted by an opposing state with an entirely different constitution and character, which regarded the Athenian power and way of life as a deadly menace to its own ambitions and security. The life of Pericles and the democratic society he led indeed have much to teach the citizens of free lands in our own time.

Pericles was an Athenian aristocrat who possessed no great private fortune. The citizen of a democratic republic, he held no office higher than that of general (*strategos*), one of ten, none of whom had greater formal powers than any of the others. He controlled no military or police forces, and he could expend no public money without a vote of the popular assembly of citizens. Unlike the presidents and prime ministers of modern representative democracies, he had no well-established, well-organized political party machinery on which to rely. Each year he had to stand for reelection and was constantly subject to public scrutiny and political challenge.

Pericles also differed from later leaders in the variety of his responsibilities and in his direct and personal execution of them. Elizabeth, Louis, and in our own time such great leaders as Franklin D. Roosevelt and Winston Churchill, were titular heads of their armed forces. But Pericles, like Caesar and, to a lesser extent, Augustus, repeatedly commanded armies and navies in battle. He was also a constitutional reformer who radically expanded Athenian democracy and brought it to fulfillment. As a diplomat, he negotiated public treaties and secret agreements and produced imaginative proposals to advance his city's fortunes. Throughout his career, he managed the public finance with unmatched skill and integrity.

Like Augustus, Lorenzo de' Medici, and Elizabeth, Pericles also sponsored a great outburst of artistic and intellectual activity. It was his idea to crown the Acropolis with the temples and statues that have made it the wonder of the world for two millennia; he also selected the architects and sculptors, and found the vast sums of money to pay for their works. He was the producer of Aeschylus' tragedy *Persians*; the friend and colleague of Sophocles; the friend of Phidias, the greatest sculptor of his day, who devised the master plan of the Parthenon. He commissioned Hippodamus of Miletus, the first city planner, and befriended Herodotus, the father of history. In moments of leisure, he debated with Zeno, Anaxagoras, and Protagoras, the leading teachers and philosophers of his time. His patronage of the arts and his personal support and encouragement of thinkers and their activities made Athens a magnet that drew to it the leading creative talents from the entire Greek world.

Two millennia after the Athenians' defeat we still marvel at what they achieved. But the visible remains, impressive as they are, do not constitute their most important legacy. Pericles confronted the problem that faces any free and democratic society: How can the citizens be persuaded to make the sacrifices necessary for its success? Tyrants and dictators can rely on mercenaries and compulsion to defend their states. Rare states like Sparta—a closed authoritarian society—could inculcate in their people a willingness to renounce their private lives almost entirely. But democracies cannot use such devices. Instead, democratic leadership involves a freer kind of public education. Pericles sought to teach the Athenians that their own interests were inextricably tied together with those of their community, that they could not be secure and prosper unless their state was secure and prosperous, that the ordinary man could achieve greatness only through the greatness of his society. All that he did and all that he sought for Athens was part of that education. Pericles tried to shape a new kind of society and a new kind of citizen, not by the use of force or terror but by the power of his ideas, the strength of his personality, the use of reason, and his genius as a uniquely persuasive rhetorician.

In ancient Athens, the people decided policy in oral debate in the open air. Skill in public speaking was essential, and Pericles was the greatest orator of his day by common consent. One of his ablest political opponents, a famous wrestler, wryly complained of his rival's skill: "Whenever I throw him," he said, "he argues that he was not thrown and convinces the very people who saw the fall." (Plutarch, *Pericles* 8.4)

Most democratic politicians are tempted to seek popularity by telling the people only good news, or by appealing to their desires and prejudices. Yet because their opinions have a strong effect on the state's actions, the people in democracies need, more than in other regimes, to understand and face reality. Even so great and powerful a leader as Franklin Roosevelt challenged the popular mood rarely, briefly, and usually indirectly, though protected by a four-year term of office. Winston Churchill, perhaps the most Periclean leader of modern times, paid a price for his political courage. But as prime minister in wartime, even he was shielded by special emergency powers and an extended term of office. Pericles, on the other hand, held office for one year at a time and could be recalled by public vote at least ten times during that year. Yet he refused to flatter the people and appeal to their prejudices. Instead, when the occasion demanded, he informed them of the realities and advised them how to cope; he called upon them to rise above their fears and short-range self-interest, and inspired them to do so. When necessary, he was willing to chastise them and risk their anger.

And provoke their anger he did. Like all democratic leaders, Pericles engaged in the rough and tumble of popular politics and was subject to every kind of attack. Throughout his years in office he confronted political conflict at home and war abroad. Domestic enemies accused him of tyranny on the one hand and demagogy on the other. Comic poets lampooned him in the public theater, made fun of the shape of his head, his Olympian aloofness, and even the woman he loved. He was forced to endure legal actions against her and many of his friends and associates, even seeing some of them driven into exile. He was accused of bringing on war to please his mistress and of imposing an inadequate and cowardly strategy on his people.

Although he successfully overcame all these trials, Pericles' career took a tragic turn, and in the last year he had reason to doubt the value of his life's work. Athens was engaged in a terrible war that he had urged the people to undertake. Then a plague broke out and killed a third of the citizens. The people of Athens held him responsible for all their miseries and removed him from office. The antidemocratic Plato could therefore dismiss him in a way that was both plausible and crushing: Pericles had sought to make the Athenians better, Plato said, yet "they imposed no shameful punishment on him when they were 'worse'; but after he had made them 'noble and good' at the end of his life they condemned him for embezzlement and almost put him to death because they thought he was a scoundrel." (*Gorgias* 515e)

Plato's judgment has influenced all subsequent opinion about Pericles and the democracy he led. Indeed, after Pericles' death, and especially after Athens had lost the war, it was easy to look upon both as a terrible failure. The Athenians lost their empire and the wealth and power that went with it; for a while they even lost their democracy and their liberty. Yet the defeat in war and the loss of empire did not mean the failure of Pericles' enterprise. He had, in fact, foreseen the possibility himself, and in a dark moment of the war urged the Athenians not to be discouraged by the prospect:

> Even if we should ever be forced to yield (for everything that grows great also decays) the memory of our greatness will be bequeathed to posterity forever; that we of all the Greeks ruled over more Greeks than anyone, that in the greatest wars we held out against enemies in alliance and individually, and that we lived in a city that was the most ingenious and the greatest. (2.64.3)

The paradox inherent in democracy is that it must create and depend on citizens who are free, autonomous, and self-reliant. Yet its success—its survival even—requires extraordinary leadership. It grants equal rights of participation to citizens of unequal training, knowledge, and wisdom, and it gives final power to the majority, which is certainly inferior in those qualities to an elite. It gives free reign to a multiplicity of parties and factions, thereby encouraging division and vacillation rather than unity and steadiness. In antiquity, this led critics to ridicule democracy as "acknowledged foolishness"; in the modern world, it has been assailed as inefficient, purposeless, soft, and incompetent. Too often in this century its citizens have lost faith in times of hardship and danger and allowed their democracies to become tyrannies of the right or left.

Germany's Weimar Republic fell victim to the Great Depression because it had no time for democratic institutions to take root and, further, because even its supporters lacked the passionate devotion to fight for their democracy in a time of crisis. They have accordingly been called *Vernunftrepublikaner*, intellectually attached to their democratic republic but not committed to its soul and spirit. A major reason for the failure of the Weimar democracy was the absence of leaders who understood and could provide the special vision needed by a democratic state.

Thucydides reports Pericles' own summary of the qualities necessary for a statesman: "to know what must be done and to be able to explain it; to love one's country and to be incorruptible." These same qualities will be needed by the leaders of the world's fragile and emerging democracies. They will have the difficult task of instilling in their people the love for their nation and the enthusiasm for their constitution that will lead them to accept risks and dangers, to endure unavoidable hardships and make necessary sacrifices. At the same time, they must restrain the people's passions, moderate their anger and ambition, and persuade them to be sober, if not rational.

It was Pericles' genius to recognize the democratic leader's obligation to educate his people in civic virtue and to have the skills needed to do so. His policies, to be sure, brought the Athenians prosperity and the practical advantages of empire. But his success and that of Athens rested on more than prosperity and rhetoric. He also had a vision for his city that offered the meanest of its citizens the opportunity to achieve, through common effort, personal dignity, honor, and the fulfillment of their highest needs. He used his talents and his character to convey that vision to his people.

If the new democracies of our time are to succeed, they too must offer more than economic prosperity. The task of their leaders will not be easy, for their people have become cynical about idealism of any kind. Like Pericles, however, they will need to give their people a noble vision that offers spiritual as well as material satisfaction so that they, too, will acquire the devotion their democracies need to carry them through the difficult challenges they will face.

In their rational and secular approach, in their commitment to political freedom and individual autonomy in a constitutional, republican and democratic public life, the Athenians of Pericles' day are closer to the values of our era than any culture that has appeared since antiquity. That is why Periclean Athens has such a powerful meaning for us. But if there is much to learn from the similarities, there is at least as much to learn from the differences between the Athenians and ourselves. Although the Athenians valued wealth and material goods as we do, they regarded economic life and status as less noble and important than distinction in public service. Although they were among the first to recognize the dignity of the individual, they could not imagine the fulfillment of their spiritual needs apart from an involvement in the life of a well-ordered political community. To understand the achievements of Pericles and his city we need to be aware of these significant differences, and we must study them with humility. For in spite of their antiquity, the Athenians may have believed things we have either forgotten or never known; and we must keep open the possibility that in some respects, at least, they were wiser than we.

# ARISTOCRAT

n the first decade of the fifth century, about 494,* the pregnant Agariste, daughter of Hippocrates, dreamed she gave birth to a lion. In a few days, as Herodotus tells the story (6.131), she presented her husband, Xanthippus, with a son, whom they named Pericles. That is the kind of dream that would be remembered only years later, when events have made it significant, but at the turn of the fifth century in Athens, the birth of a son to this couple was auspicious. The Athenian democracy was little more than a decade old, and its leaders still came exclusively from the great aristocratic families. Agariste's uncle Cleisthenes was its founder, and her family,

* All dates are B.C. unless otherwise indicated.

known as the Alcmaeonids, may have been the most famous and powerful in Athens. One legend traced their origin to the Homeric hero Nestor, king of Pylos; another made them descendants of Athens' first public officials after the end of its legendary kings. In either case, they were one of the leading families in Athenian society.

The first famous Alcmaeonid made his name at Athens more than a century before Pericles was born. A nobleman named Cylon had become famous by winning at the Olympian games, and his athletic achievements helped him to win the hand of the daughter of the tyrant who ruled Megara, the city on Athens' western frontier. It may seem strange that an athletic triumph should be the road not only to fame and fortune but also to political power, but athletic prowess meant even more to the ancient Greeks than to our own sports-obsessed world. Athletic contests were religious and cultural events of great importance that provided platforms for the display of Hellenic society's deepest values.[1]

The contests included running, the long jump, throwing the discus or javelin, wrestling, boxing, and, most prestigious of all, the chariot race. These were fierce competitions between individuals, not teams, and victory brought extraordinary honor. At Athens, winners dined at the town hall for life at public expense. Some towns tore down a section of their defensive wall to honor the victorious athlete returning from the games. Pindar, one of the greatest of Greek poets, devoted his art to commemorating such victories. Sculptors depicted the gods as young or mature athletes. All this reveals a special quality of Greek society: its powerful commitment to agon, the competition between individuals that allowed the winner to achieve excellence, fame, and heroic stature.

In the seventh century, an Olympic victor with powerful connections could pose a serious threat to the political stability of his community, and Cylon was just such a victor. The ambitious athlete aimed at seizing power in Athens and establishing a tyranny like his father-in-law's. In Cylon's time, tyranny had not yet taken on the dreadful connotations it has since acquired. It simply meant the rule of a single individual achieved by nontraditional means. It often came in the form of a popular rebellion against a ruling dynasty or an aristocracy led by a heroic leader who had gained eminence as a soldier or, as in Cylon's case, as an athlete. The early tyrant was merely carrying the tradition of competition for a leading position in the state to a new level.

In Cylon's day, it was already customary for anyone undertaking an important and risky venture to seek first the advice of the great oracle of Apollo at Delphi, which had by this time become the foremost prophet of events in the Greek world. The shrine at Delphi was thought to be the center of the earth, literally its navel (*omphalos*), and important individuals as well as representatives of cities came from all over to seek the oracle's counsel. No one would think of founding a new colony or going to war without its advice. Consulting the oracle, however, could be a tricky business. Timely access to the oracle depended on the favor of the priests, often gained by the donation of a handsome gift. The question was put by one of the male priests to the Pythia, a priestess in a drug-induced frenzy. Her answer was not intelligible and had to be interpreted by the priest, who usually put it into verse. Even then, it needed careful study, for the responses could be ambiguous.

An example every schoolchild used to know is that of Croesus, the king of the Lydian kingdom in Asia Minor in the sixth century. He wanted to conquer the powerful Persian Empire that bordered his kingdom and asked the oracle if he should attack it. The answer was: "If you march against the Persians you will destroy a great empire." (Herodotus 1.53) Filled with confidence, Croesus attacked the Persians and indeed destroyed a great empire—his own. Herodotus tells the story to illustrate the impermanence of human greatness and the deadly blindness and arrogance that threatens those who aim too high.

Cylon made a similar mistake; he must have asked what he should do to gain the mastery of Athens. The oracle told him to take advantage of the Athenians' distraction as they celebrated "the greatest festival of Zeus" and seize the Acropolis, the natural fortress above the city that held the temples of the gods. Cylon collected his supporters in Athens, added them to a force supplied by his father-in-law in Megara, and gained control of the Acropolis at the time of the Olympic games, the great festival to Zeus at Olympia in the Peloponnesus. But as Thucydides points out, the oracle may have meant the greatest festival to Zeus in Attica. That celebration would have lured most Athenians outside the city. With the people thus scattered, Cylon would have had time to entrench himself securely before his enemies could react. Cylon must have expected the shock of the coup to stun the Athenians and make them accept his control, but since most of them were in town they could rally quickly. The Athenians, therefore, fearing not only the tyranny but also subjection to their Megarian neighbors, resisted under the leadership of Megacles and his Alcmaeonid clansmen. They laid siege to the plotters on the Acropolis and soon reduced them to desperation.

The failed conspirators found sanctuary by hiding in the holy precincts of the temples, but after a while it appeared they would soon die of hunger or thirst. This presented a dilemma. The Greeks believed that the death of people in holy places brought pollution and disaster upon the whole city, as when the murder of the king of Thebes brought down a devastating plague upon that city in the myth of Oedipus. Megacles and the other archons, the aristocratic chief magistrates of the primitive Athenian state, were in charge of the siege; knowing they could not allow the plotters to die in the temples, they promised them safety if they came out. When they emerged, the archons broke their oaths and put them to death, even those who clung vainly to the altar of the Furies, the ancient goddesses who were thought to visit a terrible vengeance on murderers. For these polluting acts of sacrilege, the family of Megacles were declared accursed and sinners against the city's divine patroness, Athena. The entire family was driven from Athens, though they returned some years later when the scandal had died down. This "curse of the Alcmaeonids" passed on to Megacles' descendents and played an important role in the history of Athens.

Alcmaeon, another member of this family, was the first Athenian to win the chariot race at the Olympic games, and he gained further glory by leading the Athenian contingent in a sacred war in defense of the Delphic oracle. In competition with the leading eligible bachelors among the Greek nobility, his son won and wed the richest heiress in Greece, the daughter of the tyrant of Sicyon, and became a leading figure in Athenian politics until he and the family were driven out again by the successful tyrant Peisistratus. Alcmaeon's son, in turn, was Cleisthenes, who found a way to rid Athens of tyranny and coincidentally restore the family position. He and the other Alcmaeonids undertook the contract to rebuild the ruined temple at Delphi, and he won the gratitude of the priests there by using fine Parian marble to rebuild its facade instead of the cheaper stone stipulated in the contract. With the goodwill thus acquired, as well as a substantial bribe to the Delphian priestesss, he convinced the oracle to persuade the Spartans to expel the tyrants from Athens.

Though Peisistratus had been popular his sons were not. In the course of their reign they became harsh and tyrannical in the modern sense. In 510, a Spartan army drove out the family of Peisistratus; Cleisthenes and the Alcmaeonids returned expecting glory. When the Spartan army withdrew, however, Athens found itself in a political vacuum, which the aristocrats tried to fill with a return to the old days when political life was limited to the nobility. Cleisthenes lost out in the initial struggle for political leadership, but instead of accepting defeat and plotting to gain aristocratic support for another try, Cleisthenes broke new ground and changed the rules of the political game forever. He began to campaign outside aristocratic circles, proposing to overthrow the traditional system that favored landowners who controlled the sacred places and their priesthoods, and dominated the political and religious organizations, and to replace it with a new order that would make a place for the common man. His opponents once again invoked the "curse of the Alcmaeonids" and drove Cleisthenes, his family and supporters from the city. Cleisthenes had won the hearts of the Athenian common people. Recovering their poise after the expulsion, they took up arms, drove the Spartans out, and brought him and his faction back in triumph.

Cleisthenes fulfilled his promises and carried through the reforms that established democracy in Athens. All adult male citizens were eligible to vote for the city's magistrates and for the members of a Council of 500, which prepared legislation. They could serve on juries and attend the assembly, where final authority rested. Debate was free and open, and in theory, any Athenian could submit legislation, offer amendments, or argue the merits of any question. In practice, aristocratic political leaders did most of the talking, and it seems likely that in the first half-century of the democracy the Council of 500 had some powers that were later taken over by the assembly.

Cleisthenes, moreover, did not change the system which divided the Athenians into four classes on the basis of wealth. Only members of the two highest classes could serve as the city's top magistrates or on the Council of the Areopagus, the old aristocratic council that continued to exercise considerable political power. Members of the third class could serve on the Council of 500, but the poorest Athenians were excluded. Further, since there was no payment for public service, the poor would have found it hard to attend the assembly and serve on juries. Cleisthenes' regime has been called a "hoplite democracy" after the third class in society that formed its backbone— men who owned farms large enough to provide them with a decent living and sufficient wealth to buy the heavy armor in which they fought as soldiers. By later standards, theirs was a severely limited democracy in which the lower classes deferred to their betters. But it was, nevertheless, the first known democracy of any kind.

The new regime, therefore, had the fierce and devoted support of the people, and it quickly demonstrated the power unleashed by the new democratic constitution. The Athenians fought off several attempts by neighboring cities to take advantage of their recent civil strife, routing the combined forces of Boeotia and Chalcis. Herodotus later celebrated these victories:

> Now Athens grew more powerful. And there is not only one but there are proofs everywhere that equality before the law [isegoria] is an excellent thing. As long as the Athenians were ruled by tyrants they were no better warriors than their neighbors, but once they got rid of the tyranny they became the best of all by a long shot. This shows that while they were oppressed they were willing cowards, like slaves working for a master, but when they became free each man was eager to achieve honor for himself. (5.78)

Cleisthenes was the liberator of his city and the father of the democracy. He and his family had expelled tyranny and installed a vigorous democracy, and in the decade or so after its establishment they made political alliances that allowed them to dominate Athenian politics. Pericles' father, Xanthippus, therefore did well when in the first few years of the fifth century he married Agariste, niece of Cleisthenes. Before long he would have opportunities to exercise his outstanding forensic, political, and military talents. The union was blessed with three children: Ariphron, the oldest, named for Xanthippus' father; a daughter whose name we do not know; and the hero of our story.

Pericles grew up in a critical period for the Greek world and a turbulent time for Athens' young democracy. In 490, when he was four, the Persian king Darius sent his army to Attica to restore the tyranny and to make Athens a province of his empire. A Persian victory would soon have meant the subjection of all the Greeks. Nine thousand Athenians aided by a thousand men from the small town of Plataea defeated a much larger Persian force. The Spartans had agreed to come to Athens' aid but had delayed their departure because they were in the midst of celebrating a religious festival. Almost unaided and against all expectations, the Athenians won the battle of Marathon and drove off the Persians. The Spartan army arrived in time to inspect the battlefield and congratulate the Athenians. Almost certainly Xanthippus was among the "Men of Marathon" who soon became legendary heroes, spoken of with patriotic reverence.

After the battle, however, the rumor arose that the Alcmaeonids had plotted treason and flashed a shield during the fighting as a signal to the Persians. The story was probably a canard invented by their political enemies, eager to put an end to the strong position the Alcmaeonids and their associates had held since the revolution of Cleisthenes. The Alcmaeonids responded with an accusation of their own. Fresh from the battle, Miltiades, the mastermind of the victory of Marathon, had asked the Athenians to send him on an expedition with a fleet and army. He did not name his target but promised to enrich the Athenians. Such was his fame and influence at the moment that his request was granted without further inquiry. He attacked the island of Paros, but the Parians resisted, and in the siege that followed Miltiades was wounded and forced to return with empty hands. Xanthippus quickly brought charges against Miltiades whose sudden status made him a dangerous political competitor, and a jury convicted the dying man of deceiving the people into undertaking a disastrous expedition. They punished him with a heavy fine, and he left the great debt to his son Cimon, with whom Pericles would one day compete for political leadership.

Miltiades was gone, but a more dangerous threat soon emerged to challenge the Alcmaeonids. In 484, Xanthippus was driven from Athens for ten years by the process called "ostracism," a procedure introduced by Cleisthenes in the infancy of the democracy as a device for deterring faction and treason. Each year, probably in January, the Athenian assembly voted on the question of whether there should be an ostracism. If the majority voted no, there was none. If they voted yes, it took place on a single day in March. On that day, each citizen could write the name of the man he wanted to remove from the city on a piece of broken pottery—an *ostracon*, the scrap paper of antiquity—and bring it to the Agora. At the end of the day, the archons counted the votes to see if there were six thousand, the number required for some types of important decisions in the Athenian assembly. If six thousand Athenians had voted, the one who had received the most ballots was compelled to leave Attica for a period of ten years. The idea was to allow a popular politician like Cleisthenes, who was confident of majority support, to deter a coup by a hostile faction. The threat to a rival leader, it was thought, would serve as a deterrent to keep him and his faction in line. The institution, a kind of rough-and-ready vote of confidence, seems harsh by modern standards. But it appears to have worked, helping protect the Athenian democracy from subversion for almost a century.

Although invented by Cleisthenes in the last decade of the sixth century, the procedure had never been used until 487. In each year from 487 through 484, an Alcmaeonid or a political leader associated with the family was expelled. Then, other leading politicians were removed, the last being the upright and admirable Aristides, who had come to be called "the Just." There is a story that a rustic illiterate approached the noble Aristides on the appointed day and asked him to write the name "Aristides" on his *ostracon*. Taken aback, he asked the bumpkin what harm Aristides had ever done him. "None," was the answer; "I don't even know the man, but I am tired of hearing him called 'the Just' wherever I go." (Plutarch, *Aristides* 7)

Aristides was an outstanding statesman and general who had fought bravely at Marathon. He was recalled to help defend Athens against the Persian invasion of 480 and played a critical role in the victory. So great was his reputation for probity that he was called on to assess the contribution each member state should make when the Delian League was formed after the war, and not one of the almost two hundred states complained of unfairness. No one could have had a better claim to his title. The story is probably an invention of the critics of democracy, meant to illustrate the envy of excellence natural to that form of government. But it misrepresents the nature and purpose of the institution. Ostracism was not meant as a way of venting popular jealousy against any citizen who stood out from the crowd. It was a constitutional safeguard, a needed safety valve that helped avoid the explosion of domestic strife that might have destroyed the young democracy.

By 482, the only important politician left in Athens was Themistocles. He was inventive, a brilliant speaker, and so jealously ambitious that he said he could not sleep for thinking of the trophy won at Marathon by Miltiades. It seems likely that he was behind the ostracisms. Outside the dominant coalition established by Cleisthenes, Themistocles appears to have hit upon a plan that destroyed the ruling coalition and permitted him to achieve primacy in Athens.

In 484, when Pericles was ten, Xanthippus took his immediate family with him into exile. As members of the international Greek aristocracy, the family must have had relations of *xenia* (guest-friendship) with nobles in several other cities. Possibly they went to live in Sicyon, the home of Agariste's famous great-grandfather. Pericles was old enough to understand something of what was happening, and doubtless drew from it an early and vivid lesson of the dangers attending the competition for political power.

The return of the Persians in 481 cut short Xanthippus' exile. Xerxes, the new Great King, launched a major invasion by land and sea to punish the Athenians and to subjugate all the Greeks. The Athenians recalled all their ostracized fellow-citizens to unify their state in the face of what seemed insuperable odds. The vast Persian forces could not be stopped in central Greece, and in 480, the Athenians fled their homes and left Athens to the vengeful destruction of the Persians. The men of fighting age manned the warships, while the women and children found refuge on the island of Salamis and in some coastal cities of the Peloponnesus. The family of Xanthippus shared the common lot, and the story is told that the family dog, unable to bear his master's departure, plunged into the sea and, keeping pace with the warship, swam to Salamis where, exhausted, he died on the beach.

Salamis was the decisive naval victory that saved Greek freedom and independence and preserved the young Athenian democracy for the greatness that awaited it. But it was not until the next year that victories at Plataea and Mycale drove the Persians from Greece in headlong flight. Xanthippus commanded the Athenian contingent at Mycale, and when the Spartan forces sailed home, it was he who conducted the siege of Sestos that drove the Persians from the European shore of the Dardanelles. On his return to Athens Xanthippus was declared a hero and became a political figure of great prominence.

No modern parallel exists for the extraordinary advantages that the sons of Xanthippus and Agariste inherited. If an Adams of Massachusetts had married a near descendent of George Washington, and if the Adamses had been rich and famous aristocrats of long standing, their sons' political prospects might almost be comparable to those that lay before the young Athenians.

In almost every case, the prize for victory in the political contest in Athens was not fortune but fame. In the first half of the fifth century, political offices were unpaid. The state imposed no regular taxes and expended little money, so there was not much chance of enriching oneself through public service. The major contenders for high public office were well-to-do and well-born, and deeply imbued with the Greek ideal of competition to achieve excellence, public recognition, and the glory that it carried. The battle to gain these rewards was always fierce.

Success came in part from personal achievements in war and athletic competition and from personal qualities such as good looks, intelligence, and rhetorical skills. But powerful connections were at least as important, and Pericles and his brother had valuable contacts in the highest Athenian circles. From their father, they gained reflected military glory so recent that it still had political value. On their mother's side, they were the grand-nephews of Cleisthenes, expeller of tyrants and founder of the democracy. Probably none of their contemporaries could match so impressive a lineage in the years right after the Persian War.

At the same time, they had also inherited important liabilities. In the antagonistic world of Athenian politics, eminence provoked jealousy; thus Ariphron and Pericles could expect especially rough treatment from their competitors. Political feuds, moreover, usually passed from one generation to the next. The sons of Xanthippus could therefore expect hostility from Cimon, the very capable son of Miltiades. Further, although family membership passed through the father, the sons of Agariste would always be associated in the public mind with her notorious family—a double-edged connection. It brought fame and the support of a powerful family, but it also inspired a special strain of envy. The Alcmaeonids had held an unusual amount of power from 508 to 480, and they were viewed with particular suspicion. The charge of treachery at Marathon had never been proved, but it was still remembered. The series of ostracisms showed they had powerful enemies. Finally, there was the curse. It had been used before at convenient political moments, and it could be again. Nevertheless, the sons of Xanthippus and descendants of Cleisthenes were far more blessed than burdened by their heritage. Few young Athenians entered adulthood and public life with greater prospects.

As the older son, Ariphron might have been expected to take the lead. But there is no record of his involvement in politics or of his prominence in any other activity. The family hopes, therefore, came to rest quite early on Pericles. His mother's dream had been portentous; the young Pericles did stand out. His extraordinary powers of mind and character soon distinguished him from his contemporaries, and after the elementary instruction common to all Athenian boys, Pericles pursued his studies further.

The traditional education of Athenian youth was practical and ethical rather than intellectual. Physical training prepared the boys for the athletic contests that were a regular part of religious festivals in Athens and of Panhellenic competitions, and kept them in condition to serve as soldiers when they came of age at eighteen. Musical education taught them to sing and to play the lyre and an oboelike instrument called the *aulos*, but most of all to learn the traditional body of poetry, chiefly the epics of Homer. This, too, was practical instruction, for each year thousands of Athenian boys and men competed in choruses at religious festivals. In addition, the drinking parties, or symposia, that formed the heart of aristocratic social life usually concluded with songs from the participants.

The most important part of the traditional education involved learning the epic poems by heart, for Homer was the fountain of wisdom and the model of Greek behavior. Here the pupils found the clearest moral lessons. Protagoras, one of the great teachers of a later day, makes that point in the Platonic dialogue that bears his name. The student reads the poets because their works contain "many admonitions, and many tales, and praises and encomia of famous men, which he is required to learn by heart in order that he may imitate or emulate them and desire to become like them." They learn to play the lyre to acquire self-control; then they learn the lyric poets and hear their verses set to music so that "they may learn to be more gentle, and harmonious, and rhythmical, and so more fitted for speech and action, for the life of man in every part has need of harmony and rhythm." They learn gymnastics so that "they may not be compelled through bodily weakness to play the coward in war or on any other occasion." (326a–c)

In the early part of the fifth century, this was as much education as a young Athenian aristocrat received. It was characteristic of the archaic world of aristocratic Greece, aiming not at intellectual inquiry and understanding but at virtuous action to be achieved by imitation of good models and by training. Physical activity, both musical and gymnastic, taught competitiveness and courage, moderation, harmony, and self-control. At its core was the idea that education should shape an individual's body and character to make him fit to take his place in the community. The aristocratic ideal was of a talented amateur exercising a variety of skills but achieving a professional mastery of none.

Pericles certainly received that form of education and absorbed the lessons it taught. In Pericles' day, teachers who went beyond the usual training were few, and their doctrines were viewed with suspicion. But his exceptional intellect demanded further instruction. Even as a young man, he exhibited an intellectual talent and curiosity that made him seek out the best minds of his day, and he spent his youth and young manhood in the company of two who had important influence on his thought and development: Damon, an Athenian, and Anaxagoras of Clazomenae.

Damon must have instructed Pericles while his pupil was still young, for a comic poet speaks of him as "The Cheiron who raised Pericles" (Plutarch, *Pericles* 4.2), and in the *Iliad*, Cheiron is the centaur who educated the young Achilles. Damon earned a reputation as "a most accomplished man in every way, as well as a musician, and a companion of inestimable value for young men," and according to Plato, Damon was "in his time the wisest of all the citizens." (*Laches* 180d) His formal role was as Pericles' music teacher, but the master's instruction went far beyond singing or the lyre to include his theory of music and its relationship to ethics and politics. Damon taught that different kinds of music express different elements of human character, and Plato reports his observation that "when modes of music change, the fundamental mores of the state always change with them." (*Republic* 400b and 424c) Damon probably talked about practical political questions as well as larger issues of theory. Some of Pericles' enemies would later claim that it was Damon who advised him to use public funds to pay citizens for jury service and thereby, in their view, began the corruption of the state.

But the greatest influence on Pericles came not from a citizen but from a resident alien—what the Athenians called a metic (*metoikos*)—Anaxagoras of Clazomenae, a city in Ionia on the coast of Asia Minor. The Greek cities of that region had long been a center of intellectual inquiry of a high order. A century before the Persian War, Thales of Miletus, the first of the natural philosophers, is said to have accurately predicted an eclipse of the sun. He and another Milesian, Anaximander, sought to explain such phenomena by reference to purely natural causes without resorting to the supernatural. When Anaxagoras came to live in Athens some time after the Persian War, he brought with him the same naturalistic approach. He asked questions and proposed ideas that challenged traditional and religious beliefs, shocking and disturbing most Athenians who heard them, but exciting the impressionable young Pericles.

Anaxagoras, like the other Ionian philosophers, used reason in place of the traditional myths of Greek religion to explain the perceptible physical world, especially the heavenly bodies. He taught that they were not divine beings but that the sun was a molten mass of red-hot stone many times larger than the Peloponnesus, and that the moon was of stuff like the earth, having similar plains and ravines, its only light reflected from the sun. These rationalistic explanations ran counter to the supernatural religious beliefs of most Athenians and, in some cases, to the cults of the state. As they became known they caused scandal, and one day they would bring trouble to their proponent and his avid pupil.

At first, however, their chief result seems to have been to liberate Pericles from the superstitions common to his day. Once, the story goes, Pericles was about to launch a naval expedition. Just as the fleet was ready to sail, the sun was eclipsed in midday, darkness fell, and the men were struck with fear by what they took to be a warning from heaven. When the sun reappeared Pericles put his cloak before the eyes of his terrified steersman and asked whether he found that frightening. "No," was the reply. "Why, then, is there a difference between this and the earlier darkness, except that something bigger than my cloak caused the first one?" (Plutarch, *Pericles* 35.2) We need not believe the story, but it illustrates an aspect of Pericles' reputation for rationality and his skepticism toward common religious opinion.

Plutarch, writing more than five hundred years later, gave Anaxagoras credit for shaping Pericles' manner and style of speaking. His philosophical training gave him

> a lofty spirit and an elevated mode of speech, free from the vulgar and knavish tricks of mob-orators, but also a composed countenance that never gave way to laughter, a dignity of carriage and restraint in the arrangement of his clothing which no emotion was allowed to disturb while he was speaking, a voice that was evenly controlled, and all the other characteristics of this sort which so impressed his hearers.

These were qualities not particularly advantageous to a rising young politician in a democratic society, and the Chian poet Ion contrasts them unfavorably with the easygoing, affable, and popular style of Cimon. He describes Pericles' speaking style as "presumptuous and arrogant," revealing a haughtiness in which there was contempt and disdain for others. (Plutarch, *Pericles* 5.3) Both the friendly and the hostile view seem to portray the same man: impressive but somewhat remote and forbidding. Though these qualities may have been heightened by his study of natural philosophy, they are not surprising in a man of such lofty descent, so perilous a childhood, and so thoughtful a disposition.

Above all, Anaxorgoras influenced Pericles' political thought and practice, and his teachings helped make Pericles a unique leader under whom, according to Thucydides, "What was called a democracy was becoming, in fact, the rule of the foremost man." (2.65.9) Some philosophical rivals of Anaxagoras explained the world around us as resulting from the changes in and interaction among four primary elements: air, fire, earth, and water—elements that have always existed and are never exhausted. As the essential matter of the universe Anaxagoras instead proposed an infinite number of "seeds," also uncreated and eternal, whose combinings and separations accounted for the changing world we perceive with our senses. But why did these "seeds" combine and separate? To answer that question Anaxagoras introduced a new concept, *nous*, which we translate as "mind." The "seeds" are part of a rotation, or vortex, created and controlled by "mind." "It is the finest of all things and the purest, and it has knowledge concerning all things and the greatest power; and over everything that has souls, large or small, mind rules." (Simplicius, *In Phys.* 156, 13ff. [Diels-Kranz 59 B12])

Anaxagoras' theory was attractive to those who objected to the idea of a purely mechanical universe that operates randomly or by some unknowable necessity. Such a man was Socrates, who sought out Anaxagoras when he heard of his idea. "I was delighted with this," he said. "It seemed somehow right that mind should be the cause of all things, and I thought that if this were the case then mind, in arranging all these things, would arrange each in the way that was best for it." Socrates, in other words, hoped that Anaxagoras would explain all things in terms of a purpose with respect to which they might be judged good or bad. But Anaxagoras was no teleologist. For him, "mind" was the originator of motion, and the rotation it started produces the rest mechanistically without further intervention. Everything else was then separated from the mixture in its own time, including man, who is the wisest of the animals and himself contains "mind."

This theory presents as many philosophical problems as it solves, but it certainly excited the receptive and curious mind of the young Pericles. He was deeply impressed by what he learned from his teacher, whom his contemporaries called "Nous" after his own concept. At the height of his influence, his admirers thought of Pericles himself as *nous*, the embodiment of reason, and his reason, in turn, was the source and origin of Athenian actions. Indeed, the political world Pericles ultimately tried to create strongly resembled the physical world conceived by Anaxagoras. It was not the continuously guided and controlled movement that Socrates had sought from Anaxagoras, the political expression of which is dictatorship. Rather than imposing a single form of life upon the people from on high, which was meant to direct them to a single purpose that was not their own, it allowed the citizens of the Athenian democracy to sort themselves out, with all the freedom and unpredictability that the phrase implies.

The danger of such a system was that it might produce a dangerous instability. Its advantage was that it might unleash the latent power of thousands of individuals, joining voluntarily in a common effort to achieve unprecedented greatness. Enemies of democracy like Plato, Socrates' pupil, would find such an apparently uncontrolled political universe as unsatisfactory as his master found the physical universe of Anaxagoras. Pericles, on the contrary, seems to have been inspired by the idea to become, as Thucydides portrays him, the guiding element in his free and democratic city.

Pericles' aristocratic heritage, the influence wielded by the Alcmaeonid side of his family, and the glory of his father's achievements gave him a start in Athenian political life that few could match. None of this, however, is enough to explain why he was so different from and ultimately superior to other Athenian aristocrats of exalted background. His extraordinary intellectual training and the philosophical vision that arose from it transcended the general outlook of his peers and shaped his policies throughout his career. The young man who was about to enter Athenian public life was much more than the scion of two noble families. Like other aristocrats, he sought the victory, recognition, and glory that came with political success. Unlike the others, however, he brought to the battle unconventional ideas of greatness for his city and of the possibilities for political leadership.

# 2

# POLITICIAN

Pericles made his first major political appearance in 463 at the age of thirty-one. That was a rather late start for an aspiring Athenian politician, and it has been explained as part of a cautious and calculated strategy. Pericles apparently waited until the two political giants of an earlier generation, Themistocles and Aristides, were out of the way and Cimon was continually off on military campaigns. He also held back out of fear of the people: They said he looked like the tyrant Peisistratus, was a formidable speaker, and they thought he, too, might be aiming at tyranny. Such suspicions, when added to his family connections, would make him a likely candidate for ostracism. That explanation, however, misses the subtlety and practicality of his strategy. No doubt Pericles did calculate the steps in his political career carefully. But his actions need not be attributed to fear of competition or of popular suspicion. Instead, they reflect a keen sense of the nature of Athenian politics.

Ancient Athens had no political parties as we know them today. There were no organizations like the Republicans or Democrats in the United States or the Conservatives or Labour in Great Britain that maintain themselves over many generations, have structures independent of individual politicians, and names and symbols to which political loyalty is attached. Athenian political life centered on outstanding individuals and the supporters they gathered around them. The ancient writers referred to such factions as "those around Themistocles" or "Cimon and his friends." Sometimes they referred to a political grouping as a *stasis*, referring to those who "stood" together for some political purpose, although those who stood together one day might stand apart the next.

The formation of such a group required first and foremost a leader who could attract a following. All political leaders in Pericles' early years were aristocrats, and almost all were rich. The core of their political groups was typically formed by their relatives, their friends, and those dependent on or influenced by these people. To go beyond that circle, a political leader needed special personal qualities and achievements. Since political life in the democracy took place in the public assembly attended by some six thousand citizens, rhetorical ability of a high order was important. Popularity and political support could also be gained by good looks, a reputation for generosity, and an agreeable manner. Military success and other forms of public service helped even more to increase the political power of such groups and their leaders. Although the advancement of the fortunes of the leader and his friends was a central goal of each faction, social position and political issues were important too. Some groups had more farmers and others more city-dwellers, some concentrated their membership in one region of Athens and some in another; these distinctions made a difference. Some adhered to one foreign policy and others to its opposite. Domestic issues also divided them. Whatever his other advantages, an Athenian political leader needed to formulate and present a persuasive political program if he was to succeed.

The major Athenian politician in Pericles' early manhood was Cimon, son of that Miltiades whom Pericles' father had prosecuted. At the time of Pericles' political debut in 463, Cimon had been the dominant figure in Athens for well over a decade. He had reached that pinnacle both by his remarkable talents as a political leader and by his ability to define the issues and to persuade the Athenians to see things his way. In the personal, competitive world of Athenian politics, the faction to which Pericles belonged could advance neither its own interests nor its own political program so long as Cimon dominated the scene, and Pericles himself could not achieve his own ambitions while this powerful opponent blocked the way.

As the son of Miltiades, Cimon was a member of the great Philaid clan, wealthy and well connected. Ancient scandal accused his sister, Elpinice, of loose morals,[1] but Cimon married her off to Callias, the richest man in Athens and a member of the ancient and noble clan of Kerykes, not the sort of person to marry a woman of sordid reputation. Cimon himself married Isodice, one of the Alcmaeonids. In the years surrounding the Persian invasion Cimon had thus linked by marriage "the three most aristocratic families of early fifth-century Athens"[2] and thereby forged a political alliance of unprecedented power.

To this dynastic base Cimon brought personal qualities of great value. He was tall and impressive to look at, with a handsome head of curly hair. His manner was easy and friendly, especially pleasing in so great a nobleman. His education was old-fashioned and aristocratic, emphasizing physical education and singing rather than intellectual pursuits. A contemporary critic, Stesimbrotus of Thasos, accused him of lacking the education in poetry and the other learning appropriate to a free man and a Greek, as well as the verbal skill characteristic of Athenians. (Plutarch, *Cimon* 4.4) But Cimon, in fact, had a natural rhetorical gift that required no training and served him well in his public career.

Cimon demonstrated his personal qualities at a crucial moment for Athens. When the Persian forces were on the point of invading Athens in 480, Cimon—then only about thirty—was already showing the leadership that would soon allow him to dominate Athenian politics. The people were unsure of what to do as the Persian hordes approached. Some wanted to stay and defend their temples and homes, while Themistocles urged evacuation to Salamis and the Peloponnesus. Themistocles' strategy would have placed Athens' fate in the hands of the navy; the alternative would have relied on the army.

Among the Greeks, as in most societies before the twentieth century, enrollment in the different military branches had social and political consequences. A century and a half after the Persian War, Aristotle made that point quite clear:

Since the mass of the people is divided into four parts—farmers, crafts-men, merchants, and hired workers—and the military forces are also divided into four—cavalry, heavy infantry, light infantry, and navy—wherever the country is fit for cavalry, there it is natural to establish a strong oligarchy [or aristocracy,] (for the safety of the inhabitants depends on the power of this branch, and raising horses is possible only for those who have large estates). Where the land is suitable for heavy infantry it is natural to have [a broader form of] oligarchy (for heavy infantry is a branch limited to those who are well off rather than the poor). But reliance on light infantry and the navy is what suits democracy. (*Politics* 1321a)

Themistocles was a dangerous political opponent and a long-standing advocate of naval power. The navy consisted of oared ships manned by the poorest class of Athenians, men without land of their own. Themistocles, therefore, had strong support among the masses and was mistrusted by the aristocracy.

Cimon, on the other hand, the son of Miltiades, was a member of the great Philaid family, and rich enough to be one of the small group of aristocrats who served in the cavalry. Most Greek states, including Athens before the Persian War, relied on an army consisting chiefly of a heavy-armed infantry recruited from land-owning farmers. A man of Cimon's class could be expected to advocate land warfare when there was a choice, for there was a clear connection between the dominant form of military service and a share in political power. But he understood that Athens' only hope lay in forcing a sea battle, so he acted with the flair that would characterize his political career. He collected a group of his comrades and marched them through town up to the Acropolis. There he dedicated his horse's bridle to Athena, symbolically indicating that what the city needed at that moment was not horsemen but sailors and marines. The Greeks often took weapons and armor from fallen enemies and dedicated them at the temples of the gods as offerings of thanksgiving for the victory. Cimon took a shield so dedicated from a temple and marched directly to the ships; it was an action that "became the beginning of courage to many." (Plutarch, *Cimon* 5.2–3) It was that combination of practical wisdom and moral leadership that so endeared Cimon to the Athenians of all classes and political persuasions.

In the next year, after the great victory at Salamis, in which he had fought with conspicuous bravery and brilliance, the young Cimon was chosen as part of an embassy to Sparta, along with such seasoned veterans as Xanthippus and Aristides. The mission was an unusually important assignment for so young a man, and the friendship he developed with Sparta and its leaders as a result of this trip would be the center of his policy throughout his career.

At the time of the Persian War, Sparta was the most powerful among the Greek states and the leader of the only international organization in the Greek world, the Peloponnesian League. Sparta's power rested on its own magnificent army, trained to courage and obedience by an austere, disciplined, corporate way of life, one entirely different from the freedom and individualism of the young Athenian democracy. Distrust between such dissimilar societies was natural, especially when Athenian power had begun to grow. Cimon was the rare individual who could proudly proclaim his friendship for Sparta and still flourish in the Athenian democracy. It would be his role to explain the Athenians to the Spartans and vice versa, seeking always to maintain the precarious friendship between the two peoples.

In the years following the Persian War, Cimon played a central role in creating a structure of relations among the city-states. The flight of the Persians in 479 did not end the fighting. They had been defeated but not destroyed or rendered incapable of returning in force. Greek cities in and near Asia Minor still needed to be liberated and others, already free, needed defense. The Greeks also sought revenge and reparations for the death and destruction brought by the Persians, so they sent a force across the Aegean under Spartan leadership to achieve these goals.

The Spartans quickly earned a lasting reputation for being unable to treat their fellow-Greeks with decency and respect. The harshness and arrogance of the Spartan commander Pausanias soon alienated the other Greeks. "The commanders of the allies were treated with anger and harshness," according to Plutarch, "while he punished the soldiers with whippings or by compelling them to stand all day carring an iron anchor. No one could get bedding or food, or go down to the spring for water before the Spartans; their servants armed with whips drove away anyone who tried." (*Aristides* 23.2–3) Aristides and Cimon led the Athenian contingent, and their tactful, gentle behavior won the confidence of the allies. Accordingly, the Greeks most threatened by the prospect of a Persian return pressed the Athenians to assume the leadership, and they agreed.

The land-locked Spartans, their problems in the Peloponnesus always uppermost in their minds, soon withdrew from the leadership of a continuing war against Persia, and in the winter of 478/7, the

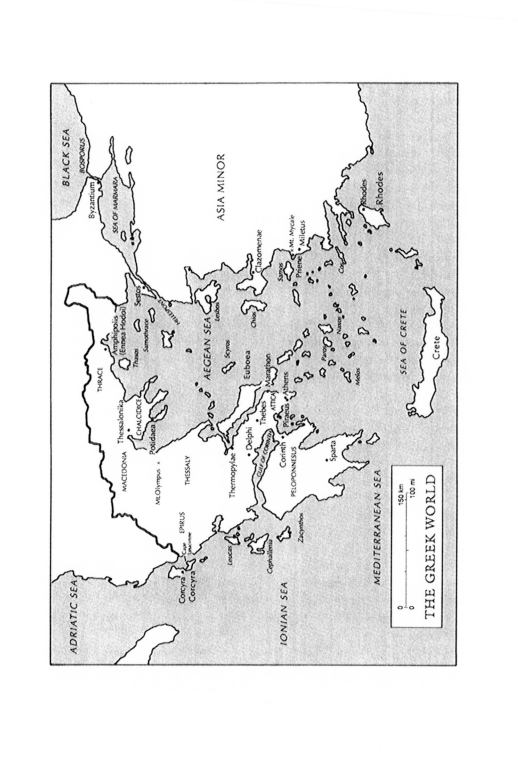

THE GREEK WORLD

ADRIATIC SEA

IONIAN SEA

MEDITERRANEAN SEA

BLACK SEA

BOSPORUS

Byzantium

SEA OF MARMARA

ASIA MINOR

Rhodes

Rhodes

SEA OF CRETE

Crete

Clazomenae

Mt. Mycale

Priene

Miletus

Samos

Chios

Lesbos

Scyros

Naxos

Paros

Melos

AEGEAN SEA

Euboea

Marathon

Athens

Piraeus

ATTICA

Thebes

Delphi

GULF OF CORINTH

Corinth

PELOPONNESUS

Sparta

Thermopylae

THESSALY

Mt. Olympus ×

MACEDONIA

Thessalonika

CHALCIDICE

Potidaea

Amphipolis
(Ennea Hodoi)

Thasos

Samothrace

Sestos

Abydus

THRACE

EPIRUS

Cape
Sounium

Corcyra

Corcyra

Leucas

Cephallenia

Zacynthos

150 km

100 mi

remaining allies met at the island of Delos in the middle of the Aegean to form a new league. Its purposes were to liberate the Greeks from Persian rule and to seek vengeance. It was to be a full offensive and defensive alliance, and membership was to be permanent. Although each state had a single vote in the common council, Athens was clearly the designated leader. An Athenian determined the contribution each state would make, the league's treasurers were Athenians, and Athenians commanded all the expenditures.

This Delian League, as it is called, had the support of all Athenian politicians and factions, but objectively it can be seen as the successful result of the policies of Themistocles. He had been one of the first to warn against the danger from Persia and to advocate a naval policy, and his strategy was chiefly responsible for victory. Now Athens was firmly committed to leading a chiefly naval war against the Persians and ready to profit from that commitment in honor, wealth, and power. That is why it is so strange to observe that Themistocles played no part in the new league and its wars. The campaign under Pausanias, the formation of the new league, the assessment of contributions, and the leadership of the league's forces were left in the hands of Aristides and Cimon—the former predominating the first but then giving way to the latter.

Why was Themistocles excluded? Domestic politics were certainly important. Aristides and Xanthippus had been ostracized in the competition for power; had Cimon been old enough and sufficiently prominent he might have shared the same fate. Themistocles' enemies had old scores to settle, and they had reason to fear a resurgence of his power. Supremely popular before the Persian invasion, Themistocles had gained even greater glory in the war. He was its greatest hero and admired not only in his native city but all over Greece. At the first Olympic games after the defeat of Persia, the spectators are reported to have neglected the contestants to stare at and applaud Themistocles. To avoid the menace of his enhanced power, his rivals joined together to check him. The marriage alliances created by Cimon and his close association with Aristides proved strong enough to keep Themistocles from using his new opportunities and ultimately defeated him.

The isolation of Themistocles, however, was not merely personal and factional. Part of the contest was a serious disagreement about foreign policy. The trouble began just after the Persian withdrawal. Athens was in a shambles and almost nothing was left of its defensive walls, so the Athenians set to work rebuilding both. The Spartans did not like walled cities, since the superiority of their army made defensive walls unnecessary for them, and they found siege warfare difficult. The power and daring the Athenians had shown in the recent war, moreover, made Sparta's allies nervous, and they urged the Spartans to object. Themistocles, the driving force behind the building of the walls, tricked the Spartans into inaction until the walls were high enough to defend. He then made a defiant speech, rejecting Sparta's claim to leadership and asserting Athenian independence from and equality with the Spartans. Officially, the Spartans made no complaint, but "secretly they were angry." (Thucydides 1.92) This was the beginning of a Spartan hostility to Themistocles that would follow him until he was driven from Greece.

The possession of strong walls was a necessary part of the new role Athens would have to play. But hostility to Sparta was not. The Spartans were divided among themselves as to their policy after the war, and the majority were ready to accept Athenian hegemony in the Aegean under friendly leadership in Athens. They liked and supported Cimon, who reciprocated their attitude completely. Cimon constantly praised the Spartans' simplicity and manners and ostentatiously emulated them. He named one of his sons Lacedaemonius ("Spartan") and at some point became Sparta's diplomatic representative, or *proxenos* (proxy), in Athens. The Spartans publicly favored him, and he took pride in their support. His policy was to maintain friendly and respectful relations with Sparta while vigorously pursuing the war against the Persians. Themistocles, of course, knew there was a Spartan faction suspicious and jealous of the growing power of Athens, and he feared the threat they represented. But Cimon believed in the peaceful intentions of most Spartans and their tolerant acceptance of Athens' leadership of the Delian League. Cimon's policy was more attractive and won the day. Themistocles lost out in the political struggle in Athens and in 473 he was ostracized. The following year, at Spartan instigation, Leobotes (an Alcmaeonid) brought charges of treason against Themistocles, who fled to Persia where he died. Athens was thus firmly committed to Cimon's Spartan policy and, thereby, to Cimon.

Events quickly justified both. Victory followed victory as Cimon led expeditions that solidified the league, cleared the sea of pirates, and drove the Persians from the Aegean. His campaigns brought Athens safety, wealth, and power. They also brought Cimon wealth, glory, and popularity, all of which fortified his political position. The wealth especially he used to good political effect. Wherever he went he was accompanied by young men in fine suits of clothes, which they exchanged with any needy and aged citizen they came upon. They also carried large quantities of change and slipped a few coins into the hands of poor men they encountered. For his own fellow-demesmen, the residents of his home district, he did even more and in a more public and spectacular manner.

> He removed the fences from his fields so that both foreigners and citizens could help themselves to the fruit without fear; and each day he gave a dinner at his house, plain, but enough for many people, to which any poor men who liked came and gained their daily sustenance without trouble, with leisure to devote themselves only to public business. (Plutarch, *Cimon* 10.1)

Cimon was by nature a generous man, but these actions went far beyond private generosity into the realm of shrewd political calculation. For all his advantages, Cimon was a conservative politician in a democratic state where the successes of the Delian League and the naval power on which they rested gave increasing influence to the men of the lower classes who rowed the ships. Continued political success required their support, and Cimon's plan was to befriend the poorer citizens and to seem generous in meeting their needs. He had thus found a way to build a base among the poor to rival that of their natural leader Themistocles and others in his faction. Like the old-time political bosses of Boston, New York, and Chicago he won a loyal following among poor voters by taking care of their personal wants and seeing to it that they voted when needed.

In this way he could carry out a domestic policy that was remarkably conservative. The democratic constitution introduced by Cleisthenes three decades before the great Persian invasion had not changed the property requirement limiting the archonship, the highest office in the state, to the upper classes. The Council of 500, which he invented to prepare bills for the assembly, among other duties, probably excluded the lowest class. The Council of the Areopagus, moreover, was left untouched. This body went back to legendary times, and it was the chief instrument of government in the days when Athens was a purely aristocratic republic. Each year the Athenians elected ten archons from among the rich and noble, and at the end of that year the ten graduated into the Areopagus, where they served for life. A body so composed inevitably had great prestige and influence; even after the reforms of Cleisthenes, it was thought to have ill-defined, but nonetheless real, powers of oversight concerning the magistrates and the constitution.

In the year 487/6, however, a new law provided that the archons should be chosen by a procedure ending in a lottery. Henceforth, these officials would be selected by chance and not because of their special qualities of lineage, mind, or character. This democratic innovation was bound to reduce the prestige of the office and of the council in which former archons served. A telling blow against the upper classes, it was probably the work of Themistocles and his faction, perhaps one of the issues leading to the ostracism of his opponents in the surrounding years. It was part of the personal contest among political leaders but also a maneuver in the continuing struggle between aristocracy and democracy in Athens.

The critical and heroic role played by Themistocles and by the poor men who rowed Athens' warships at Salamis and Mycale during the Persian War might have been expected to increase the influence of the masses still further at the expense of the upper classes. Instead, Aristotle reports that "After the Persian Wars the Council of the Areopagus grew strong again and controlled the city. . . . For seventeen years the constitution remained the same, with the Areopagites in charge." (Aristotle, *Ath.Pol.* 23.1; 25.1) These seventeen years (479–462) were the period when Cimon came to exercise the dominant position in Athens. Right after the Persian War, most Areopagites had still been elected rather than allotted, and their prestige had been enhanced by their good service in the war. They passed no new laws; they merely began to exercise their old informal rights, shielded by a favorable political climate, especially the support of the increasingly popular Cimon.

There can be no doubt that it was Cimon's policy to check the growing political role of the lower classes and to restore a degree of aristocratic influence. When the great revolution to full democracy came in 462, Cimon tried to defend the expanded powers of the Areopagus "and to revive the aristocracy [as it has been] in the times of Cleisthenes." (Plutarch, *Cimon* 14.2) The Athens of Cleisthenes, of course, was not an aristocracy but a limited and deferential democracy. It did not consider every citizen capable to serve in the highest offices. While it left final decisions to the assembly of all citizens, it expected them to be guided to a good one by their betters. By means of the "Areopagite constitution," Cimon wanted to restore the Athenian democracy to its first form and hold it there. It was a tribute to his great abilities that he was able to do so for so long in the face of changed political, military, and social conditions. As the years passed, Athens' power, wealth, and security depended more and more on its lower classes, yet they cheerfully accepted a political system that did not fully recognize their new status. The power and pride they had gained from their naval victories and the prosperity of their burgeoning empire help explain this long complaisance. But a great deal of the credit must go to Cimon himself, whose achievements and talents gave him a popularity that sustained his policies at home and abroad and seemed to make him unassailable.

Such were the circumstances in which Pericles began his own political career. But his first appearance as a distinct figure in Athenian history was not political (at least not openly so), but rather religious and artistic. Each year, the chief archon of Athens chose three poets to whom he granted a chorus and chief actor to perform their plays in a competition at the forthcoming festival. Earlier the chief archon would have chosen three wealthy Athenians to serve as *choregoi*, or producers, one for each poet, whose job was to hire a chorus and a chorus-master to train them. (The competition for the glory of victory was no less keen among *choregoi* than among poets and actors, and their names were inscribed on victory lists alongside them.) At the great annual festival of Dionysus in 472, the poet Aeschylus was one of the three poets chosen and he presented three related tragedies and an associated satyr play, as was then the custom. The *choregus* assigned to Aeschylus that year was Pericles, son of Xanthippus. Auspiciously for their sponsor, Aeschylus' plays won the first prize. One of them, *Persians*, survives.

That Pericles had the resources to pay for a chorus is unmistakable evidence that his father had died and that he had come into his patrimony, probably only a short time earlier. The Athenians had no direct taxation, even in time of war. To pay for choruses at festivals— as well as for the outfitting of warships—the city imposed a public duty called a "liturgy" (*leiturgia*) on their richest citizens. During the prosperous fifth century, these periodic levies were seen as opportunities for gaining public favor, and wealthy men often volunteered to undertake more liturgies than were required of them, vying with one another to carry them out most splendidly. It is unlikely that chance happened to impose this public service on Pericles so soon after he came into his inheritance; the ambitious young man probably seized the first available opportunity to bring himself to public attention.

The assignment of poets to *choregoi* appears not to have been random, at least not always. Themistocles had once been a *choregus* for the poet Phrynichus who, unlike most tragedians, wrote on contemporary subjects. Herodotus tells us that soon after the fall of Miletus put an end to the rebellion of the Ionian Greeks against Persia, Phrynichus put on a tragedy called *The Taking of Miletus*. Everyone in the theater was driven to tears, and the Athenians, we are told, were so distressed that they fined the poet and forbade the production of the play ever again. (6.21) But the anti-Persian feeling thereby evoked fit perfectly with the policy of Themistocles, leading us to think that he may well have been the *choregus* on that occasion. It is also quite possible that Themistocles' enemies were responsible for the playwright's punishment—the contentious world of Athenian politics could be a dangerous place even for poets.

*Persians* is the only play of Aeschylus' that we know to have treated a contemporary subject instead of a mythological theme. It dealt with the battle of Salamis, fought only seven years earlier, and showed the suffering of the Persian women (who formed its chorus) on learning of the terrible defeat. But it also celebrated the Athenians' glory, a subject certain to please the audience and judges at the great Dionysia of the city. Pericles must have been glad to provide a chorus for such a play and may have taken the initiative. It may seem surprising that Pericles should have been eager to celebrate a battle whose great hero was Themistocles, considering his rivalry with Pericles' father. But there is no reason to assume Pericles held any hostility toward Themistocles at this time. Besides, Themistocles was no longer a problem for Athenian politicians. He had been ostracized the year before, would soon be condemned as a traitor in absentia, and would never see Athens again. *Persians*, moreover, would have reminded the audience not only of Salamis but of the great victory over Persia by the Greeks, a victory whose last battle had been won by an Athenian general, Xanthippus, the recently deceased father of the play's *choregus*. Pericles evidently sponsored Aeschylus' play as an act of piety to the state and toward the glorious memory of his father. To present such a play and win first prize with it was not a bad way for an ambitious young man to introduce himself to the people of Athens.

After this brilliant debut, Pericles devoted himself to military service and took part in several expeditions where he showed himself "brave and fond of danger." (Plutarch, *Pericles* 7.1) In the busy and exciting early years of the Delian League, a military career was natural for a young man of his class and expectations. The training and experience he acquired on land and sea would serve him well in his many years as an Athenian general. But these and a reputation for bravery were also essential for a political future. The Greeks expected their leaders to show physical courage, whether in the athletic arena or in battle, as well as piety, generosity, and nobility. Cimon had risen to power chiefly because of his military prowess, and any rival must be able to show at least honorable service and military competence. By this time, moreover, the generals were coming to be the most important political figures in Athens. Archons served only for one year and, since 487/6, they were chosen by lot. Generals, on the other hand, were chosen by direct election and could be reelected without limit. The formation of the Delian League also meant that Athenian generals would be active every year, busy driving off the barbarian, gaining booty for Athens, freeing the seas, and winning glory. It was inevitable that in time the generals would become the truly important people in Athenian politics, and Cimon's brilliant military career surely hastened the process. By the 460s, it was evident that the road to political leadership passed through military service. It appears that Pericles was elected general when he reached thirty, the minimum age for the position, and that he commanded a fleet of fifty ships on an expedition to the neighborhood of Cyprus.

This success and early prominence may help explain why he was chosen to lead the first direct attack on Cimon, whose overwhelming eminence had not entirely crushed all opposition. The leader of the opposing faction was Ephialtes, a man known for his justice and incorruptible honesty, who appears to have begun as an ally of Themistocles and to have taken control of the opposition after his ostracism. Ephialtes and his associates wanted to destroy Cimon's power, and that of the aristocratic forces he represented, and to broaden Athenian democracy by giving greater power to the lower classes. A serious problem in the empire appeared to provide the opportunity.

In 465, a quarrel arose between Thasos, an important island in the northern Aegean and a charter member of the Delian League, and Athens over the control of a gold mine and some trading posts on the Thracian mainland across from the island. The Thasian uprising marks a turning point in the league's history, for it is the first occasion when its forces were used for what seem to be purely Athenian purposes. Cimon quickly defeated the enemy fleet and settled down for what proved to be a long and difficult siege of the island. At the same time, he landed a community of ten thousand Athenians and allies to establish a colony nearby at Ennea Hodoi, a location both economically and militarily strategic. The colony was ill-fated, for the settlers were soon wiped out by an army of natives. Meanwhile, the Thasians held out for more than two years against an expensive siege that was increasingly frustrating to the Athenians. Despite the ultimate surrender and punishment of Thasos, the entire campaign was the least glorious and successful of all those led by Cimon and undoubtedly caused much grumbling and dissatisfaction in Athens.

Ephialtes and his faction chose this opportunity to strike, and they fiercely attacked what Cimon stood for—Areopagite power, limited democracy, and friendship with Sparta. In the years before the Thasian rebellion, Cimon's popularity protected these policies. But with the disappointment arising from that campaign, and Cimon's prolonged absence in command of it, there was a chance of weakening his popularity.

Ephialtes and Pericles were elected generals, probably during the siege of Thasos, and it was most likely in the same period that Ephialtes launched his attack on the Areopagus. The time was not ripe for an assault on the institution itself or its powers, so he went after its individual members as a way of discrediting the council. It was a feature of Athens' democratic constitution that at the end of their year in office Athenian officials had to submit an account of their service, financial and otherwise, to public scrutiny. Ephialtes took the opportunity to bring charges of peculation against the outgoing archons who were about to enter the Areopagus and succeeded in having them removed from that council. He probably made similar charges against individuals already on the council with equal success.

These trials must have weakened the prestige of the Areopagus and encouraged Ephialtes and his supporters to try the same tactic against their main target. Their opportunity came when Thasos surrendered in 463. As soon as Cimon returned to Athens he was charged with misbehavior. The formal complaint was that he had been in a good position to conquer Macedonia for the Athenians but that he had accepted a bribe from the Macedonian king to hold back. The nature of the charge shows how difficult it was to make a substantial complaint against Cimon and how eager his opponents were to use the present opportunity against him. Invading Macedonia had been no part of his assignment, and the idea of the fabulously wealthy Cimon accepting a bribe was laughable. But the specifics of the charge were not important. Everyone understood that this was a political trial testing the strength of Cimon and his opponents—another wrestling match in the endless contest of Athenian politics. Ephialtes and his faction apparently believed that the annihilation of an Athenian colony, the long siege, and the embarrassment of the Areopagites had weakened Cimon enough to bring him down.

Athenian law knew no public prosecutor. In cases affecting the community as a whole, such as the alleged malfeasance of a general, any citizen could bring and prosecute an action. In this case, the enemies of Cimon selected several men to prosecute, of whom the leading figure and the most eager was Pericles. There were several good reasons for the choice. The most obvious was Xanthippus' successful prosecution of Cimon's father, Miltiades, for misbehavior as a general. The coincidence was sure to be noticed and the old memory revived, along with the old prejudices. Cimon had healed the rift between his family and the Alcmaeonids by means of marriage alliances, but his prosecution by the son of an Alcmaeonid mother could serve as a sign that the truce among competing aristocratic families was over. Finally, Pericles' personal qualities, his eloquence, lineage, and austere and noble bearing, recommended him to the radical democrats as an ideal prosecutor of the aristocratic Cimon.

Pericles, just over thirty years old, must have been glad to accept this opportunity. The eyes of all Athens, indeed of Sparta and the rest of the Greek world, too, would focus on the trial of the greatest man in Greece. Regardless of the verdict, a prosecutor who performed well would win fame and rise in the estimation of his faction and of many other Athenians.

One report of Cimon's defense survives, and it shows how his accusers connected his failure to press Athenian imperial interests with his well-known friendship for Sparta. Cimon defended himself and his policy without apology: "I am not a representative of rich Ionians and Thessalians, as are some others so they may be courted and paid," he said. "I am a representative of the Spartans and imitate and love their thrift and self-control, which I honor above any wealth, glorifying my city with wealth won from her enemies." It was a stinging and effective defense both of aggressive war against Persia and friendship with Sparta. Since that policy, despite the recent campaign, had brought consistent and unprecedented success, and since the specific charges against him were manifestly absurd, Cimon won acquittal.

In spite of his zeal for the assignment, Pericles was not particularly aggressive during the trial. In fact, he was "very gentle" with Cimon, according to Plutarch (*Cimon* 14.4), acting like a man who was only doing his duty. A fifth-century writer provides a romantic explanation for Pericles' restraint, reporting that Cimon's sister Elpinice had come to Pericles's house—an astonishingly bold and imprudent act for a respectable Athenian lady—to plead for her brother. Pericles supposedly replied, properly if not gallantly, "You are too old, Elpinice, to involve yourself in these affairs." Nonetheless, the story goes, Pericles made only a perfunctory case at the trial. In fact, Pericles must have known from the beginning that there was little chance to convict Cimon on such trumped-up charges. He still had strong support, and a too-vigorous attack could easily backfire. Since Pericles' main goal was to bring himself to public attention as a rising young member of the opposition, a dignified and not excessive prosecution was just what was needed. Prudence, not romance, therefore, explains his performance.

There is no telling how long Cimon might have maintained his position had not events abroad once more given his enemies an opening. In 464, during Athens' siege of Thasos, Sparta had suffered a terrible earthquake, which in turn encouraged her serflike subjects, the helots, to launch a major uprising. Defeated in battle, the rebels took refuge in a mountain stronghold where the Spartans could not get at them, and stubbornly held out there. At last, in 462, the Spartans called upon their allies for help, especially the Athenians. The old Greek alliance under Spartan leadership sworn in 481 against the Persians had never been formally renounced. Meanwhile, the Athenians had succeeded in many sieges and gained a great reputation for skill in that kind of warfare, in which the Spartans had little experience. It seemed natural, therefore, to ask for their help, especially under the leadership of Sparta's devoted friend Cimon.

The proposal provoked a heated debate in the Athenian assembly that plainly showed the continued existence and energy of a faction opposed to Cimon and his policies. The Spartan envoy who made the formal request was called Pericleidas, and many years later Aristophanes lampooned the scene in his comedy Lysistrata: "Don't you remember," his heroine says to the Spartans, "when once Pericleidas the Spartan, pale in his red coat, came here and knelt at these Athenian altars, begging for an army?" (1137–1141) Leading the opposition, Ephialtes spoke vehemently against the proposal, urging the Athenians "not to help or restore a city that was a rival to Athens but to let the pride of Sparta lie low and be trampled underfoot." (Plutarch, Cimon 16.8) The violence of his language reveals how much Ephialtes and at least some of his faction hated the Spartans. Part of the reason for this hatred was an adherence to the foreign policy of Themistocles, who had sought to make Athens sole leader among the

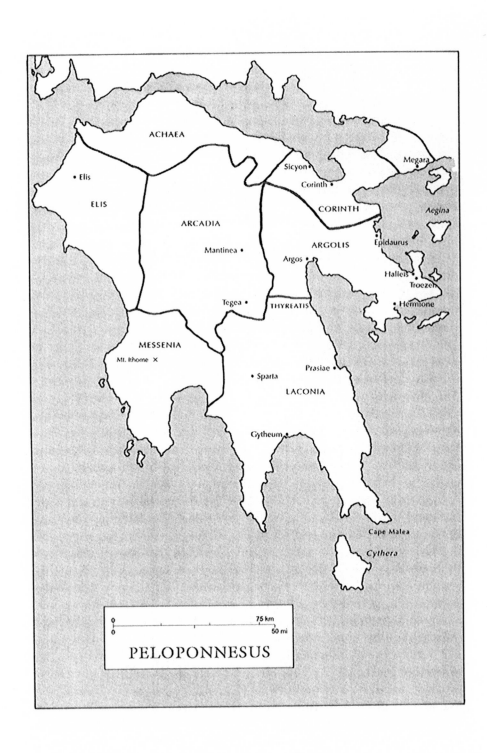

ACHAEA

Megara

Sicyon

• Elis

Corinth

ELIS

CORINTH

Aegina

ARCADIA

Epidaurus

Mantinea •

ARGOLIS

Argos •

Halieis •

Troezen

Tegea •

THYREATIS

• Hermione

MESSENIA

Mt. Ithome ✕

• Sparta

Prasiae •

LACONIA

Gytheum •

Cape Malea

Cythera

0                75 km

0                50 mi

# PELOPONNESUS

Greeks and resented Sparta's jealousy of her new power and influence. Still another cause was Sparta's firm support of Cimon's faction and its successful resistance to the advance of democracy in Athens.

Cimon and his policies, however, were still popular, and he made an effective reply to the opposition, urging the Athenians "not to leave Greece lame nor see their city deprived of its yokefellow." It was a homely but powerful metaphor, comparing Athens and Sparta to a team of oxen pulling the Greek plow, and it strongly appealed to an assembly made up chiefly of farmers. It also appealed to warm memories of cooperation in the common cause against the Persians and to the Panhellenic spirit of that time. The assembly accordingly voted to send Cimon with four thousand hoplites to help the Spartans against the rebels.

The Athenians were not in Sparta long before they wore out their welcome. For no obvious reason, the Spartans singled the Athenians out among their allies, sending them home on the ground that they were not needed after their first attempt to take the rebels' fortress on Mt. Ithome had failed. But Thucydides discloses the real reason behind this flimsy pretext: "the Spartans were afraid of the boldness and the revolutionary spirit of the Athenians, thinking that . . . if they remained they might be persuaded by the men on Ithome to change sides." (1.102.3) Sparta was a closed society that normally did not allow outsiders to move about their territory freely, even as individuals. Although commanded by Cimon, four thousand Athenians, raised in the free air, formed by the variety and prosperity of democratic Athens, proud of their constitution and of the power and glory of their state, were bound to be shocked by the austerity and material backwardness of Sparta. They must also have been struck by the rigidity and subordination, the absence of freedom they found, and, as was customary in their own state, they undoubtedly expressed their unfavorable impressions openly, frequently, and loudly. It is easy to imagine how such behavior might have bothered the Spartans, who were already suspicious and jealous of the Athenian democracy and its power. Their confidence, moreover, was especially unsteady at a moment when a natural calamity, and a dangerous revolution, had exposed Spartan weakness.

The Athenians quite naturally looked upon their dismissal as an insult, a disgrace, and proof of Spartan hostility. It was a terrible blow to Cimon and his policy, which was based on a contrary assumption. News of the cool treatment the Athenian expeditionary force was receiving must have reached Athens before its return, for by the time

Cimon led his men back his opponents had carried out a major constitutional revolution.

The hoplites were men of at least moderate property who had
benefited most from the democratic revolution of Cleisthenes. Most
of them were content under the conservative democracy of Cimon,
and were a significant part of the core of Cimon's political support.
Ephialtes and his colleagues, therefore, took advantage of their absence from Athens to propose that the Areopagus be deprived of the
"additional" powers that they alleged it had usurped. There can be no
doubt that the Areopagus had placed serious restraints on the sovereignty of the people, and that the removal of most of its powers was
the decisive act in moving Athens from limited to full democracy.
With so many middle-class hoplites away, the political power of the
unpropertied, largely dissatisfied lower class, the thetes, was temporarily great. The rump assembly passed a law transferring almost all
the powers of the Areopagus to the more democratic Council of 500,
which already existed, and to the popular law courts. The Areopagus
was left with its ancient jurisdiction over cases of homicide but little
else.

On his return, Cimon vainly tried to undo this legislative revolution, arguing for a restoration of the constitution of Cleisthenes. But
the insulting action of his Spartan friends had destroyed his support
in Athens. Even his own soldiers must have been angry at their
treatment in Sparta and disenchanted with Cimon. For the foresee-
able future, therefore, his revolutionary opponents would control the
Athenian assembly and the destiny of Athens. The next spring, in
461, they felt strong enough to call for an ostracism and succeeded in
making Cimon the victim. The "radical" democrats, as Cimon would
have thought of them, were firmly in control.

Pericles took part in this victory for his faction, but he remained
subordinate to its leader, Ephialtes. He was only two or three years
past thirty, and in the normal course of events he had several years as
a "junior partner" still ahead of him before he could seek the leading
position. But the revolutionary year 462/1 was not normal. Passions
ran high, and hatred for Ephialtes must have been strong and widespread among the friends of Cimon, for in the same year as Cimon's
ostracism Ephialtes was murdered in one of the very few political
assassinations in the history of Athenian democracy.

The identity of Ephialtes' murderer remains one of history's un-
solved mysteries. Plutarch rightly dismisses the improbable slander
that Pericles had killed him out of jealousy and envy. Aristotle names

a certain Aristodicus of Tanagra, of whom we know nothing, and other writers say that the assassin was never known. In any case, the democratic faction lost its leader at the very moment of victory. The man who would take his place was very young and relatively inexperienced. He could not at once hope to exercise as much influence as the fallen leader, but he could benefit from his martyrdom. We are not told how and why Pericles became head of the faction led by the fallen Ephialtes, but he was well prepared by family tradition and associations, by his unusual education, and by his native abilities to lead the movement toward a fuller democracy and a greater Athens.

# 3

# DEMOCRAT

After Ephialtes' death, Pericles rose from being a secondary member of a dissident political faction to a position as the uniquely powerful leader of a great democratic city ruling over a rich naval empire. He achieved this, first, through a series of constitutional reforms that gave a greater political role to the lower classes, and then by creating a powerful coalition with the great majority of Athenian farmers who fought in the heavy infantry. His rhetorical talent, political sense and organization, and the success he achieved allowed him to meet challenges from all directions. He also gained important support because of the power of his ennobling, carefully conceived, and forcefully communicated vision of a great city that gave meaning to the lives of all its citizens.

In the 450s, under Pericles' leadership, the Athenian assembly passed a series of laws that went far toward establishing a constitution as thoroughly democratic as the world has ever seen. It gave direct and ultimate power to its citizens in the assembly and the popular law courts, where they made all decisions by a simple majority vote, and it provided for the selection of most public offices by lot, for the direct election of a special few, and for short terms of office and close control over all public officials. This constitution reflected Pericles' vision of government, and within its confines he was able to achieve and maintain a position as leader and foremost citizen.

In 458, members of the class of small farmers (*zeugitai*) who fought as hoplites became eligible for the archonship, previously limited to rich men in the top two economic classes. Therefore, they would join the Areopagus and put an end to its domination by the rich and well-born. This step further reduced the influence of the archons and Areopagus to the advantage of the randomly chosen Council of 500, of the assembly, and of the popular law courts (*dikasteria*).

In 451/450, Pericles himself introduced a law imposing a stricter definition of Athenian citizenship. Up to then, children of an Athenian father and a foreign mother were legitimate Athenian citizens; the new law required that both parents be Athenian. The purposes of the new definition are far from clear, but whatever its other consequences, the new law meant that henceforth political membership in the community would be determined not by traditionally aristocratic religious bodies, or even by individual local townships, but by the people as a whole. It was an assertion of the sovereign power of the Athenian assembly as the seat of the democracy.

Another important change arose from the new burden carried by the popular courts. The growth of the Athenian population, the burgeoning commercial economy, the increased number of disputes arising from contact with foreigners, and the growth of the litigious spirit common to democracies put great pressure on the existing judicial system. Later in the century, Aristophanes plausibly estimated that the six thousand jurors (*dikastai*) empaneled annually heard cases on three hundred days each year. (*Wasps* 661ff.)

The democratic ideal required that the majority of citizens take part in public decisions, but the poor could not do so without pay. To meet the problem, Pericles introduced a law authorizing such payments. It was not long before the democratic policy of payments for service extended beyond jurors to the five hundred men who served on the council, to the archons, to all public officials chosen by lot, and to soldiers and sailors on duty. Aristotle calculated the number of citizens receiving pay at the same time for public services, military and civilian, domestic and imperial, at over twenty thousand. Pericles' introduction of payment for public service made many Athenians full citizens for the first time, and the life of the full Athenian democracy begins with his reforms.

It is important to have a clear understanding of the kind of regime Pericles' reforms produced, for it is not easy even for citizens of what are called democracies in the twentieth century to comprehend its nature. To a degree hard for us to grasp, politics was primary in the ancient Greek city, and the form of the constitution was understood and expected to shape the character of its citizens. The art, the literature, the philosophy, and all the great achievements of Periclean Athens cannot be fully understood apart from their political and constitutional context in the democracy established by Cleisthenes about 508 and extended by Pericles a half-century later.

The place to start a description of the Athenian democracy is with a definition of the term. Developments in the modern world, however, make that a difficult task, for the word has become debased and almost meaningless. Few modern states will admit to being anything but democratic. States as different as the United States, the Soviet Union, Great Britain, China, Switzerland, Cuba, South Africa and Nigeria all assert that they are democracies. That is confusing enough, but there are further complications. Many people today would insist that to qualify as a democracy a state must offer full constitutional and political protections and opportunities to all who have legal permanent residence within its borders and desire citizenship. But the Athenians limited the right to vote, hold office, and serve on juries to adult males who were citizens. Slaves, resident aliens, women, and male citizens under the age of twenty were denied these privileges. Modern critics question the democratic character of the Periclean regime because of the presence of slavery and the exclusion of women from political life. In excluding such groups, the Athenians were like every other society since the invention of civilization about 3000 B.C. until just recently. What sets Athenians apart are not these exclusions but the unusually large degree of inclusion, as well as the extraordinarily significant and rewarding participation of those included. It is useful to remember that what has been called the Jacksonian democracy in America co-existed with slavery, that women were everywhere denied the right to vote until this century, and that we continue to limit political participation to those of a specified age. To deny the title of democracy to Periclean Athens because of those excluded would be to employ a parochial and anachronistic set of criteria that produce paradoxical results. Certainly, no contemporary Greek doubted that Athens was a democracy; the only argument was whether democracy was good or bad, an argument almost unthinkable in our time.

The Athenians, on the other hand, would have been astonished at the claims of modern states to that title, even such states as the United States and Great Britain, for to them an essential feature of democracy was the direct and full sovereignty of the majority of citizens. Government by elected representatives, checks and balances, separation of powers, appointment to important offices, unelected bureaucracies, judicial life tenure, terms for elective office of more than one year—all these would have seemed clear and deadly enemies of what reasonable people might understand as democracy. These differences require a brief examination of how the Athenian democracy worked if we are to shed our modern prejudices and grasp its true character.

To use a helpful if anachronistic device, let us consider the three familiar branches of government: legislative, executive, and judiciary. At the heart of what we would call the legislative branch of the Athenian democracy was the assembly (*ekklesia*). It was open to all adult male citizens of Athens, during Pericles' lifetime perhaps as many as forty thousand men. Most Athenians lived many miles from the city and few owned horses, so attendance required a long walk to town. As a result, the number taking part was probably from five to six thousand, although some actions required a quorum of six thousand. The meetings took place on a hill called the Pnyx, not far from the Acropolis and overlooking the Agora. The citizens sat on the earth of the sharply sloping hill, and the speakers stood on a low platform. It was not easy for them to make themselves heard; Demosthenes, the great fourth-century orator, is said to have practiced speaking by the seashore over the crashing surf to make his voice strong enough for his work on the Pnyx.

We can get some idea of the opening of these meetings from a comic version in Aristophanes' *Acharnians*, performed in 425. The first speaker is a typical Aristophanic comic hero, an old-fashioned farmer who complains about the war because it keeps him in Athens, away from his farm in the country:

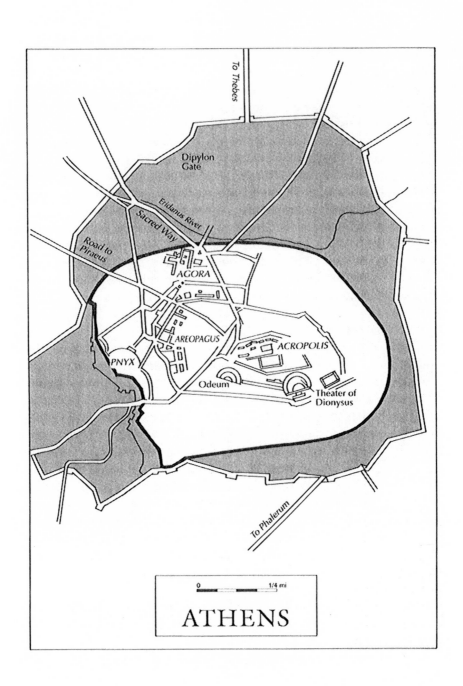

To Thebes

Dipylon
Gate

Eridanus River

Sacred Way

Road to
Piraeus

AGORA

AREOPAGUS

ACROPOLIS

PNYX

Odeum

Theater of
Dionysus

To Phalerum

0          1/4 mi

ATHENS

It is the day of an assembly and already morning, but the Pnyx is deserted. They are chattering in the Agora, dodging the rope dripping with red dye.[1] Even the Presidents of the Assembly have not arrived. They will be late, and when they finally come they will push and fight each other for a seat in the front row, streaming down all together, you can't imagine how; but they will say nothing about making peace. Oh my Athens! I am always the first to make the return voyage to the assembly and take my seat. And since I am alone, I groan, I yawn, I stretch my legs, I fart, I don't know what to do, I write, pull out my loose hairs, add up my accounts, looking off at my fields, longing for peace, hating the town, sick for my village-home, which never said "buy my charcoal, my vinegar, my oil"; the word "buy" is unknown there where everything is free. And so, I have come here fully prepared to shout, to interrupt and abuse the speakers if they talk about anything but peace. But here come these noon-time Presidents. Didn't I tell you? Didn't I predict how they would come? Everyone jostling for the front seat!

Next, the herald of the assembly says, "Move up! Move up within the consecrated area!" Then he recites the formula that regularly began debate in the assembly: "Who wishes to speak?" (19–45)

The scene in *Acharnians* omits the prayer that began sessions of the assembly and preceded the beginning of business. We can get an idea of what that was like from the parody Aristophanes presents in another of his comedies, the *Thesmophoriazusae*. The humor in the passage derives from the hilarious idea of women holding a political assembly and from Euripides' reputation as a misogynist. The herald recites the opening prayer, which included a curse on those who would subvert the democratic constitition:

Let there be silence, let there be silence. Pray to the Thesmophorae, Demeter and Kore, and to Plutus and Calligeneia and to Earth the foster mother, and to Hermes and the Graces that this present assembly and meeting may do what is finest and best, bringing advantage and good fortune both to Athens and to ourselves. And let the woman who acts and speaks best for the Athenian people and for Womankind win out. Pray for this and for good things for yourselves. Io Paean! Io Paean! Let us rejoice. (295–311)

The assembly of women responds with a choral song of prayer. Then the herald recites the curse:

Pray to the Olympian and Pythian and Delian gods and goddesses, and to the other gods that if anyone plots evil against the people of Wom-

ankind or is negotiating with Euripides or the Persians to the harm of
the people of Womankind, or aims at becoming a tyrant or at restoring
a tyrant, or denounces a woman for palming off someone else's baby as
her own, or if there is a slave who is an accomplice in her mistress'
intrigues and betrays her secret to her master, or who does not deliver
messages faithfully, or if there is a lover who gets what he wants from
a woman with lies but never carries out his promises . . . may he and
his family die a horrible death; and pray that the gods give many good
things to all the rest of you women. (330–51)

Again the chorus responds with a prayerful song. Then the herald
turns to business:

Listen all! Approved by the Council of Women, moved by Sostrata,
Timoclea was president and Lysilla secretary: to hold an assembly on
the middle day of the Festival of Thesmorphoria in the morning, when
we all have most leisure; the first item on the agenda will be: what
should be done with Euripides, since it is clear that he wrongs us all?
Who wishes to speak?

If we put aside the jokes at the expense of women, substitute "the
people of Athens" for "the people of Womankind," and add "those
who bring false reports and those who deceive the people" to the list
of those accursed we will be left with a fair approximation of the form
in which the assembly began its business.

But the real meetings on the Pnyx were rarely comic; they dealt
with serious questions. The assembly had four fixed meetings in each
of the ten periods into which the official year was divided, and special
meetings were called when needed. Topics included approval or disapproval of treaties and making declarations of war, assigning generals to campaigns and deciding what forces and resources they should
command, confirmation of officials or their removal from office,
whether or not to hold an ostracism, questions concerning religion,
questions of inheritance, and, in fact, everything else. In the second
meeting of each period "anyone who wishes can address the people
on whatever subject he likes, whether private or public," and the
third and fourth meetings discussed "all other kinds of business,"
whatever that might be.[2]

It is especially impressive for a citizen of a modern representative democracy to read of these great town meetings dealing directly
with questions of foreign policy—questions that could mean life or
death for those present at the debate and for their city. Many such

dramatic assemblies met in Pericles' time, but the one best described took place almost a century after his death. Philip of Macedon had marched into central Greece, only three days' march from Athens, one of his greatest enemies. What to do, whether to resist or try to negotiate such terms as they could, these decisions could determine the fate of Athens and its people, and they would be decided on the Pnyx by the assembled masses. Demosthenes, leader of the resistance to Philip, gives his version of the meeting.

> It was evening when a messenger came to the presidents of the Council to report that Elatea had been taken. In the midst of their dinner they got up at once and cleared the booths in the market-place . . . while others sent for the generals and called for the trumpeter, and the city was filled with commotion. At dawn on the next day the presidents called the Council to the Council House, and you [the Athenian people] went to the assembly, and before the Council began proceedings and made any proposal the whole people was seated up on the Pynx. Then the Council arrived, the presidents reported the news it had received and introduced the messenger who had brought it. When he had spoken the herald asked, "Who wishes to speak?" And no one came forward. (*De Corona* 169–70)

To get an idea of the distance between ancient and modern democracy we need only consider how an emergency—like the seizure of an American embassy—would be dealt with today in the United States. It would probably arrive first as secret information at some bureau of the government's vast and complex intelligence service. It would be treated as highly confidential and revealed only to a few people in the White House and the State and Defense departments. Policy would be discussed in a small, closed group, and the decision made by one man, the president. If there were no leaks, the people would hear of it only when the die had been cast.

Questions no less grave than the one confronting the Athenians of Demosthenes' time arose more than once in Periclean Athens. Each time, the popular assembly held a full debate and made the decision by raising their hands in a vote determined by a simple majority. There can be no stronger evidence of the full and final sovereignty of the Athenian people.

An assembly of thousands, of course, could not do its business without help. For that it relied on the Council of 500, chosen by lot from all the Athenian citizens. Although it performed many public functions that the larger body could not handle efficiently, its main responsibility was to prepare legislation for consideration by the people. In this respect, as in all others, the council was the servant of the assembly. The assembly could vote down a bill drafted by the council, change it on the floor, send it back with instructions for redrafting, or replace it with an entirely different bill. Full sovereignty and the real exercise of public authority rested directly with these great mass meetings. Almost no constitutional barrier prevented a majority of the citizens assembled on the Pnyx on a particular day from doing anything they liked.

In Athens, the executive was severely limited in extent, discretion, and power, and the distinction between legislative and judicial authority was far less clear than in our own society. To begin with, there was no president or prime minister, no cabinet or any elected official responsible for the management of the state in general, for formulating or proposing a general policy. There was nothing that Americans would call an "administration" or that the British would call a "government." The chief elected officials were the ten generals all serving one-year terms. As their title indicates, they were basically military officials who commanded the army and navy. They could be reelected without limit, and extraordinary men like Cimon and Pericles were elected almost every year. But they were most exceptional. The political power such men exercised was limited by their personal ability to persuade their fellow-citizens in the assembly to follow their advice. They had no special political or civil authority, and, except on military and naval campaigns, they could give no orders.

Even in military matters, the powers of the generals were severely limited. Leaders of expeditions were selected by vote of the full Athenian assembly, which also determined the size of the force and its goals. Before the generals took office they were subjected to a scrutiny of their qualifications by the Council of 500. After completing their year of service, their performance on the job, and especially their financial accounts, were subject to audit in a process called *euthyna*. Aristotle describes how the process could continue, even after that hearing:

> Officials called Examiners sit during the regular market hours at the statue of the eponymous hero of each tribe. If any citizen wishes to prefer a charge, either of a private or public nature, against any of the officials who have rendered their accounts at an *euthyna*, within three days he must write on a whitened board his own name, and the name of the man he accuses, the offense with which he charges him, and the fine he considers appropriate. (*Ath. Pol.* 48.4)

If the examiner decides the charge has any merit, he passes it on to the appropriate popular law court for final judgment. This was not the only control the people had over the few officials chosen by election. Ten times a year the popular assembly voted "to determine whether [the generals'] conduct of military affairs appears satisfactory; and if the people vote against someone's confirmation in office he is tried in a law court. If he is found guilty they assess his punishment or fine; if he is acquitted he resumes office." (61.2) Since elected office conferred prestige, elected officials were carefully watched lest they undermine the rule of the people.

Even with these severe controls, the Athenians filled only a few public offices by election, choosing their military officials, naval architects, some of their treasurers, and the superintendents of the water supply in that manner. All other officials were chosen by lot, in accordance with the democratic principle that any citizen was capable of performing civic responsibilities well enough, and its corollary that feared the fall of executive or administrative power into the hands of a few men, even those with experience or special abilities.

A partial list of the allotted offices in Athens indicates the kinds of public services that were entrusted to the average citizen chosen at random. First came the Council of 500, whose members could not serve more than two terms and whose duties included preparing legislation for the assembly and receiving foreign heralds and ambassadors. From this group came a board of presidents of the council, a foreman of that board, the officials who presided over meetings of the assembly, and the chairman of each day's meeting. The Treasurers of Athena, officials who supervised the great public imperial treasury that contained vast amounts of money, were also chosen by lot. So, too, were the vendors, who farmed out public contracts to work the publicly owned mines and to collect the state's taxes; the receivers, who collected public revenues and distributed them to the appropriate officials; the accountants, who checked the accounts of those officials; the examiners, already mentioned, who sat in the Agora to receive public complaints against public officials; and commissioners, who were responsible for maintaining public sanctuaries.

It is worth quoting Aristotle's description of the duties of another board of allotted officials, the city commissioners, for it provides a picture of Athenian life not often discussed:

They see to it that the flute-girls, harp-girls, and lyre-girls are not hired for more than two drachmas, and if several men are eager to hire the same girl they cast lots between them and assign her to the winner. They also take care that none of the dung-collectors deposits the dung within ten stadia of the city walls. They don't allow people to let their buildings encroach on the street, to build balconies that extend out over the street, to make drain-pipes that discharge into the street from above, or to have windows that open onto the street. They also remove the bodies of people who die in the streets, using public slaves [owned by the Athenian state] for the purpose. (50.2)

The Athenians also chose their market inspectors by lot; their duties included inspecting the purity of articles for sale. Commissioners of weights and measures supervised the honesty of purveyors, grain commissioners saw to it that there was no price gouging for grain and bread and that the loaves were of full weight, and there were many others. To a degree that is amazing to the modern mind the Athenians kept the management of their public life in the hands of the ordinary citizen, away from professionals, experts, bureaucrats, and politicians.

The Athenian judicial system may appear even stranger to the modern eye than the rest of the constitution. The distinction between assembly and law courts, for example, is almost a technicality. The idea behind both institutions was the same: full, direct, popular sovereignty. The panel of six thousand jurors who enlisted to serve in the courts each year, in fact, was called the Heliaea, a name given in other states to the assembly. From this panel on any given day jurors were assigned to specific courts and specific cases. The usual size of a jury was 501, although there were juries of from 51 to as many as 1501, depending on whether the case was public or private and how important it was. To avoid any possibility of bribery or partiality, the Athenians evolved an astonishingly complicated system of assignments that effectively prevented tampering.

Legal procedure was remarkably different from what takes place in a modern American court. The first surprise is the absence of any public prosecutor or state's attorney. There were, in fact, no lawyers at all. Complaints, whether civil or criminal, public or private, large or small, were registered and argued by private citizens. Plaintiff and defendant, suer and sued, each made his case in his own voice, if not in his own language. Anyone was free to hire a speechwriter to help him prepare his case, and the profession flourished, although it didn't reach its peak until many years after the days of Pericles. Another surprise is the lack of any judge. The jury was everything. No self-respecting Athenian democrat would allow some individual, whatever his qualifications, to tell him what was relevant evidence and what was not, or which laws and precedents applied. That would give too much weight to learning and expertise; it would also increase the danger of corruption and of undemocratic prejudice. It was, therefore, up to the contestants in the case to cite the relevant laws and precedents and up to the jurors to decide between them. Thus, in fundamental matters of justice and fairness, the Athenian democrat put little faith in experts.

In the courtroom, the plaintiff and defendant each had an opportunity to present his case, rebut his opponent, cite the law, produce witnesses, and sum up. Each phase was limited to a specific amount of time, which was kept by an official using a water clock, and no trial lasted more than a single day. Finally, the case went to the jury, which received no charge or instruction. It did not deliberate but just voted by secret ballot. A simple majority decided the issue. If a penalty was called for and not prescribed by law (as few were) the following procedure was used: the plaintiff proposed one penalty, the defendant a different one; the jury voted to choose one of these but could not propose any other. Normally, this process led both sides to suggest moderate penalties, for the jury would be put off by an unreasonable suggestion. Although critics complained that democracy made the Athenians litigious, the system contained a device meant to promote restraint: If the plaintiff did not win a stated percentage of the jurors' votes he was required to pay a considerable fine—to the state in public prosecutions, to the defendant in private ones. This must have served as a significant deterrent to frivolous, malevolent, and merely adventurous suits.

The Athenian system of justice had obvious flaws. Decisions could be quirky and unpredictable since they were unchecked by precedent. Juries could be prejudiced, and the jurors had no defense, except their own intelligence and knowledge, against speakers who cited laws incorrectly and distorted history. Speeches—unhampered by rules of evidence and relevance, and without the discipline imposed by judges—could be fanciful, false, and sophistical. Yet from a modern perspective, the Athenian system has a number of attractions. The American legal system and court procedure have been blamed for being excessively technical, verging on incomprehensibility, and for giving lawyers and judges the central role, which yield an enormous advantage to the rich who can afford to pay the burgeoning costs of litigation. The absence of a sufficient deterrent to unfounded lawsuits has helped to crowd court calendars. Time spent in jury selection and wrangling over legal technicalities stretches out still further a process that has no time limit. It is not uncommon for participants in a lawsuit to wait for many years before coming to trial; sometimes the plaintiff has died before his day in court. Not everyone is convinced that what is gained in the scrupulous protection of the participants' rights in an increasingly complex code of legal procedure is worth the resulting delay. And often decisions are made by judges on recondite legal or procedural grounds that are incomprehensible to the ordinary citizen.

For all its flaws, the Athenian system was simple, speedy, open, and easily understood by its citizens. It contained provisions aimed at producing moderate penalties and at deterring unreasonable lawsuits. It placed no barriers of legal technicalities or expertise between the citizens and their laws, counting as always on the common sense of the ordinary Athenian.

The Athenian democratic system, brought to its height in the time of Pericles, has been harshly criticized through the ages. Ancient writers directed most of their attacks against the idea of government by mass meeting and the selection of public officials by lot. The Athenian renegade Alcibiades told a Spartan audience: "As for democracy . . . nothing new can be said about an acknowledged foolishness." (Thucydides 6.89) Plato has Socrates make the same point more fully and seriously. He observes that when it is a matter of building a house or a ship the Athenian assembly listens only to experts. If someone without expert qualifications tries to give advice in such matters, "even if he is very handsome and rich and noble," they refuse to listen to him. Instead, "they laugh and hoot at him until either he is shouted down and withdraws of his own accord or the sergeants-at-arms drag him off or he is expelled by order of the presidents." But when the discussion is about affairs of state, "anyone can get up to speak—carpenter, tinker, cobbler, passenger and shipowner, rich and poor, noble and commoner—and nobody rebukes him, as they did in the earlier case, for trying to give advice when he has no knowledge and has not been taught." (*Protagoras* 319D–E)

The Athenians did, in fact, appreciate the importance of knowledge, skill, talent, and experience where they thought these things existed and could be used in the public interest. Thus they elected military officers, treasurers, naval architects, and managers of the water supply. If they did not elect professors of political science or philosophers or lawyers to govern and judge them, it was because they were skeptical that there was a useful expertise in these areas, and that if it did exist, it could safely and profitably be employed for the public good. It is not clear that the experience of the last twenty-five hundred years has shown them to be wrong.

Second, it is most unlikely that many fools or incompetents played a significant role in public affairs, perhaps no more so than today. The assembly itself was a far less unwieldy or incompetent body than is generally assumed. If a citizen attended no more than half the minimum number of yearly sessions, he would still hear twenty sets of debates by the ablest people in the state, chiefly elected officials or those formerly holding elective office, the leading politicians in all factions, and a considerable number of experts on a variety of subjects. Moreover, these were true debates in which it was not possible to hold to prepared remarks; speakers had to respond extemporaneously to hard questions and arguments from the opposition; nor were they irresponsible displays but serious controversies leading immediately to votes that had important consequences for the orators and their audience. If each attendant at the assembly had been listening to such discussions for an average of only ten years, such experiences alone must have fashioned a remarkable body of voters, probably more enlightened and sophisticated than any comparable group in history. Furthermore, each year five hundred Athenians served on the council, where every day they gained experience in the management of Athens' affairs, from the most trivial to the most serious, producing bills that served as the basis for the debates and votes of the assembly. In any assembly, therefore, thousands of those attending, perhaps a majority of them, would have had that kind of training on the council. In light of such experience, the notion that decisions were made by an ignorant multitude is not persuasive.

But were debates in the assembly carried on by ordinary Athenians, citizens without the necessary special knowledge and capacity for informed advice? The evidence suggests not, for there were impressive deterrents that would make an inexperienced, ill-informed, poorly educated man reluctant to speak up.

Years of attendance at meetings of the faculties of great American universities suggests that few, generally the same few, are bold enough to speak for or against some not very controversial policy argued in a group of fewer than one hundred, not to mention those rare larger meetings when subjects arousing passion are at issue. The people involved have extraordinary educations, unusual intellectual ability, and belong to a profession where public speaking is part of the trade. The meetings are conducted in the decorum of established rules of order that forbid interruption and personal attacks, yet most of those attending speak rarely, if ever; they are deterred by shyness and fear of embarrassment.

Meetings of the Athenian assembly, on the other hand, were not always quiet, seemly occasions. We should not forget Dicaeopolis' threat "to shout, to interrupt and abuse the speakers" or Plato's report of how the Athenians laughed and hooted or shouted down speakers who lacked what they thought was the necessary expertise. These informal deterrents alone sharply limited the number of speakers in the assembly. But there was also a formal device that encouraged them to take thought before speaking. At some time, perhaps during the career of Pericles but certainly not more than fifteen years after his death, the Athenians introduced a procedure called the *graphe paranomon* that had the effect of making the citizens in the assembly guardians of the constitution. Any citizen could object to a proposal made in the council or the assembly by asserting that it contradicted an existing law. This stopped action on the proposal or suspended its enactment if it had already been passed. The proposer was then taken before a popular court. If the jury decided against him, his proposal was disallowed and he was fined. Three findings of this kind deprived the proposer of his rights as a citizen. The expectations of the assembly and its procedures, therefore, make it most unlikely that ignorant incompetents played a significant role in its deliberations.

An even graver charge has been leveled through the ages against the kind of democracy promoted by Pericles. It is said to be inherently unstable, inviting faction and class warfare, to be careless of the rights of property, and to result in the rule of the poor, who are the majority, over the rich minority. The "Old Oligarch," the name given to the unknown author of an antidemocratic pamphlet written a few years after the death of Pericles, simply assumes that democracy promotes the interests of the poor at the expense of the rich. According to this writer, the Athenians chose democracy because "they preferred that the masses should do better than the regular citizens." (Pseudo-Xenophon, *Constitution of the Athenians* 1.1)

Plato says that "democracy originates when the poor win, kill or exile their opponents, and give the rest an equal share in the citizenship and in opportunities of office, and most of the magistrates are chosen by lot." (*Republic* 557A) He goes on to describe how democracy, after a time, degenerates into tyranny: The group that is most numerous and powerful is "the mass of the people, who work with their own hands, take little interest in politics, and possess very little." They come to the assembly only to get their share of the loot: "their leaders deprive the rich of their property, give some to the masses, keeping most of it for themselves." (565A) The attacks on the propertied lead them to defect from the democracy, which, in turn, causes the people to become a bloodthirsty mob. They rally to a leader and support him as he carries out "exiles and executions, hinting all the while at cancellations of debts and redistributions of lands until he reaches the point where he must either be killed by his enemies or become a wolf instead of a man—that is, a tyrant." (565E–566A)

The same charges were made by Aristotle and Polybius in antiquity, and by the eighteenth century they formed a powerful body of received opinion about ancient democracy. James Madison, holding views typical of the founders of the American republic, said that "democracies have ever been spectacles of turbulence and contention; have ever been found incompatible with personal security or the rights of property; and have in general been as short in their lives as they have been violent in their deaths."

Madison and his colleagues may be forgiven for mistaking the character of a regime brought to an end more than two thousand years earlier. But there is no such excuse for Plato's misrepresentation of the Athenian democracy. Starting with the fuller democracy instituted by Ephialtes and Pericles from 461, we discover an almost unbroken, orderly regime that lasted 140 years. Twice it was interrupted by oligarchic episodes. The first resulted from a coup in the midst of a long and difficult war and lasted four months. The second was imposed by the Spartans after the Peloponnesian War and lasted less than a year. On each occasion the full democracy was restored without turmoil—without class warfare, revenge, or confiscation of property. Through many years of hard warfare, military defeat, foreign occupation, and oligarchic agitation, the Athenian democracy persisted and showed a restraint and moderation rarely equaled by any regime.

This behavior is all the more remarkable in light of the political and constitutional conditions that prevailed in the Periclean democracy and thereafter. The mass of Athenians were not faced with the power of what has been called a military-industrial complex, thwarted by the complexities of representative government, checks and balances, and machinations of unscrupulous lobbyists, or manipulated by the irresistible deceptions of mass media. They had only to walk up to the Pnyx on assembly day, make speeches, and vote in order to bring about the most radical social and economic changes: the abolition of debt, confiscatory taxation of the rich, the simple expropriation of the wealthy few. But this they never did. Although political equality was a fundamental principle of democracy, economic equality had no place in the Athens of Pericles. On the contrary, the democracy he led defended the right of private property and made no effort to change its unequal distribution. The oath taken by jurors included the following clause: "I will not allow private debts to be cancelled, nor lands or houses belonging to Athenian citizens to be redistributed." (*Against Timocrates* 149) In addition, the chief magistrate each year swore that "whatever anyone owns before I enter this office he will have and hold the same until I leave it." (Aristotle, *Ath.Pol.* 56.2)

The last thirty years of the century were terrible times of war, plague, impoverishment, and defeat. Yet neither during or after the war did the Athenian masses interfere with private property or seek economic leveling. In the Periclean democracy, the Athenian citizen demanded only equality before the law, full political rights, and the kind of even chance these provided. By these rules he was willing to abide in the face of the greatest disasters and the greatest temptations. It was this politically equal, individualistic, law-abiding, and tolerant understanding of democracy that Pericles had done much to create and to which he could appeal and point with pride, confident that his fellow-citizens shared it.

We need not be surprised that ancient writers, hostile to democracy, blamed Pericles for his part in bringing it into existence. They accused him of corrupting the masses by bribing them with payment for public service and of using democratic reforms only for the purpose of increasing his own power. What does seem surprising from our perspective is that some of them denied that Athens in his time was truly a democracy at all. Under Pericles' leadership, says the historian Thucydides, his contemporary and admirer, Athens was a democracy in name only. (2.65.7) Plutarch, Pericles' ancient biographer, suggests that the Athenian statesman was not truly a democrat. Instead, he used a democratic platform to achieve power and then ruled the people, benevolently but firmly. After he had achieved a secure political position Pericles

was not the same man, submissive to the people and ready to obey and give in to the desires of the masses as a steersman yields to the winds. Instead he gave up this lax and effeminate demagogy . . . and tightened up the management of the state in an aristocratic and royal way. He used his leadership for the best interests of all in a straight and upright manner. In most things he led a willing people, persuading and teaching the masses, but sometimes, when they were very angry with him, he tightened the reins and compelled them to do what was good for them, very much like a physician who treats a complicated and chronic illness, sometimes with harmless goodies that please his patient, but sometimes with bitter medicine that brings them salvation. (15.2–3)

What are we to make of these suggestions? Thucydides' language calls to mind for modern readers the principate of Augustus at Rome. But to suggest the analogy with Periclean Athens is at once to see its inadequacy. The rule of Augustus rested on his absolute control of an enormously powerful military force, the only one left in the Mediterranean world. Pericles controlled no army, not even a police force. He depended entirely on the continued and freely expressed support of the Athenian people. All decisions of the state were decided by a majority in the assembly, where all elections were also held without coercion. His only office was that of general, subject to yearly elections, public inspection of his accounts, and constantly open to recall and public trial. There can be no doubt that such a regime was a true democracy.

What of the charge of insincerity—that Pericles used the democracy to achieve his own ends without believing in its principles? Pericles' political behavior is a sufficient refutation. He remained active for more than thirty years after acquiring the leadership of the dominant faction in Athens, and his prestige and influence grew with the years. At times his policies were rejected. On occasion he was compelled to stand by while his friends and loved ones came under attack by political enemies. In the year before his death, the assembly rejected his policy, removed him from office, and punished him with a heavy fine. They could have done the same at any time in the previous three decades, but of course they did not. Nor did Pericles ever try to protect himself against this democratic constitution or to place himself above it by changing its rules.

But why should such a man, who could live as a lord in an aristocracy or as the master in a despotism, prefer a democracy? In the case of Pericles several answers suggest themselves. First, support of popular government was part of a family tradition. His maternal grandfather, Cleisthenes, was the founder of democracy, and it was natural that his descendants should be imbued with respect for it. Second was the teaching of Anaxagoras. If we have understood it correctly, it provided a philosophical support for the democratic system of government as against the more hierarchical traditional beliefs, and Pericles was a man much influenced by rational, philosophic analysis.

Finally, we may speculate that Pericles was devoted to democracy because he saw better than any contemporary its capacity for greatness. Pericles, as we shall see, wanted to move his city toward a vision of unmatched quality. Athens' safety, wealth, and power depended on control of the sea and the men of the lower classes who were its oarsmen. It was their enthusiastic allegiance that the democracy had won. Other regimes, which excluded great numbers from active citizenship, thereby wasted a considerable portion of their potential strength. The need for oppressive regimes to keep watch on the excluded masses further sapped their potential power. Only democracy held the prospect of releasing the full energy of all the people, thereby creating a polis of unprecedented potential. Perhaps that prospect, more than anything else, made Pericles the convinced democrat that he always was.

# 4

# SOLDIER

The triumph of democracy in Athens produced a sharp change in the city's foreign policy and unleashed a war that threatened the new regime, Athens' control of its empire, even the autonomy of the city. Modern scholars call it the First Peloponnesian War, a contest between the Delian League led by Athens and the Peloponnesian League under Spartan hegemony. The two sides fought intermittently on land and sea between about 460 and 445. At the peak of the Athenians' power their forces stretched from Sicily to the Nile delta, and their armies controlled Central Greece and access to the Peloponnesus. At other times they were compelled to defend the frontiers of their homeland and the very walls of their city. During this war, Pericles was required to act not only as political leader

65  □

and constitutional reformer but also as diplomat, strategist, and the commander of fleets and armies. To all these activities he brought his unusual talents as well as an even rarer understanding of their interrelationships.

The political revolution in Athens brought with it a diplomatic revolution in the relations among the Greek states. On the dismissal of their army from Sparta the Athenians broke off the alliance they had made with the Spartans at the time of the Persian War. They also concluded full offensive and defensive alliances with Argos, Sparta's neighbor and bitter enemy, and with the Thessalians in northern Greece, famed for the strength and excellence of their cavalry. The first alliance clearly implied a threat to Sparta; the second increased the military power supporting that threat. The new hostility revealed how tenuous had been the previous peace and friendship wrought by Cimon: It was really more an alliance between factions than states. A hard core of Spartans was suspicious, jealous, and fearful of the power of Athens and unwilling to share Sparta's position of leadership among the Greeks. Sparta's Athenian enemies were aware of Spartan hostility and unwilling to overlook the obvious threat to their interests. They chose to extend Athenian involvement to the mainland of Greece, thereby challenging Sparta's heretofore unquestioned control of the Peloponnesus and its superiority in land warfare.

Infantry was the dominant military arm throughout the classical period, and the Spartans, with their well-trained and superbly disciplined hoplite phalanx, had the best infantry there was. The hoplite was a heavily armed infantryman who had a short sword at his waist but whose chief weapon was a pike of from seven and a half to nine feet in length. He was protected by a breastplate, helmet, and greaves; on his left arm he carried a large, round, heavy shield that protected his front and his left side and extended some distance beyond his left shoulder. This extension protected the exposed right side of his neighbor, so each hoplite sought to protect his own right by moving behind the extending shield of his neighbor. The shield was large enough to serve as a stretcher for a wounded man or a pall for a dead one. A terrible encumbrance in flight, they were discarded whenever the hoplites retreated. The soldiers were formed into a phalanx that was organized in close order, usually at least eight ranks deep. So long as the hoplites fought bravely and held their ground, there would be few casualties and no defeat. But if even a small number gave way, the result was generally a rout.

The usual hoplite battle in Greece was between the armies of two poleis quarreling over a piece of land. One army invaded the territory of the other when the crops were almost ready for harvest. The defending army had no choice but to protect its fields or surrender; otherwise its crops would be destroyed and its people would go hungry. The phalanx was a community effort that relied on the courage, discipline, and dedication of the individual soldier. Each citizen's survival depended on the cooperation of his comrades, and the city, in turn, could not exist without the efforts of every citizen.

In its subordination of the individual to the community, Sparta seemed closest to the ideal polis. At first, the Spartans were not very different from the other Greeks, but about 725 the pressure of a growing population led them to launch a war of conquest against their neighbor Messenia. Victory gave them as much land as they would ever need. They reduced the conquered people to slaves (helots) so that the Spartans would be freed from having to work the land that supported them. But a revolt of the helots in the third quarter of the seventh century, aided by neighboring states in the Peloponnesus, turned into a long and bitter war that threatened the very existence of Sparta. This was the turning point in Spartan history. The Spartans could not hope to keep down the helots, who outnumbered them perhaps ten to one, without making fundamental changes in their way of life.

The new system exerted control over each Spartan from birth, when state officials decided which infants were physically fit to survive. At the age of seven, each Spartan boy was taken from his mother and turned over to instructors who trained him in athletics and the military arts and taught him to endure privation, bear physical pain, and live off the country, by theft if necessary. At twenty, the Spartan youth was enrolled in the army and lived in barracks with his companions until the age of thirty. Bonding between generations was achieved by a homosexual liaison between a young man and an older man in which the physical relationship was supposed to be subordinate to the improvement of the younger man's character by his older mentor. When this rite of passage was complete, the physical relationship ended; the personal bond, however, was meant to last and helped tie the community together.

Marriage was permitted for these young men, but it was a strange sort of marriage. A young Spartan man could visit his wife only infrequently and then only by stealth. At thirty, the Spartan man became a full citizen, an "equal" (*homoios*). He took his meals at a public mess in the company of fourteen comrades. His food, a simple diet, often consisted of a kind of black soup that appalled the other Greeks. Military service was required to the age of sixty; only then could the Spartan retire to his home and family.

This regimen extended to the women, too. They did not take military training, but female infants were examined for fitness in the same way as males. Girls were taught gymnastics, were permitted greater freedom than other Greek women, and were equally indoctrinated with the Spartan ideals. It was a commonplace among the Greeks that the Spartan women were even fiercer than the men. Spartan mothers sent their sons into battle telling them to come back either with their shields or on them.

The entire system was designed to change the natural feelings of devotion to wife, children, and family into a more powerful commitment to the polis. Privacy, luxury, and even comfort were sacrificed to the purpose of producing soldiers whose physical powers, training, and discipline made them the best in the world. Nothing that might turn the mind away from duty was permitted. Neither family nor money—coin itself was forbidden lest it corrupt the desires of Spartans—were allowed to interfere with the only permitted ambition: to win glory and respect by bravery in war.

Although the Athenians, like most Greeks, cherished the same ideals as the Spartans, they had no reason to abandon the normal adherence to individual and family values even before the arrival of democracy. The coming of popular government and the wealth from their empire made them even more devoted to personal liberty than before. The contrast between the leaders of the two alliances could not be greater. The wars between Sparta and Athens that dominated the last six decades of the fifth century represented a struggle not only between great states but between competing ideas, political systems, and ways of life.

No less different were their approaches to war. Sparta was a military state with the best hoplite army anywhere, and its allies provided contingents of such numbers and quality that no one could match a Peloponnesian army under Spartan command. The Athenians commanded a naval empire that dominated the sea as the Spartans did the land, and their allies contributed ships or money. Although the Athenians themselves fought well in their phalanx, as they had shown against Greek opponents and at Marathon, as well as during the Persian invasion of 480, they could not hope to match Peloponnesian numbers in a full-scale battle. This made Athens vulnerable to attack from the land. If an enemy could destroy the Athenian army or force it to take refuge behind the city walls, the great imperial navy would be of no avail. A besieging army could destroy the Athenian farms, olive trees, and grape vines; cut the city off from its port; and starve the people into submission. The Spartans and their Peloponnesian League were the only Greeks capable of such a strategy. Cimon had avoided the problem by staying on good terms with the Spartans, but when his opponents rejected his policy they were faced with the need for a new one. Alliances with Sparta's Peloponnesian enemies offered one tempting possibility, and the democrats seized on it after the ostracism of Cimon. When that strategy failed, Pericles confronted the next great challenge of his career: to devise a way of dealing with Sparta's great military power.

The new Athenian alliances with Argos and Thessaly threw down the gauntlet to the Spartans, but very soon the Athenians took actions that were still more provocative. After some years of holding out on Mt. Ithome, the rebellious helots surrendered on condition that they be allowed to leave the Peloponnesus unharmed. The Spartans must have expected that they would scatter throughout the Greek world and pose no further threat, but the Athenians arranged matters otherwise. Having lately acquired the port of Naupactus, near the narrows on the northern shore of the Corinthian Gulf, they now offered it as a home for the departing helots, who gladly accepted. Naupactus was a fine naval base, ideally located to interfere with the commercial and naval operations of many of Sparta's allies, especially Corinth, and the grateful helots could be relied upon to make it available to Athens. But these strategic considerations were secondary. The Athenians became the benefactors of the helots "because of the hatred for the Spartans they already felt." (Thucydides 1.103.3)

Next, the Athenians took a step that troubled the Spartans even more. Two allies of Sparta, Corinth and Megara, were embroiled in a war over a piece of border territory between them. The Megarians were losing, so they offered to secede from Sparta's Peloponnesian League and make an alliance with Athens in return for help against the Corinthians. The proposal was both opportune and dangerous. The Megarians inhabited a small, infertile plain, with mountains at both ends, on the Isthmus of Corinth. It could not produce enough grain to feed the 25,000 to 40,000 Megarians, but the highlands had enough vegetation to feed the flocks of sheep that produced Megara's chief export: coarse, low-priced woolen coats. They also raised pigs, and among their other exports were garlic and a strong-tasting salt. During the great Peloponnesian War, when the Megarians were suffering from interference with their trade and devastations of their land, Aristophanes made fun of their misery and starvation. Informers "kept denouncing Megara's little coats; and if anyone ever saw a cucumber, a hare, a suckling pig, a clove of garlic, or a lump of salt, all were denounced as Megarian and confiscated." (*Acharnians*, 519–22)

Caught between two powerful neighbors, the Megarians had nonetheless remained independent through the centuries, strong enough to fight off the Corinthians and the Athenians in turn. By the beginning of the sixth century, however, they had lost disputed border territory on the west to Corinth and the island of Salamis in the Saronic Gulf to Athens, and these losses must have made the Spartan offer of alliance a welcome protection against both threats. The Megarians remained loyal until the Spartans, distracted by the earthquake and helot rebellion, abandoned them to the mercies of the opportunistic Corinthians. The Spartans' ensuing breach with Athens offered them a way out. If the Spartans abandoned them they would change sides and offer themselves to the Athenians in return for support against Corinth.

Megara, on Athens' western border, had enormous strategic importance. Its western port, Pegae, gave access to the Corinthian Gulf, which the Athenians could only reach by a long and dangerous route around the whole Peloponnesus. Its eastern port, Nisaea, lay on the Saronic Gulf, where an enemy could use it to launch a swift attack on Piraeus, the Athenian home port. Even more important, Athenian control of the mountain passes of the Megarid, possible only with a friendly Megara, would make it very difficult, if not impossible, for a Peloponnesian army to invade Attica. An alliance with Megara would bring security against attack and thereby provide freedom to pursue opportunities wherever they arose. On the other hand, the alliance would mean war with Corinth, a rich and powerful state not to be taken lightly.

From the time of Homer, Corinth had earned the epithet "wealthy," in part because of its excellent craftsmen who made and sold beautiful pottery, bronzes, and objets d'art, but chiefly because of its geographical position, which gave it enormous advantages in commerce. The Corinthians had taken advantage of their position to build a stone causeway across the isthmus. A ship traveling the east-west route could be hauled across from one port to the other, thereby avoiding the voyage around the Peloponnesus and making Corinth the Suez or the Panama of its day. Few ships failed to stop there, for

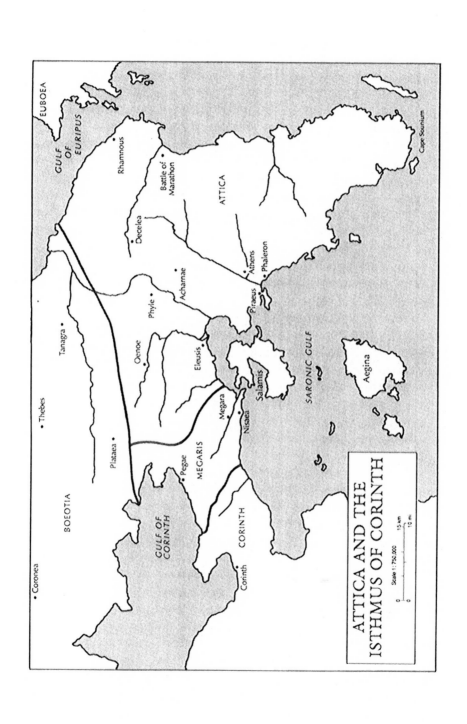

ATTICA AND THE
ISTHMUS OF CORINTH

Scale 1: 750,000

15 km

10 mi

EUBOEA

GULF OF EURIPUS

Rhamnous

Battle of Marathon

ATTICA

Decelea

Athens

Phaleron

Praeus

Coronea

Thebes

Tanagra

BOEOTIA

Phyle

Acharnae

Oenoe

Eleusis

Plataea

Pegae

MEGARIS

Megara

Nisaea

Salamis

SARONIC GULF

Aegina

GULF OF CORINTH

Corinth

CORINTH

Cape Sounium

not only was the route around the Peloponnesus long and dangerous, especially in the seas around its southern tip, Cape Malea, but the city was located on an isthmus that was the only land route from the Peloponnesus in the south to central and northern Greece. Control of the north-south route by land and the east-west route by sea allowed the Corinthians to impose a tax on trade passing through their territory in all directions, thereby swelling the city's coffers.

Nor was that all, for Corinth was also a tourist attraction and a sailor's town. The Isthmian Games, one of the four great religious-athletic festivals of the Greek world, were held in Corinthian territory and attracted large crowds. So did the Temple of Aphrodite, which was "so rich that it owned more than a thousand temple-slaves, prostitutes whom both men and women had dedicated to the goddess of love." (Strabo 378) These attractions brought crowds of tourists to the city and enriched the local merchants, craftsmen, and shopkeepers; and they were costly, whence arose the proverb "not for every man is the voyage to Corinth."

The Corinthians were the richest of Sparta's Peloponnesian allies and the most independent. In many ways they resembled the commercial republic of Venice in the late middle ages. They had colonies in the west and in the Aegean, in the midst of the Athenian Empire. They had a well-established, oligarchic government lead by men with long experience in diplomacy and negotiation. Their position as a center of trade gave them excellent access to information and to the ears of leading figures from other states. They would be formidable opponents.

Even more serious than alienating Corinth, accepting a state in rebellion from Sparta into an Athenian alliance amounted to an act of war against the Peloponnesian League. Nevertheless, the Athenians did not hesitate to make the alliance, to place a garrison in Nisaea, and to build long walls connecting the port to Megara. As far as they were concerned, the war was a fact and the Megarian alliance a heaven-sent chance to fight it safely and successfully.

The Megarian alliance, Thucydides tells us, was the reason that "the bitter hatred of the Corinthians for the Athenians first came into being" (1.103.4), and before long Athens was fighting Corinth and her Peloponnesian allies in a struggle that modern scholars call the First Peloponnesian War. Even as they prepared for that great conflict, the Athenians were drawn into another major commitment far from home. An Athenian imperial fleet of considerable size was already engaged in a campaign at Cyprus as part of the war against Persia and the effort to gain command of the sea. The expedition may have been sent out before the fall of Cimon; but well after that event, when the Ephialtic faction had gained control, a rebellion broke out in the Persian province of Egypt. Responding to pleas for help from the rebel King Inaros of Libya, the Athenians abandoned Cyprus and sent their powerful fleet of two hundred ships to the Nile. Just as they were facing a serious war in Greece they undertook a major campaign against the Persians in Egypt, an act that appears more than a little reckless.

Pericles undoubtedly approved the policies adopted by his faction, and since he was its foremost spokesman, he surely took the lead in persuading the Athenians to accept them. Hostility to Sparta was at the center of the martyred Ephialtes' policy and had brought his faction to power. It was inconceivable that his collaborator and heir would not continue to promote it. As for the attack on a Persian province, that was fully in accord with the program supported by all Athenians since 479. Pericles' father had helped begin it, and Pericles himself had led a fleet far to the east into waters controlled by the Persians in the late 460s. Egypt, moreover, was the most tempting of targets, rich in wheat and treasure. A victory for the rebels would weaken the Persians and strengthen the Athenians. Thus we may well believe that Pericles favored aid to the Egyptian rebels, too.

In 460, the Athenian Empire was still new. It had won an amazing series of victories over foreigners and Greeks with barely a setback. The regime of the completed democracy was even newer, and its leaders, like those of the young French and Russian revolutions, may have thought that free men inspired by a noble cause would sweep all before them. Events would prove them too optimistic, but only after a long time and very great success. Pericles himself was still young, and he, more than most, had known nothing but astonishing success. He was ready to run risks to achieve great results.

The strategy of the Athenians can only be deduced from their actions, for no ancient writer discusses it. The Athenians were committed to helping the Megarians, so they must have planned to join their allies in defeating Corinth. The Corinthians would be sure to call on Sparta and the rest of the Peloponnesian League for help, and the full Peloponnesian levy far outnumbered any army the Athenians and their allies could put into the field. Part of the Athenian hopes may have rested on Sparta's continued weakness resulting from the helot rebellion, which might delay her reaction until it was too late. But the key to Athenian strategy must have been Argos.

The Argives had once been the dominant power in the Peloponnesus. Their tyrant Pheidon had defeated the Spartans in a great battle and gained control of the Olympic festival and of the strategically important island of Aegina. He imposed a uniform system of weights and measures on the whole Peloponnesus, and tradition credits him with minting the first silver coins in Greece. Over the centuries, however, the Spartans had gained the upper hand. They won control over the disputed border area of the Thyreatis, which has been called the Alsace-Lorraine of the Peloponnesus and which remained a source of friction between the two states. Early in the fifth century, the Spartans won a crushing victory in battle, almost destroying the Argive state. After the Persian War, from which Argos had stood aloof rather than fight under Spartan command, the Argives recovered their strength and took advantage of Spartan distraction to dominate the small cities of the Argolid and its boundaries. Under a new democratic constitution and with a unified home territory, Argos was determined to restore its power and prestige and to challenge Sparta again for control of the Peloponnesus. The Argives' alliance with Athens in 461 proves they were confident and ready to fight.

The emergence of a strong and independent Argos hostile to Sparta offered the Athenians a way to overcome the military inferiority that threatened the safety of Athens and seemed to prevent the victory of a naval power over Greece's dominant power on land. By making alliances with Sparta's Peloponnesian enemies, the Athenians could in effect fight the war in Sparta's home territory, keeping Athens safe.

The strategy the Athenians adopted under Pericles is similar to the one used by his ward Alcibiades four decades later, about which we are much better informed. His goal, too, was to dismantle the Peloponnesian League without pitting the Athenian army against the much stronger infantry of the enemy. In 461, as in 421, alliance with Argos was the starting point. That city was encouraged to seek resumption of its ancient role as master of the Peloponnesus by attracting Peloponnesian states away from the Spartans and bringing them over to a new alliance led by Argos.

The time was ripe for such a plan, for the winds of change were blowing in the northern and western Peloponnesus. Elis and Mantinea had each become a unified state instead of a collection of villages, and each adopted a democratic constitution certain to cause suspicion in Sparta and to create sympathy for democratic Argos. Elis had gone so far as to expand its power to the borders of Messenia,

Sparta's chief granary and the home of most of her helots, much to the alarm of Sparta. Tegea and other cities in the region of Arcadia, to the north of Sparta, had fought and lost wars against Sparta a decade or so earlier. It is plausible to think that they still carried a grudge and might be swept along in a new movement against the Spartans. Coastal states might be torn away from them by means of interference with their trade and attacks on their lands and cities launched from the sea. Distracted by the Argives and such allies as they could gather, and without a navy to fight at sea, the Spartans could give no help. As a result, the coastal states might fall away like ripe fruit from a tree.

Such was the strategy of Alcibiades in the later period, but in the years following 461, the Argives never achieved leadership of such an alliance, as they did in the years following 421. The strategy suggested for the Athenians in 461, therefore, must remain a hypothesis. Yet their actions in the First Peloponnesian War are consistent with it, and none better has been put forth.

Athens' role in this strategy was primarily naval but partly military. First and foremost, Athens had to be able to support Argos in case of attack by Sparta and her allies. This required the ability to get forces there quickly and securely, which meant by sea. The first engagements of the war are best understood as part of an attempt to protect Argos and to gain control of the coast between Athens and the port of Argos to assure this vital line of communication. Perhaps about 460, the Athenians and the Argives defeated the Spartans at the little town of Oenoe in Argive territory on the road from Sparta. The Spartan expedition probably came in response to the Argive alliance with Athens and the trouble it promised, but the Argive and Athenian armies were ready and won the victory. It was not a great battle, but to win any battle on land against the Spartans was a remarkable achievement. The Argives dedicated a group of sculptures to commemorate it at Delphi, and the Athenians put up a commemorative painting on the famous Painted Porch (*Stoa Poikile*) in the Agora, near the painting of the battle of Marathon.

Not much later, the Athenians attacked the Argolic peninsula to the east of Argos to gain control of the sea route between them. They took some coastal towns but were checked at Halieis, which has the best harbor between Athens and Argos. In Athenian hands, it would also serve as a base of operations against Epidaurus, the major Peloponnesian city on the Saronic Gulf. Understanding the threat, the Corinthians and their Sicyonian neighbors along with the Epidaurians came to Halieis and prevented its fall. In a companion battle, the Athenian fleet crushed its Peloponnesian opponents in the waters of the Saronic Gulf. These early battles were inconclusive: Argos was safe and Athens ruled the sea, but the route between them was not fully secure.

Athenian activities on the western shore of the Saronic Gulf were also aimed at the island of Aegina, long threatened by Athens' location on its eastern shore. Aegina had once been the leading naval power in Greece and a major commercial center. Herodotus mentions an "ancient hatred" between Athens and Aegina, and whatever the origin, they often fought one another because of it. By the 460s, Athenian trade and naval strength had easily surpassed Aegina's, but Pericles still regarded the hostile island in the Saronic Gulf, easily visible from Attica, as a threat. In one of his more memorable remarks he called it "the eyesore of the Piraeus" and urged that it be removed. In 458, the Athenians and their allies fought and won a great naval battle against the Aeginetan and Peloponnesian fleets off Aegina. They landed and besieged the city, which surrendered the following spring. The Aeginetans were compelled to destroy their walls, surrender their fleet, and become subjects in the Athenian Empire, paying the highest tribute of all. The Saronic Gulf was becoming an Athenian lake.

While the siege was still under way the Corinthians invaded Megarian territory. They hoped to relieve the pressure on Aegina and, perhaps, to capture Megara, for the Athenian forces were stretched very thin at the time. A large force was tied up at Aegina and another large contingent was still off in Egypt. In a remarkable display of determination, the Athenians withdrew no troops from either theater. Instead, they sent the conservative general Myronides with a force composed of those normally excused from service in the field because of age: boys under twenty and men over fifty. This unprepossessing corps marched into the Megarid and won a smashing and humiliating victory that made Megara safe. In later years, the comic poets would celebrate Myronides as a sturdy representative of the "good old days," before the corruption of the extreme democracy took hold: "When noble Myronides was in charge no one would have dared to take pay for doing his civic duty." (Aristophanes, *Lysistrata* 302–6)

The first few years of the war were notable for the lack of Spartan participation. At most, some Spartans may have been among the three hundred Peloponnesians sent to help Aegina in its siege. But that was a trivial commitment to the defense of their allies. Why were the Spartans so inactive? If Athenian control of the routes through Megara prevented an invasion of Attica, why didn't the Spartans launch a serious attack against Argos, or send significant help to Corinth or Aegina? If they were still weakened and distracted by the helot rebellion, how were they able to send a substantial force farther from home into central Greece, as they did in 458?

The explanation for Spartan inactivity is less material than political. Throughout the entire history of the rivalry with Athens in the fifth century, opinion in Sparta was divided. There was always a faction eager to destroy Athenian power, and willing to fight a war to do so. Normally they were in the minority and failed to get their way. In 475, alarmed by Athens' growing power as head of the Delian League, this faction proposed a war against Athens to regain leadership at sea, but the decision went against them. The majority of Spartans wanted peace and trusted Cimon to lead Athens along a safe path. In 465, at least some Spartans agreed to an invasion of Attica during the Thasian rebellion against Athens. We cannot know whether they could have persuaded the Spartan people to keep that promise, for the great earthquake and helot rebellion made that impossible.

It must have been this same faction that raised the alarm in 461, leading to the expulsion of Cimon's Athenian army from the Peloponnesus. Whatever the motives for that insult, the majority of Spartans must quickly have seen it as a great mistake when it led to the overthrow of Cimon, the victory of his enemies, and the diplomatic revolution that confronted Sparta with a dangerous hostile alliance. The troubling Megarian alliance with Athens resulted from Corinthian actions in behalf of Corinthian interests that were of no intrinsic concern to Sparta. The pacific majority of Spartans must have asked why they should enter a dangerous war on behalf of Corinth. They seem to have chosen to let the Corinthians and their friends in Sicyon and Epidaurus fight the battle on their own behalf, no doubt underestimating the capacity and determination of the Athenians to fight successfully on so many fronts at once. Both Spartan kings, moreover, were of a peaceful persuasion. Archidamus, the senior of them, took no part in any campaign in this First Peloponnesian War. He was a personal friend of Pericles, and he still resisted the proposal to rush into war against Athens in the great Peloponnesian War three decades later. Pleistoanax, the younger king, would be notorious throughout his life for his eagerness for peace with Athens. Under these circumstances, it is not surprising that the Spartans held back from serious fighting in the first years of the war.

By 458, however, the situation had changed. Aggressive Athenian actions vindicated the suspicions of the anti-Athenian faction: The Athenians were aiming at the destruction of Spartan power. They had seized port cities in the eastern Peloponnesus, attacked Aegina, and humiliated the Corinthian army. When Aegina fell, as it surely would, the Athenians would have destroyed the only major fleet available to challenge them at sea, gained new financial resources, and acquired a convenient base for launching attacks on the ports of Corinth, Epidaurus, and other Spartan allies on and near the Saronic Gulf. If the Spartans remained inert some of their allies might fall to Athens; even if they held out, Sparta's incapacity to help them would undermine her position as leader of the league that was the basis for her security. It was clear, therefore, that the Spartans had to act.

In the spring of 457, the Spartans loaded an army of fifteen hundred of their own men and ten thousand allies on to ships and sent them across the Corinthian Gulf into central Greece. A Spartan army was usually commanded by a king, but this one was led by the regent Nicomedes on behalf of Pleistoanax, who was still too young. (Archidamus was also available, but he must have disapproved of the campaign.) The action took the Athenians by surprise, for they had no fleet in place to prevent the crossing.

The ostensible reason for the expedition was to defend the little central Greek state of Doris from an attack by the neighboring Phocians. Doris was the legendary home of the Dorian family of Greeks, of which Sparta was the most powerful member. Legend made it the point from which the sons of Heracles launched the invasion that brought the Peloponnesus under Dorian control, and the Spartans regarded it as their mother city. But putting down the Phocians, which the Spartans quickly did, did not require so large a force, and companion events suggest an ulterior motive.

The Spartans did not go directly home from the Dorian campaign; they lingered, instead, at the town of Tanagra in Boeotia, on the frontier of Attica. This large, populous, and fertile region was chiefly agricultural. Its plains encouraged the use of horses and the development of cavalry, but its people knew little of ships, and its cities had no navies. By Athenian standards, Boeotia was a backward area full of country bumpkins who produced wonderfully good things to eat but ate too much of it themselves. The Athenians thought of them as uneducated, slow, and stupid and fixed on them the epithet

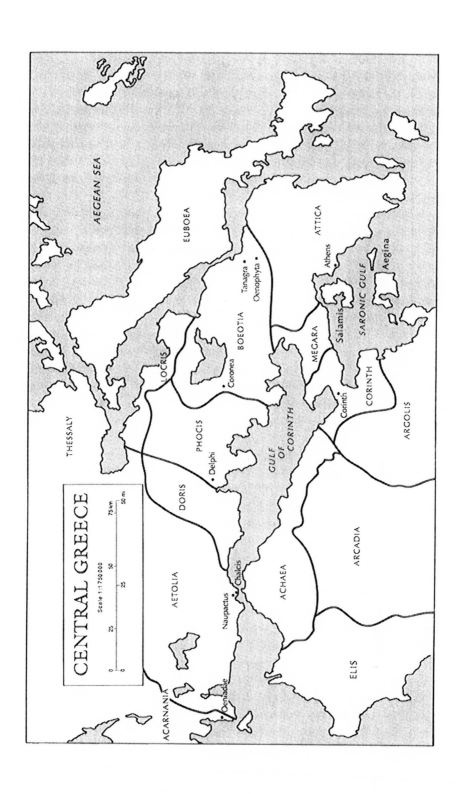

CENTRAL GREECE

Scale 1:1,750,000

AEGEAN SEA

THESSALY

EUBOEA

LOCRIS

BOEOTIA

Tanagra
Oenophyta

Coronea

PHOCIS

Delphi

DORIS

GULF
OF
CORINTH

ATTICA

Athens

MEGARA

Salamis

SARONIC GULF

Aegina

CORINTH

Corinth

ARGOLIS

AETOLIA

Naupactus

Chalcis

ACHAEA

ARCADIA

ELIS

ACARNANIA

Oeniadae

"Boeotian swine." This unflattering name had already become well known by the first part of the fifth century, as we learn from a verse by the greatest of Boeotian poets, who wrote: "Rouse up your comrades, Aeneas, first to proclaim the name of Hera Parthenia, and then to know if, with true words, we can escape that ancient rebuke, Boeotian swine." (Pindar, *Olympian* 6) The Boeotians may have been less quick than the Athenians, but they were numerous and good fighters. Together with the Spartans and their Peloponnesian allies, they posed a serious threat to Athens.

Thucydides tells us that the Spartans stayed at Tanagra because the Athenians, aware of their location, would now send a fleet to block the sea route and that Athens' control of Megara already blocked the way by land. These facts, however, should have been predictable. When the Spartans left home they must have known that they might have to fight their way back—and they must have been willing to do so.

Thucydides also supplies a better explanation. The Spartans moved to the Boeotian frontier of Attica in part because "some Athenians secretly invited them in, hoping to put an end to the democracy and to the building of the long walls." (1.107.4) These walls—one connecting the fortification wall that ringed Athens with the one that protected its port and naval base at Piraeus, another running from Athens to the old harbor at Phalerum, and a third, built a dozen or so years after the first two, running parallel to the first and less than two hundred yards from it—were built specifically upon the advice of Pericles. They allow us to see for the first time the new strategy he was planning for the defense of Athens and her empire. When the walls were completed they would turn the area between Athens, Piraeus, and Phalerum into an island unassailable by land and invincible so long as Athens maintained control of the sea and the empire and revenues it provided. If the Athenians were prepared to abandon their homes and farms in the country when an enemy army invaded, they could not be defeated, since their empire would allow them to hold out indefinitely. Pericles had devised a revolutionary strategy, but it was ahead of its time. The Athenians were far from ready to make the sacrifice in 457 or soon thereafter. The possibility existed, however, and would serve them well in the future.

If the Athenians had adopted Pericles' new strategy they would also have strengthened the newly extended democracy by emphasizing its navy at the expense of the more conservative infantry and the aristocratic cavalry. That prospect may well be what prompted this

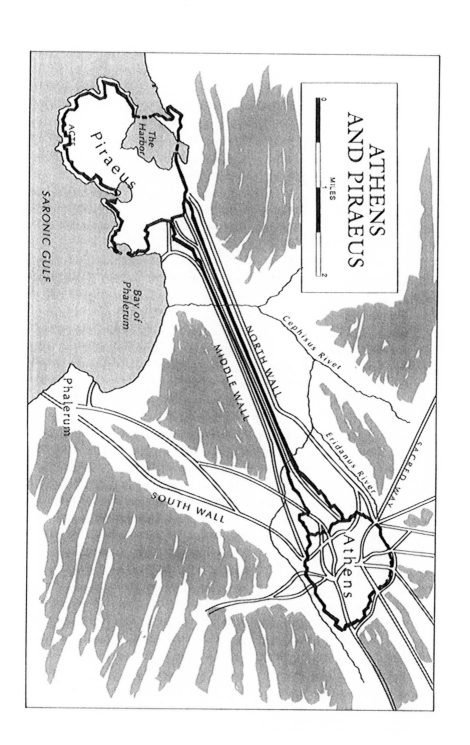

ATHENS
AND PIRAEUS

MILES

SARONIC GULF

Piraeus

The Harbor

ACT

Bay of
Phalerum

Phalerum

NORTH WALL

MIDDLE WALL

SOUTH WALL

Cephisus River

Eridanus River

SACRED WAY

Athens

rare case of a treasonous conspiracy in Athenian history. Cimon was in exile, and in his absence his supporters were leaderless, frightened, and, as a result, irresponsible. Had Cimon been present it seems certain that he would have discouraged and prevented their activities. All we know of him shows that he was comfortable with the Athenian democracy; he preferred a more moderate variety, but he could live happily even under the constitution created by Ephialtes and Pericles. He never allowed partisanship to stand in the way of patriotism, but he was absent and could not control the more reckless elements of his faction. Probably these extremists had communicated with the Spartans even before they left the Peloponnesus, and it is certain that they urged Nicomedes to attack the Athenians before they could complete their long walls.

But the Spartan commander had more to rely on than the exhortations and promises of Athenian traitors. Thebes, the chief city of Boeotia and the proud home of the legendary and tragic Oedipus, had been at odds with the Athenians since the previous century. Although the Thebans had long wanted to bring all the Boeotian towns under their control, they had never succeeded. During the Persian invasion, the Thebans had sided with the invader. So when the Persian army fled, their city was disgraced, their confederation broken up, and the Boeotian cities under Theban control made autonomous. Since the Persian War, Thebes had recovered some of her strength and had begun to restore the confederation. When the Thebans learned of Sparta's impending expedition into central Greece, they sought to use the opportunity to their own advantage. After the ensuing battle of Tanagra, they asked the Spartans "to help their city to gain the entire hegemony of Boeotia," in return for which "They would themselves make war on the Athenians so that there would be no need for the Spartans to bring an army outside of the Peloponnesus." (Diodorus of Sicily 11.81.1–4) Before the expedition, the Spartans must have promised to join them in fighting the Athenians on their way home from Doris and to carry the fight to the Athenians thereafter.

The appearance of a large force of Spartan and Theban soldiers on the northern frontier of Attica was cause for serious concern. When the Athenians learned that the Peloponnesians and Boeotians were at Tanagra, they went out to confront them. Their long walls were not complete, but they were not prepared to let the enemy ravage their land. The Athenian infantry was bolstered by contingents from the empire and by a thousand men from Argos. In addition, the

Thessalians sent a force of cavalry, which turned out to be no great favor. Although the Athenians outnumbered the enemy slightly, the Thessalians deserted to the Spartans in the course of the fighting, allowing the Spartans to win.

The definition of victory in a Greek battle was control of the field that allowed the victor to set up a trophy and bury his dead while requiring the loser to ask for a truce to collect and bury his soldiers killed in battle. In that technical sense, the Spartans won the battle at Tanagra. But casualties on both sides were heavy, and the Spartans were unable to exploit their victory by ravaging the fields of Attica, much less by attacking the city or forcing the Athenians to surrender. Instead, they marched through the Megarid, where the Athenians made no effort to stop their return to Sparta.

The Athenians had lost the battle in large part because of the treason of their Thessalian allies, an ironic turn of events, because they entered it fearful of betrayal within their own ranks. As the Athenians were encamped at Tanagra, Cimon, still under the ban of ostracism, came into the ranks of his tribe in battle armor, ready to fight on behalf of his city and "by his deeds to free himself from the charge of Laconism." (Plutarch, *Pericles* 10.1) But Cimon's enemies accused him of trying to cause confusion in the ranks and then lead the Spartans against the city of Athens, so the Council of 500 drove him away on the grounds of his exile. Instead of stalking off in anger or sulking, he urged his friends, especially those most suspected of friendship with Sparta, to fight stoutly and so dispel those suspicions and charges. His friends took his suit of armor and placed it in the midst of their company, fought with extraordinary bravery, and were cut down to a man.

Pericles, too, had fought vigorously at Tanagra. His later well-deserved reputation as a cautious general, sparing of the lives of his men, should not obscure his own daring and courage in battle. At Tanagra he was "the most conspicuous of all in taking no care for his safety." (Plutarch, *Pericles* 10.2)

The outcome of the battle and the loyal bravery with which the Cimonians had fought changed the thinking of the Athenians. Their fears of treason had proved to be misplaced. Although the Spartans had withdrawn they might return the next spring, joined by the Thebans, who were strengthened by their control of Boeotia. Pericles' supporters had been among the council members who had driven Cimon off, but after his demonstration of loyalty and mindful of the common danger, they decided to end factional strife and plot a new course.

The time had come to seek peace with Sparta, and the man best suited to conduct negotiations was Cimon. If Cimon was prepared to accept the new constitution, and his subsequent behavior showed that he was, and if Pericles was ready to make peace with the Spartans, as his actions suggest, why not use Cimon's unique attributes to achieve an armistice and possibly a true peace treaty? Any time gained could be used to complete the walls and increase Athenian security in case the war resumed. Pericles, therefore, proposed a decree that recalled Cimon to Athens six years before his exile was scheduled to expire. The Spartans must have been unhappy with the results of Tanagra and the belligerent policy it represented. They had suffered heavy losses without gain to anyone but the Thebans, and they had no reason to believe that continued fighting would bring better success. News of Cimon's return to Athens at Pericles' invitation suggested that the Athenians might be ready to abandon their hostility and return to the old partnership with Sparta. The result was a truce of four months, probably negotiated by Cimon.

The Athenians were ready to make peace, but many of them were annoyed and threatened by the new Theban power the Spartans had helped create in Boeotia. They had enlarged the walls around Thebes and forced reluctant Boeotian cities into her confederation. The Thebans had proven their hostility at Tanagra, the Boeotians were numerous and tough fighters, and a Boeotian confederation under Theban control on the long northern border of Athens represented a great potential danger. Just about two months after the battle at Tanagra, therefore, the Athenians sent a large army into Boeotia under Myronides' command. They met the Boeotians under Theban leadership at Oenophyta, not far from Tanagra, and won a great victory. They gained control of all Boeotia except Thebes itself, installing the democrats who had invited their invasion to lead the governments in the towns, and overran Phocis and Locris beyond it. In a single campaign, the Athenians had become masters of central Greece. At the same time, they completed the northern and southern long walls, and the island of Aegina surrendered.

The victory at Oenophyta brought the Athenians to the height of their power. In the summer of 457, the Athenian fleet dominated the Aegean without challenge; the empire was loyal and secure and provided an annual revenue to support that fleet. Vigilance and the Megarian alliance guarded them against invasion from the Peloponnesus, and control of Boeotia guaranteed safety from attack from that direction. The fall of Aegina gave them full control of their home waters. Few states have enjoyed a better strategic situation, for the Athenians were free to attack the enemy from the sea but could not themselves be readily attacked at all. The price of victory at Oenophyta, however, was the end of peace negotiations with Sparta. Success encouraged the aggressive faction at Athens to Pericles' left that pressed for imperial expansion.

In 457, Pericles was still under forty and far from unchallenged in Athenian politics. Myronides was the victor of Oenophyta and had great influence. He clearly favored an aggressive policy against Thebes and spoke for a majority of Athenians. The attack on Boeotia was technically not a violation of the truce, which governed relations with Sparta only. But the extraordinary success it achieved put an end to hopes for peace. Although Pericles did not favor the policy, he had to accept what he could not alter. With this shift in Athenian policy, Cimon decided that the political climate in Athens was not to his liking and withdrew once again into exile until events might change the mood. The war against the Peloponnesians would resume, and Pericles had to play his part in it.

The Athenians next reverted to the strategy of putting pressure on the Spartans by attacking her Peloponnesian allies and even the Spartan homeland of Laconia from the sea. In 456, Tolmides took a force of Athenian ships and soldiers around the Peloponnesus. In a daring attack that must have shocked the enemy, he landed at Gytheum, the Spartans' chief port, ravaged its lands and burned the docks and the city. From there he sailed to the northern shore of the Corinthian Gulf, where he captured the Corinthian colony of Chalcis, and then to the southern shore, where he defeated the army of Corinth's neighbor Sicyon.

Two years later, Pericles was general and led another seaborne expedition into the Corinthian Gulf. Leaving from Megara's western port at Pegae, he delivered another defeat to the army of the Sicyonians. From there he moved on to Achaea, already allied to Athens, picking up reinforcements for his assault on Acarnania on the northern shore of the entrance to the gulf. There he ravaged the territory and besieged the important city of Oeniadae, though he failed to take it, and sailed home, "having showed himself to be formidable to the enemy but a safe and effective commander to his fellow-citizens. For no misfortunes struck the men on the expedition." This expedition was characteristic of others Pericles would lead and plan: it was seaborne, without avoiding specific missions on land; it had limited goals and duration; and it was carried out with great regard for the safety of the men involved. This last element was especially characteristic of Pericles as a general:

> In his generalships he was especially famous for his caution. He never willingly undertook a battle that involved great risk or uncertainty, nor did he envy or emulate those who took great risks, won brilliant success, and were admired as great generals. He always said to his fellow-citizens that as far as it was in his power they would live forever and be immortals. (Plutarch, *Pericles* 18.1)

Pericles was a "soldier's general," an Omar Bradley rather than a George Patton. He lacked the flair and boldness of a Cimon, the daring and ruthlessness that seeks victory at any cost. As a soldier he fought well and had great personal courage, but his generalship, like his politics, was calculating and rational. He never lost sight of the relationship between ends and means, and Athens' means in manpower were limited in comparison with the demands made upon them. Whenever possible he preferred to achieve his goals by diplomacy rather than by war. If fighting was necessary, he preferred to use allied troops, especially on land, rather than Athenians, putting his faith in the superior training and skill of the Athenian navy. Because of Athens' unique imperial and financial resources, he always thought that time was on Athens' side; so he avoided hasty actions and set battles on land, where the Athenians lacked the advantages they held at sea. First and foremost, moreover, Pericles was a political leader, and it can never be helpful to a politician to return from battle with a decimated army and a long casualty list. His competence and his caution, at any rate, earned him a good reputation, although he never won the kind of brilliant victory that brought others greater glory.

Neither the conquest of central Greece nor the naval expeditions of Tolmides and Pericles provoked a response from Sparta. With an Athenian fleet alert in the gulf and Megarian and Athenian forces on guard at the passes through the Megarid, the Spartans were locked into the Peloponnesus. Without a significant fleet they could not defend their coastal allies or even their own coastal towns. If this situation had continued much longer the Peloponnesian League might have begun to crumble and with it the power of Sparta. Events in Egypt, however, changed everything. Since 461, Athenian forces had been supporting a native rebellion in Egypt against the Persians. Finally, the Persian king had sent a large army against the rebels and their Athenian allies. In 454, after a long siege, the entire Greek force of the Athenians and their allies was destroyed and Egypt restored to Persian control.

This terrible disaster cost the Athenians and their allies no fewer than forty ships and eight thousand men. It broke an uninterrupted series of Athenian victories over Persia, caused serious unrest in the Aegean, and put a stop to Athenian efforts on the Greek mainland. The threat to their maritime empire made them abandon their war against the Peloponnesians, and there are no reports of Athenian actions against them from 454 to 451.

In 451, Cimon's period of ostracism came to an end and he returned to Athens. Pericles had already shown himself willing to collaborate with his former rival in the interests of peace, and by now the need for such cooperation was even greater than it had been in 457. Cimon was still a powerful potential opponent, but he was less dangerous than before. Pericles' popularity and influence had grown during Cimon's absence. Cimon, moreover, accepted the constitutional changes that had by now been in place for up to a decade, and circumstances had brought Pericles around to a Cimonian foreign policy: peace with Sparta and war against Persia. In the aftermath of the Egyptian disaster, the empire could not be held without the defeat of Persia, and Athenian resources were not great enough to wage war against the Persians and the Peloponnesians at the same time.

In 451, Cimon negotiated a Five Years' Peace with Sparta. The Spartans were glad to escape from the frustration and dangers of a war in which they could strike no effective blow, and they must have been heartened by the return to Athens of their good friend Cimon. The price they exacted was the end of Athens's alliance with Argos and the threat it posed to Sparta. Peace would also end the attacks on Sparta's allies and the pressure it put on Sparta's hegemony in the Peloponnesus. In return, the Athenians were allowed to keep what they had gained, which included the unprecedented security produced by the Megarian alliance, domination of Boeotia, and control of Aegina. Beyond that, the peace freed them to deal with Persia and the trouble in the Aegean empire. They must have hoped that before the five years expired, outstanding problems would be settled, the old friendly relations between Athens and Sparta restored, and a new, long-lasting peace established among the Greeks.

In the next year, the Athenians sent Cimon to sea in what was clearly intended as a major counterattack against the Persians. He led two hundred ships into the eastern Mediterranean, sending sixty to the rebels still holding out in Egypt and taking the rest to Cyprus, now a major Persian naval base, where the Athenians settled down to a siege of the town of Citium. There Cimon died, either of wounds or disease.

For thirty years, Cimon had been a great figure in Athens; he made a major contribution to unity and victory in the Persian War, and by his diplomatic and military talents he helped to found the Delian League and to convert it into an Athenian Empire. A conservative in temperament, an aristocrat by birth, training, and inclination, he nevertheless felt comfortable in Athens' democratic society, even in the extended one created by Ephialtes and Pericles. His influence did much to reconcile the aristocracy to Athenian democracy and thus avoid the bloody civil wars that accompanied the appearance of democracy in other Greek states. Small wonder that Plato, who had rejected the Athenian democracy as a place where a noble soul could practice political virtue, treated him as a demagogue no different from Themistocles and Pericles. (*Gorgias* 515 d–e) Cimon, however, was no demagogue, but a practical politician willing to make his homeland as good as possible in an imperfect world rather than destroy it in the search for perfection.

After his death the Athenians withdrew their forces from Egypt and Cyprus, but the expedition had not been in vain. Off Cyprus they encountered the combined Persian fleet of Phoenicians, Cypriotes, and Cilicians. They defeated them at sea and then put in to the island to deliver another blow in a battle on land. The Athenians had accomplished their main purpose of inflicting a serious defeat on the Persians, reclaiming control of the sea, discouraging their allies from rebelling and deterring the Persians from venturing into the Aegean to help them.

With Cimon no longer a factor in Athenian politics, Pericles had a free hand to pursue his own policies. Events would soon show that he had decided on a new foreign policy that he would try to pursue for the rest of his life. The program of aggressive war against Persia had accomplished as much as it could, but the disaster in Egypt showed that all the gains could be endangered by seeking to expand too far. Whatever he might have thought of the war with the Peloponnesians and expansion on the Greek mainland, that, too, had achieved as much as was reasonable. Since the conquest of central Greece, the Athenians had twice tried and failed to push forward into Thessaly. Seaborne raids had not yet dissolved the Peloponnesian

League, and Tanagra had shown the high price of a direct conflict with the Spartan army. All this led Pericles to seek an end to war with Sparta, as well as with Persia. He knew that Athens needed peace to restore control of the cities whose loyalty had been shaken by the Egyptian disaster and to give a new and firm basis to the empire.

# 5

# IMPERIALIST

imon's death made it easier for Pericles to seek a peace with Persia and thereby achieve an end to the fighting everywhere. This general peace, in turn, would allow Athens to make its empire safe, a central goal for Pericles and the Athenians. The empire itself was, in fact, the key to Athens' defense. It represented security against a renewal of the Persian threat, and it provided the means for warding off any future challenge from Sparta. Beyond that, its revenues were essential to Pericles' plans for making Athens the most prosperous, beautiful, and civilized city the Greeks had ever known. The glory it reflected was an essential part of his vision for Athens.

Pericles and his Athenians, then, regarded their empire as necessary. But it also raised serious questions. Could an empire limit its growth and ambition and maintain itself in safety? Or did rule over others inevitably lead the imperial power to overreach and bring about its own ruin? Was empire, especially by Greek over Greek, morally legitimate? Or was it evidence of hubris, the violent arrogance that was sure to bring on the justified destruction of those who dared to rule over others as though they were gods?

It fell to Pericles, as leader of the Athenian people, to guide their policy into safe channels and to justify the empire in the eyes of the other Greeks as well as their own. In both tasks Pericles broke a sharply new path. He put an end to imperial expansion and moderated Athenian ambitions. He also put forward powerful arguments, by word as well as deed, to show that the empire was both legitimate and in the common interest of all the Greeks.

It is important to recall that the Athenians did not set out to acquire an empire, and that the Delian League that was its forerunner came into being only because of Sparta's default. The caution the Athenians showed in accepting the offer of leadership did not mean that they were reluctant to head the war against the Persians. If the Spartans had good reasons for rejecting the hegemony, the Athenians had even better ones for accepting it. First and foremost was the fear and expectation that the Persians would come again to conquer the Greeks. The Persians had attacked them three times in two decades, and there was no reason to believe that they would permanently accept the latest defeat. Second, the Athenians had hardly begun to repair the damage done by the latest Persian attack; they knew another would surely make Athens a target again. In addition, the Aegean and the lands to its east were important to Athenian trade. Their dependence on imported grain from the Ukraine, which had to travel from the Black Sea, meant that even a very limited Persian campaign that gained control of the Bosporus or the Dardanelles cut their life line. Finally, the Athenians had ties of common ancestry, religion, and tradition with the Ionian Greeks, who made up most of the endangered cities. Athenian security, prosperity, and sentiment all pointed toward driving the Persians from all the coasts and islands of the Aegean, the Dardanelles, the Sea of Marmora, the Bosporus, and the Black Sea.

The new alliance was one of three interstate organizations in the Greek world, alongside the Peloponnesian League and the Hellenic League formed against Persia, which had by no means lapsed when the Spartans withdrew from the Aegean. After the founding of the

Delian League, the Hellenic League had an increasingly shadowy existence and collapsed at the first real test. The important, effective, and active alliances were the Peloponnesian League, led by Sparta, on the mainland and the Delian League, led by Athens, in the Aegean.

From the first, the Delian League was more effective than the others because it was enthusiastically voluntary; its purposes were essential to its members and its organization was clear and simple. Athens was the leader: all the members, about 140 in the beginning, swore a perpetual oath to have the same friends and enemies as Athens—that is, a permanent offensive and defensive alliance under Athenian leadership. Hegemony, however, was not domination. In the early years of the league, the Athenians were "leaders of autonomous allies who took part in common synods." (Thucydides 1.97.1) In those years, policy was determined and decisions made in those synods meeting at Delos, and Athens had only one vote.

In theory, Athens was only an equal partner in the synod with the same single vote as Samos, Lesbos, Chios, or even tiny Seriphos. In fact, the system worked in Athens' favor. Athenian military and naval power, the enormous relative size of Athens' contribution, and her immense prestige as hegemon guaranteed that the many small and powerless states would be under her influence, while the larger states that might have challenged the Athenians were easily outvoted. Many years later, the embittered and rebellious Mytileneans would say, "The allies were unable to unite and defend themselves because of the great number of voters." (Thucydides 3.10.5) In the early years, however, there appears to have been harmony and agreement among the members, large and small, and the degree of Athens' influence was proportionate to her contribution. From the beginning, then, Athens was in the happy position of controlling the Delian League without the appearance of illegality or tyranny.

The early actions of the league must have won unanimous and enthusiastic support: The Persians were driven from their remaining strongholds in Europe, and the sea lanes of the Aegean were made safe by the expulsion of a nest of pirates from the island of Scyros. As victory followed victory and the Persian threat seemed more remote, some allies thought the league and its burdensome obligations were no longer needed—a way of thinking common throughout history. No sooner has the danger abated than the allies wish to abandon their efforts. In such cases, it is usually the hegemonic power that takes a more sober view, and so it was with the Athenians. They rightly saw that the Persian threat was not gone. Indeed, it would increase to the degree that Greek vigilance waned. Thucydides makes it clear that the chief causes for the later rebellions was the allies' refusal to provide the agreed-upon ships or money and to perform the required military service. The Athenians held them strictly to account and

> were no longer equally pleasant as leaders. They no longer behaved as equals on campaigns, and they found it easy to reduce states that rebelled. The blame for this belonged to the allies themselves: for most of them had themselves assessed in quotas of money instead of ships because they shrank from military service so that they need not be away from home. As a result, the Athenian fleet was increased by means of the money they paid in, while when the allies tried to revolt, they went to war without the means or the experience. (1.99.2–3)

Less than a decade after its formation, perhaps in 469, the forces of the Delian League won smashing victories over the Persian fleet and army at the mouth of the Eurymedon River in Asia Minor. The decisive Persian defeat intensified the restlessness of the allies and the harshness and unpopularity of the Athenians. The rebellion and siege of Thasos from 465 to 463, which arose from a quarrel between the Athenians and the Thasians and had no clear connection with the purposes of the league, must have had the same effect.

The first Peloponnesian War strained Athenian resources to the limit and encouraged defection. The destruction of the expedition to Egypt in the mid 450s provided the shock that hastened the transformation from league to empire. To many, it must have seemed the beginning of the collapse of Athenian power, so it provoked new rebellions. The Athenians responded swiftly and effectively to put them down and then took measures to ensure they would not be repeated. In some places they installed democratic governments friendly to and dependent upon themselves. Sometimes they posted military garrisons, sometimes they assigned Athenian officials to oversee the conduct of the formerly rebellious state, and sometimes they used a combination. All were violations of the autonomy of the subject state.

The Athenians tightened their control of the empire even more in the 440s. They imposed the use of Athenian weights, measures, and coins, closing the local mints and so depriving the allies of a visible symbol of their sovereignty and autonomy. They tightened the rules for collection and delivery of tribute payments, requiring that the trials for those accused of violations be held in Athens. Colonies that rebelled or refused to pay tribute were suppressed by military action. Sometimes the Athenians confiscated territory from the offending state and gave it as a colony to loyal allies or Athenian citizens. When such a colony was composed of Athenians it was called a cleruchy. Its settlers did not form a new, independent city but remained Athenian citizens. When the Athenians suppressed a rebellion they usually installed a democratic regime and made the natives swear an oath of loyalty. The following is the oath imposed upon the people of Colophon:

> I will do and say and plan whatever good I can with regard to the people of the Athenians and their allies, and I will not revolt from the people of the Athenians either in word or deed, either myself or in obedience to another. And I will love the people of the Athenians and I will not desert. And I will not destroy the democracy at Colophon, either myself or in obedience to another, either by going off to another city or by intriguing there. I will carry out these things according to the oath truly, without deceit and without harm, by Zeus, Apollo, and Demeter. And if I transgress may I and my descendants be destroyed for all time, but if I keep my oath may great prosperity come to me.[1]

A bit later a similar oath was imposed on the Chalcidians, but in this one allegiance was sworn not to the alliance but to the Athenian people alone.

A critical step in the transition from league to empire was taken in the year 454/3 when the treasury was moved from Delos to the Acropolis in Athens. Fear that the Persians might send a fleet into the Aegean was the reason given. We do not know whether that fear was real or merely a pretext, but the Athenians did not waste time in turning the transfer to their advantage. From that year until late in the Peloponnesian War, the Athenians took one-sixtieth of the tribute paid by the allies as first fruits for the goddess Athena Polias, patroness of the city and, now, of the reconstituted league. The Athenians were free to use the goddess' share as they liked, not necessarily for league purposes, and Pericles, as we shall see, had very definite ideas as to how it should be spent.

Changes so important and radical that they transformed a voluntary league of allies to a largely involuntary empire ruled by Athens demanded justification, even in the ancient world of the Greeks. In most respects, the Greeks resembled other ancient peoples in their attitudes toward power, conquest, empire, and the benefits that came with them. They viewed the world as a place of intense competition in which victory and domination, which brought fame and glory, were the highest goals, while defeat and subordination brought ignominy and shame. They always honored the creed espoused by Achilles, the greatest hero of Greek legend: "Always to be the best and foremost over all others." When the legendary world of aristocratic heroes gave way to the world of city-states, the sphere of competition was elevated from contests between individuals, households, and clans to contests and wars between cities. In 416, more than a decade after the death of Pericles, Athenian spokesmen explained to some Melian officials their view of international relations: "Of the gods we believe, and of men we know, that by a necessity of their nature they always rule wherever they have the power." (Thucydides 5.105) Although their language was shockingly blunt, it was not far from the views of most Greeks.

Yet the Melian Dialogue, in which this statement appears, was a dramatic presentation of the morally problematic status of the Athenian Empire. The Athenians' harsh statement is provoked by the Melians' claim that the gods will be on their side, because the Athenians are behaving unjustly. The Melian complaint may refer to the specific actions taken or contemplated by the Athenians, but it would have struck a deeper vein of sympathy among the Greeks. The Greeks were free from the modern prejudice against power and the security and glory it could bring, but their own historical experience was different from that of other ancient nations. Their culture had been shaped not by great empires but by small, autonomous, independent poleis, and they came to think that freedom was the natural condition for men raised in such an environment. Citizens should be free in their persons; free to maintain their own constitutions, laws, and customs; and their cities should be free to conduct their own foreign relations and to compete with others for power and glory. The Greeks also believed that the freedom made possible by the life of the polis created a superior kind of citizen and a special kind of power. The free, autonomous polis, they thought, was greater than the mightiest powers in the world. The sixth-century poet Phocylides was prepared to compare it to the great Assyrian Empire: "A little polis living orderly in a high place is greater than block-headed Nineveh." (Fragment 5)

When poleis fought one another, the victor typically took control of a piece of borderland that was usually the source of the dispute. The enemy was not normally enslaved nor was his land annexed or occupied. In such matters, as in many, the Greeks employed a double standard by which they distinguished themselves from alien peoples who did not speak Greek and were not shaped by the Greek cultural tradition. These people were barbarians (*barbaroi*), because their speech sounded to the Greeks like "bar bar." Since they had not been raised as free men in free communities, but lived as subjects to a ruler, they were manifestly slaves by nature; so it was perfectly all right to dominate and enslave them in reality. Greeks, on the other hand, were naturally free, as they demonstrated by creating and living in the liberal institutions of the polis. To rule over such people, to deny them their freedom and autonomy, would clearly be wrong.

This was what the Greeks thought, but they did not always act accordingly. At a very early time, the Spartans had conquered the Greeks residing in their own region of Laconia and neighboring Messenia and made them slaves of the state. In the sixth century, they formed the alliance that we call the Peloponnesian League, which gave the Spartans considerable control over the foreign policy of their allies. But the Spartans generally did not interfere with the internal arrangements of the allied cities, which continued to have the appearance of autonomy. In the two decades after the Persian War, the Argives appear to have obliterated some towns in the Argolid and annexed their territory; yet such deviations from the pattern remained unusual and did not overcome the general expectation that Greeks should live as free men in autonomous poleis, not as subjects in great empires.

The Greeks shared still another belief that interfered with the comfortable enjoyment of great power and empire. They thought that any good thing amassed by men to an excessive degree led, through a series of stages, to what they called *hubris*. Such men were thought to have overstepped the limits established for human beings, and thereby to have incurred *nemesis*, divine anger and retribution. These were the main ideas emerging from the oracle at Apollo's shrine at Delphi, where could be found the pair of divine warnings to man to avoid *hubris*: "know thyself" and "nothing in excess." The great example to the Greeks of the fifth century of *hubris* and *nemesis* was the fate of Xerxes, Great King of the Persian Empire. His power filled him with a blind arrogance that led him to try to extend his rule over the Greek mainland and so brought disaster to himself and his people.

Therefore, when the Athenians undertook the leadership of a Greek alliance after the Persian War, and that leadership brought wealth and power and, in fact, turned into what was frankly acknowledged as an empire, traditional ways of thinking provided no firm guidelines. The advantages of empire to the Athenians, tangible and intangible, were many. The most obvious was financial. Revenues paid directly by the allies in the form of tribute, indemnities, and other unspecified payments came to 600* talents annually at the beginning of the Peloponnesian War. Of the 400 talents of home income that came in each year, a large part also resulted from the empire, for import and other harbor duties at Piraeus and court fees paid by allied citizens whose cases were heard in Athens. Other similar items made up a considerable portion of that figure. Athenians also profited in the private sphere by providing services for the many visitors drawn to Piraeus and Athens by judicial and other imperial business and by the greatness of Athens itself, which the empire made possible.

The imperial revenues are sometimes thought to have been necessary for the maintenance of the democracy, providing the money to pay for the performance of public duties. But the evidence argues otherwise. Pay was introduced, after all, before the Athenians began to keep a sixtieth of the tribute for themselves. Even more telling is the fact that the Athenians continued to pay for these services even after the empire and its revenues were gone. On the other hand, it cannot be irrelevant that these payments were inaugurated when the success of the empire had brought great wealth to Athens in the form of booty and increased trade and that they spread beyond jury pay in the years surrounding the introduction of Athena's tithe. It seems likely, in any case, that in Pericles' time the people of Athens connected the growth and flourishing of the democracy with the benefits of empire.

Apart from direct financial gain and, as they thought, the financial support for their democracy, the people of Athens also received benefits in what it is now fashionable to call the quality of life. The empire, according to the "Old Oligarch," allowed Athenians to mingle with people from many places, and so they discovered

> various gastronomic luxuries; the specialties of Sicily, Italy, Cyprus, Egypt, Lydia, Pontus, the Peloponnesus or any other area have all been brought back to Athens because of their control of the sea. They hear all dialects, and pick one thing from one, another from another; the other Greeks tend to adhere to their own dialect and way of life and

---

* It is impossible to compare the value of ancient money with modern equivalents. It may be helpful to know that 1 talent would pay the two-hundred-man crew who manned an Athenian warship for a month.

dress, but the Athenians have mingled elements from all Greeks and foreigners. (2.7–8)

A contemporary comic poet provides a more detailed list of the exotic delicacies and useful wares that the empire made available to the Athenians:

> From Cyrene silphium and ox hides, from the Hellespont mackerel and all kinds of salted fish, from Italy, salt and ribs of beef . . . from Egypt sails and rope, from Syria frankincense, from Crete cypress for the gods; Libya provides abundant ivory to buy, Rhodes raisins and sweet figs, but from Euboea pears and sweet apples. Slaves from Phrygia . . . Pagasae provides tattooed slaves, Paphlagonia dates and oily almonds, Phoenicia dates and fine wheat-flour, Carthage rugs and many-colored cushions. (Hermippus in Athenaeus 1.27e–28a)

These, as the "Old Oligarch" observes, are "less important matters," but they helped bring home to the Athenians the advantages of empire and the rule of the sea that it made possible.

Perhaps the greatest attraction of the empire was less tangible than any of these things, appealing to an aspect of human nature common to many cultures across the centuries. Most people prefer to think of themselves as leaders rather than followers, as rulers rather than ruled. As even the poorest cockneys took great personal pride in the thought that the sun never set on the British Empire and that Britannia ruled the waves, so each Athenian took pride in the greatness of his state. The "Old Oligarch," explaining how the Athenians benefit from having allied citizens come to the courts in Athens for justice, shows how the ordinary citizen enjoyed such feelings:

> If the allies did not come for trials, they would only respect those Athenians who go abroad—the generals, the trierarchs and the ambassadors; but as it is, each individual ally is compelled to flatter the common people of Athens, realizing that, having come to Athens, the penalty or satisfaction that he receives at law depends solely upon the common people; such is the law at Athens. Therefore he is compelled to plead humbly in the courts and to seize people's hands as a suppliant as they enter. This situation has increased the subjugation of the allies to the people of Athens. (1.18)

For all the benefits it brought to the Athenians, the imperial ledger was not entirely unbalanced, for the allies also received much value

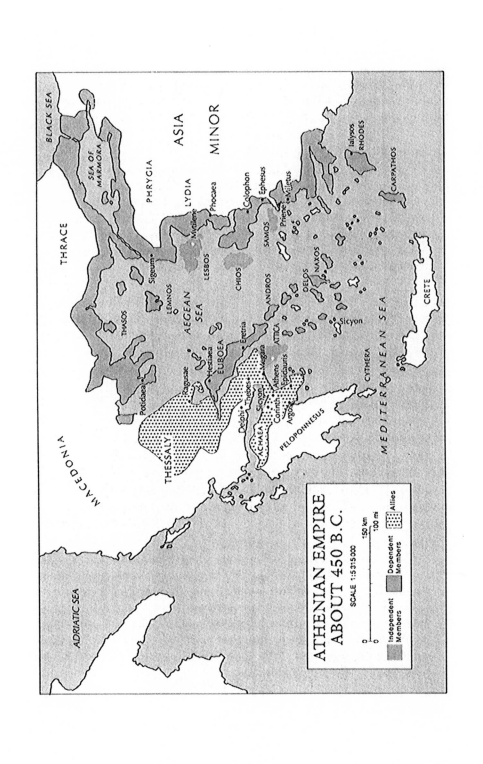

ATHENIAN EMPIRE
ABOUT 450 B.C.

SCALE 1:5,315,000

150 km
100 mi

Independent
Members

Dependent
Members

Allies

BLACK SEA

SEA OF MARMORA

THRACE

MACEDONIA

ADRIATIC SEA

PHRYGIA

ASIA

MINOR

LYDIA

Sigeum

Phocaea

Mytilene

Colophon

Ephesus

Priene

Miletus

Talysos

RHODES

CARPATHOS

LESBOS

CHIOS

SAMOS

NAXOS

DELOS

ANDROS

AEGEAN SEA

THASOS

LEMNOS

Potidaea

Aragusae

Hestiaea

EUBOEA

Eretria

ATTICA

Sicyon

Delphi

Thebes

Megara

Athens

Sicyon

Corinth

Epidauris

Argos

ACHAEA

THESSALY

PELOPONNESUS

CYTHERA

MEDITERRANEAN SEA

CRETE

for their participation. Foremost among these advantages was freedom from Persian rule, the chief purpose for which the league had been formed, and the peace that the Athenian Callias, son of Hipponicus, had negotiated with the Persian Empire. Ionian cities had either been under barbarian rule or fighting to be free of it for well over a century, so these achievements were not insignificant. The success of the league and empire had also brought an unprecedented freedom to sail in the waters of the Aegean. In addition, the campaigns against Persia had brought a percentage of booty to the allies who had taken part in them, and the commercial boom that enriched Athens also brought wealth to many of their allies. In short, the Athenians had brought freedom from Persian rule, peace, and prosperity to all Greeks in and around the Aegean Sea.

To many, Athenian intervention also brought democracy, but that was not its aim. Pericles and the Athenians, when they could, left the existing regime in place, even when it was oligarchic or tyrannical. Only when rebellions forced them to intervene did they impose democracies, and even then not always. Pericles' imperial policy was prudent and pragmatic, not ideological. Nevertheless, over the years, the Athenians instituted and supported many democracies against oligarchic or tyrannical opponents throughout the empire. From a twentieth-century perspective, this might seem like an unalloyed benefit of the empire, but it was not so viewed by everyone in the time of Pericles. Aristocrats and members of the upper classes in general regarded democracy as a novel, unnatural, unjust, incompetent, and vulgar form of government, and they were not alone in resenting the Athenian role in support of it. In many cities, probably in most, even members of the lower classes regarded Athenian intervention in their political and constitutional affairs as a curtailment of their freedom and autonomy, and would have preferred a nondemocratic constitution without Athenian interference to a democratic government with it.

Modern scholars have tried to argue that this Athenian support for democracy made the empire popular with the masses in the allied cities, and that the hostility with which they reportedly came to view it was the result of distortions caused by the aristocratic bias of the ancient writers. The consensus, however, has rightly continued to emphasize the empire's fundamental unpopularity with all classes except the small groups of democratic politicians who benefited directly from Athenian support. There is no reason to doubt the ancient opinion that Greeks outside, and especially inside, the Athenian Empire were hostile to it. Even some Athenians objected to what they deemed the immorality of Athens' behavior toward the imperial allies.

Pericles undertook to justify to each constituency Athenian rule and Athens' continued collection of the tribute. For the cities in the empire he provided justification by claiming a change in the concept behind the league. From the beginning, some league members were colonies that had been founded by Athens. Among the Greeks, colonial status implied a proud familial relationship, not inferiority. Beyond that, the Athenians had long claimed to be the founders of the Ionian cities; the Ionians not only accepted the claim but had used it to persuade the Athenians to accept the leadership in the first place. The time of the treasury's transfer was the year that had been scheduled for the quadrennial celebration of the Great Panathenaic Festival in Athens—ties between colony and mother city were normally warm and were celebrated by such religious observances. It was customary for Athens' allies to bring a cow and a full suit of armor to this festival as a symbol of allegiance. It was not a heavy burden, and it gave the colony the honor of participating in the grand procession to the sacred shrine of Athena on the Acropolis. Henceforth, all the allies of Athens would share the honor.

We need not believe that all were grateful for the honor or that they found the trappings of a colonial relationship a satisfactory reason for continuing their contributions in circumstances so different from what they had been. Their doubts were surely increased by the terms of the peace treaty with the Persian Empire negotiated by Callias in 449: "All the Greek cities of Asia are to be autonomous; no Persian satrap is to come closer than a three days' journey from the sea; no Persian warship is to sail in the waters between Phaselis and the Cyanean rocks; if the King and his generals respect these terms, the Athenians are not to send any expedition against the country over which the King rules." (Diodorus of Sicily 12.4.5–6)[2] By this agreement, the Persians gave up their claim to the Greek states on the Aegean and its coasts, as well as the Athenian lifeline through the Dardanelles to the Black Sea. The Persian Wars were now truly over, and the Athenians could claim to have completed the victory left unfinished by the Spartans.

It was a great moment, but it raised serious questions. Although Cimon—the indefatigable prosecutor of the war against Persia—was dead, his example, his memory, and his friends remained to raise doubts about a peace with what had become the traditional enemy. If there was peace with Persia, moreover, would that mean the end of allied contributions, of the league, of Athenian hegemony?

To the first problem, a question of Athenian politics, Pericles applied a skillful touch. The choice of Callias as the Athenian negotiator had been significant. He was the brother-in-law of Cimon, the husband of Elpinice. His central role was evidence that the recent friendship between Pericles and Cimon lived on after the latter's death, and he must have done much to help win the Cimonian faction over to the new policy. By various other connections, Pericles had associated himself with the Cimonians, and he continued to do so throughout the years. As a modern scholar has put it: "Behind the public politics of the Athenian state was the family-politics of the great houses; here Pericles was an adept."[3]

Pericles' political operations appear to have had a public aspect as well, if the reconstruction of events by a great modern historian is correct. After their victory at Cyprus, the Athenians made a thanksgiving dedication of a tenth of the booty and commissioned the poet Simonides to commemorate the Persian defeat. It "praised the struggles on Cyprus as the most glorious deed that the world had ever seen. At the same time, it was a monument to the whole Persian War, the inclination to which had been embodied in the person of Cimon."[4] We may assume that Pericles was behind this propaganda, which implied that the war had been won by a glorious Athenian victory instead of by a negotiated peace, and which tied Cimon to the new Periclean policy. At the same time, the memorial to Cimon was a gesture meant to attract and conciliate his friends.

Pericles had need of conciliation and unity in Athens. For in spite of the peace, he had no thoughts of abandoning the league that had become an empire. Nor did he wish to sacrifice the glory, the political and military power, and the money that went with it. Athens needed the empire to protect its own security and to support the creation and maintenance of the great democratic society Pericles had in mind. Part of that greatness would involve a vastly expensive building program that would need to draw on the imperial treasury for nonmilitary and purely Athenian purposes. Pericles and the Athenians therefore needed to justify the continuation of allied payments as well as their diversion to new purposes.

But already there was trouble in the empire. In 454/3, 208 cities appear on the tribute list and are assessed more than 498 talents. Four years later, only 163 cities are assessed at 432 talents; but some made only partial payment, some paid late, and some surely did not pay at all. Hesitation, uncertainty, and resistance threatened the empire's existence. At the same time, the threat of Sparta loomed. The truce negotiated by Cimon would run out in a few years, but he was no longer there to calm Spartan fears. Great differences remained between the two powers, and there was no certainty that they could be overcome without war. Yet Pericles' plans required peace.

Not long after Callias' peace was concluded, Pericles tried to solve his problems with a most imaginative proposal. He introduced a bill,

> to invite all Greeks, wherever they lived, whether in Europe or in Asia, whether small cities or large, to send representatives to a congress at Athens, to deliberate about the holy places that the barbarians had destroyed, and about the sacrifices that they [the Greeks] owed, having promised them to the gods when they fought against the barbarians, and about the sea, so that all might sail it without fear and keep the peace. (Plutarch, *Pericles* 17.1)[5]

Messengers were sent to all corners of the Greek world to deliver an invitation to "share in the plans for the peace and common interests of Greece." Pericles, as one scholar has put it, was "calling on the Greek world to set up another organization to do what the Spartan-led Greek alliance of 480 should have done but had failed to do, and to provide for the peacetime needs which the Delian League had hitherto satisfied."[6] Beyond that, the invitation presented an Athenian claim to Greek leadership on a new foundation. While war had brought the Greeks together originally, let the maintenance of peace and security cement their union from then on. Religious piety, Panhellenism, and the common good were now to justify continued loyalty and sacrifice.

Was Pericles sincere? The temples burned by the Persians were almost all in Attica, and the fleet that would keep the peace would be chiefly Athenian. Pericles may therefore have expected the Spartans and their allies to reject his proposal and thus provide him with a new justification for consolidating the empire. On the other hand, Pericles could honestly have been trying to achieve Greek freedom, security, and unity by this device. The cynical view ignores the facts of Pericles' recall of and rapprochement with Cimon, and the truce with Sparta, plainly intended to be a preliminary to a new policy of lasting peace. But the picture of Pericles as a disinterested devotee of Panhellenic cooperation neglects the great advantages to Athens if the congress should meet and approve his proposals.

Pericles could well have thought there was a chance the Spartans would accept the invitation. The policy of its militant party had brought disaster to Sparta and raised Athens to new heights. Sparta's agreement to the Five Years' Peace of 451 shows that this faction had been discredited. It was not unreasonable to expect that the peace faction, impressed by Pericles' unexpected alliance with Cimon and his apparent conversion to a new foreign policy, might take advantage of the troubles in Athens' maritime empire to negotiate a lasting peace, as in Cimon's time. Such a development would achieve Pericles' goals and represent a diplomatic victory for his new policy of pacific imperialism.

If Sparta refused, nothing would have been lost and much gained. Athens would have shown its Panhellenic spirit, its religious devotion, and its willingness to lead the Greeks for the common benefit; it would thus have gained a clear moral basis for pursuing its own goals without hindrance or complaint from others.

The situation is similar to what the United States faced after World War II. Europe was already well on the road toward being divided into two spheres of influence. The U.S. Marshall Plan, which would have made aid available to all Europe including the Soviet Union and its satellites, would have given the United States considerable influence and weakened that of the U.S.S.R. While its chief goal was political—to strengthen Western Europe—it is too cynical to deny that the United States was also moved by the suffering of Europe. Fortunately, helping to relieve the suffering also helped to accomplish the political aims. They could not be sure the Russians would refuse their aid and, in fact, for some time it appeared that they, too, would accept. The United States was ready regardless of what they decided. The Russians' eventual refusal was certainly not surprising.

Like the Russians, the Spartans declined the invitation to participate in the new plan for international cooperation, and as a result, the congress did not go forward. The Spartan refusal, however, was a great propaganda victory for Athens, for the Athenians could now blame their rivals for being indifferent to the welfare of the Greeks and unwilling to fulfill their sacred vows and duties. Even though the congress never met, this episode announced to the Greek world that Athens was ready to take the lead in carrying out a sacred responsibility. It also provided Athens with a justification for rebuilding its own temples. Pericles was now free to restore order to the empire, to continue collecting tribute on a new basis, and to use the revenue for the projects he had in mind.

A mutilated papyrus now located in Strasbourg provides a good idea of these plans. The papyrus apparently reports a decree proposed by Pericles in the summer of 449, soon after the failure of the congress. Five thousand talents were to be taken from the treasury at once to be used for the construction of new temples on the Acropolis, with another two hundred transferred annually for the next fifteen years to complete the work. The building program, however, would not interfere with the maintenance of the fleet, which justified the payment of tribute. The council would see to it that the old ships would be kept in good repair and ten new ships added annually.[7] If there had been any question before, there could be none now: The Delian League, the alliance (*symmachia*) of autonomous states, had become what the Athenians themselves were increasingly willing to call an empire (*arche*), an organization that still produced common benefits but was dominated by the Athenians and brought them unique advantages.

This new imperial policy was the work of Pericles. If the evidence already given were not enough, the attacks launched by Pericles' political enemies provide clinching proof. A few years after the new program had begun, Pericles found himself challenged by a formidable political faction led by Thucydides, son of Melesias. A relative of Cimon's, possibly his brother-in-law, this Thucydides was a brilliant orator and political organizer. He used the usual personal attacks to win support, alleging that Pericles was trying to establish himself as tyrant. This he cleverly combined with an assault on the use of imperial funds for the Periclean building program. Plutarch reports the essence of the complaints that were made in the assembly:

> The people is dishonored and in bad repute because it has removed the common money of the Hellenes from Delos to Athens. Pericles has deprived it of the most fitting excuse that it was possible to offer to its accusers, that it removed the common funds to this place out of fear of the barbarian and in order to protect it. Hellas certainly is outraged by a terrible arrogance [*hubris*] and is manifestly tyrannized when it sees that we are gilding and adorning our city like a wanton woman, dressing it with expensive stones and statues and temples worth millions, with money extorted from them for fighting a war. (*Pericles* 12.2)

The attack was shrewd, subtle, and broad in its appeal. It was not against the empire itself or the tribute derived from it, which would have alienated most Athenians. Instead it complained, on the one hand, about the misdirection of funds to the domestic program of Pericles. This reminded the friends of Cimon who were now part of the Periclean coalition that the original Cimonian policy had been abandoned and perverted. On the other hand, it reached out to a broader constituency by taking a high moral tone. Employing the language of traditional religion and old-fashioned morality, it played on the ambiguity many Athenians felt toward their rule over fellow-Greeks.

Thucydides' attacks forced Pericles to defend the empire and his new imperial policy before the Athenians themselves. In answer to the main complaint he offered no apology. The Athenians, he said, need make no account of the money they receive from their allies so long as they protect them from the barbarian:

> They furnish no horse, no ship, no hoplite, but only money, which does not belong to the giver but to the receiver if he carries out his part of the bargain. But now that the city has prepared itself sufficiently with the things necessary for war, it is proper to employ its resources for such works as will bring it eternal fame when they are completed, and while they are being completed will maintain its prosperity, for all kinds of industries and a variety of demands will arise which will waken every art, put in motion every hand, provide a salary for almost the entire city from which at the same time it may be beautified and nourished. (12.3–4)

The first part of this rebuttal answered the moral attack: The use of imperial funds for Athenian purposes was not analogous to tyranny, Pericles asserted, but to the untrammeled use of wages or profits by a man who has entered a contract. If there was any moral breach, it must be on the part of any allies that shrank from paying the tribute while Athens continued to provide protection. The second part was aimed especially at the lower classes who benefited from the empire most directly, and reminded them in the plainest terms what it meant to them. Harry Truman made a similar argument in the presidential contest of 1948. Charging that his opponents intended to undo the New Deal, he used the slogan, "Don't let them take it away." The people he addressed understood him and voted accordingly.

The Athenians understood Pericles equally well, and in 443, when he was sure of the result, he called for an ostracism that served both as a vote of confidence in his leadership and as a referendum on his policies. Thucydides was expelled, and Pericles reached new heights of political influence. The people supported him not least because of the powerful stake they had in the empire.

The concept of "empire" does not win favor in the world today, and the word "imperialism" derived from it has carried a powerfully pejorative meaning from its very invention in the nineteenth century. Both words imply domination imposed by force or the threat of force over an alien people in a system that exploits the ruled for the benefit of the rulers. Although tendentious attempts are made to apply the term "imperialism" to any large and powerful nation that is able to influence weaker ones, a more neutral definition based on historical experience requires political and military control to justify its use. In that sense, there seems to be only one empire in the contemporary world—the domination of the Russians over the other nationalities that comprise the Soviet Union—and even that one appears to be crumbling. But even before its decay, the Russians had taken no public pride in their unique achievement; instead, they would regard this description as a canard and an insult—such is the contemporary dislike for these terms.

Yet holding such views, the people of our time are unique among those who have lived since the birth of civilization. A major source for this opinion is the Christian religious tradition, especially the New Testament, which deprecates power and worldly glory and praises humility. But an understanding of Christianity that is hostile to power and empire is far from inevitable, for Christianity took control of the Roman Empire only three centuries after its birth and has been able to live comfortably with various empires down to our own century when, for the first time, hostility to empire has come to the fore. Perhaps the rise of democracy and nationalism in the last two centuries are more important sources, since they place the highest values on the freedom and autonomy of a people. Possibly the modern attitude arises most from the extraordinary horror of modern warfare and the historical experience that competition for empire often leads to war. Yet there is also something uncanny in this attitude, for it rejects not only empire but the use of power itself as inherently evil. Nevertheless, power is merely "the ability or capacity to act or perform effectively,"[8] and its use is inescapable.

If, however, we are to understand the empire ruled by the Athenians of Pericles' time and their attitudes toward it, we must be alert to the great gap that separates their views from the opinions of our own time. These developments were a source of pride and gratification, but in some respects they also caused embarrassment and, at least to some Athenians, shame. Pericles himself, as we shall see, confronted the problem more than once and addressed it with extraordinary honesty and directness, although neither he nor the Athenians were ever able to resolve its ambiguities.

The Athenians themselves repeatedly acknowledged the unpopularity of their rule, and the historian Thucydides, a contemporary of outstanding perceptiveness, makes the point in his own voice. At the beginning of the war, he tells us,

> Good will was thoroughly on the side of the Spartans, especially since they proclaimed that they were liberating Greece. Every individual and every state was powerfully moved to help them by word or deed in any way they could. . . . So great was the anger of the majority against the Athenians, some wanting to be liberated from their rule, the others fearing that they would come under it. (2.8.4)

Pericles was fully aware of these feelings, and he understood both the ethical problems and practical dangers they presented. Yet he never wavered in his defense of the empire.

In 432, when the threat of war was imminent, an Athenian embassy arrived at Sparta, ostensibly "on other business" but really to present Athens' position to the Spartans and their assembled allies. Their arguments were fully in accord with those of Pericles. The ambassadors argued that the Athenians acquired their empire as a result of circumstances they did not set in motion and of the natural workings of human nature. On the one hand, they point out,

> we did not acquire this empire by force, but only after you [Spartans] refused to stand your ground against what was left of the barbarian, and the allies came to us and begged us to become their leaders. It was the course of events that forced us to develop our empire to its present status, moved chiefly by fear, then by honor, and later by advantage. Then, when we had become hated by most of the allies and some of them had rebelled and been subdued, and you were no longer as friendly to us as you had been but were suspicious and at odds with us, it was no longer safe to let go, for all rebels would go over to your side. And no one can be blamed for looking to his own advantage in the face of the greatest dangers. (1.75.3–5)

On the contrary, they continue, the Athenians had only done as the Spartans would have had to do had they continued their leadership. In that case, they would have become equally hated. "Thus we have done nothing remarkable or contrary to human nature in accepting the empire when it was offered to us and then refusing to give it up, conquered by the greatest motives, honor, fear, and advantage." (1.76.2)

Pericles certainly thought that circumstances had made the Empire inevitable, and the mainspring of Athenian action after Plataea and Mycale had been the general fear that the Persians would return. As the league achieved success and the allies' commitment waned, the Athenians feared the dissolution of the league and the return of the Persians. When the Spartans became hostile, they feared allied defections to the new enemy. The compulsion that was needed to deal with these problems created a degree of hatred that made it too dangerous to give up control, as Pericles would explain to the Athenians later on:

> Do not think that we are fighting only over the question of freedom or slavery; on the contrary, the loss of our empire is also at stake and the danger from those in the empire who hate us. And it is no longer possible to give it up, if any among you, moved in the panic of the moment to the abandonment of responsible action, wants to put on the trappings of virtue. For by now you hold this empire as a tyranny, which it may have been wrong to acquire but is too dangerous to let go. (2.63.1–2)

Pericles clearly saw the dangers that argued for the maintenance of the empire, but he was moved by the claims of honor and advantage as well. In the great Funeral Oration of 431, he called attention to the tangible advantages brought by the empire and its revenues:

> We have provided for the spirit many relaxations from labor with games and festivals regularly throughout the year, and our homes are furnished with beauty and good taste, and our enjoyment of them drives away care. All the good things of the earth flow into our city because of its greatness, and we are blessed with the opportunity to enjoy products from the rest of the world no less than those we harvest here at home. (2.38)

But these pleasures and advantages were far less important to Pericles than the honor and glory the Athenians derived from the empire, rewards that justified the risk of their lives. He asked his fellow-citizens "every day to look upon the power of our city and become lovers [*erastai*] of her, and when you have appreciated her greatness consider that all this has been established by brave men who knew their duty and were moved to great deeds by a sense of honor." (2.43.1) At a darker moment, in the next year, when the possibility of ultimate defeat could not be ignored, Pericles once again called the Athenians' attention to the power and glory of their imperial achievement and to its lasting value:

> To be sure, the man who does not like our activities will find fault with all this, but the man who, like us, wants to accomplish something will make it his goal, and those who do not achieve it will be jealous of us. To be hated and unpopular for the time being has always been the fate of those who have undertaken to rule over others, but whoever aims at the greatest goals must accept the ill-will and is right to do so. For hatred does not last long, but the brilliance of the present moment is also the glory of the future passed on in everlasting memory. With this foreknowledge of future glory you must behave with honor at this time and by the zeal of your efforts obtain both now. (2.64.3–6)

It would be wrong to regard such arguments as mere rhetoric. Pericles spoke at critical moments in Athenian history, reaching out to the deepest and most important values cherished by his fellow-citizens, and everything we know of him indicates that he cherished them too. But he also valued the empire for reasons that were not so important and appealing to the average Athenian. He wanted to create a new kind of state, a place for the development of the aesthetic and intellectual greatness inherent in humanity and especially in Greek culture. Athens was to be the "education of Greece," and toward that end she had to attract the greatest poets, painters, sculptors, philosophers, artists, and teachers of every kind. The power and wealth brought by empire was needed for that purpose and also to pay for the staging and performance of the great poems and plays they wrote, the magnificent buildings they erected, and the beautiful paintings and sculptures with which they enriched the city.

This was a vision that required an empire, but an empire different from any that had ever existed and even from the one created by Cimon. This new kind of empire needed the security and income for nonmilitary purposes that could only come in time of peace. Yet the Athenian Empire, like all its predecessors, had been achieved by war, and many people could not conceive of one without the other. The problem was intensified by the character of the Cimonian empire, which was already an historical novelty: a power based not on a great army dominating vast stretches of land but on a navy that dominated the sea. This unusual empire dazzled perceptive contemporaries. The "Old Oligarch" pointed out some of its special advantages:

> It is possible for small subject cities on the mainland to unite and form a single army, but in a sea empire it is not possible for islanders to combine their forces, for the sea divides them, and their rulers control the sea. Even if it is possible for islanders to assemble unnoticed on one island, they will die of starvation. Of the mainland cities which Athens controls, the large ones are ruled by fear, the small by sheer necessity; there is no city which does not need to import or export something, but this will not be possible unless they submit to those who control the sea. (1.2–3)

Naval powers, moreover, can make hit-and-run raids on enemy territory, doing damage without casualties; they can travel distances impossible for armies; they can sail past hostile territory safely, while armies must fight their way through; they need not fear crop failure, for they can import what they need. In the Greek world, besides, all their enemies are vulnerable: "every mainland state has either a projecting headland or an offshore island or a narrow strait where it is possible for those who control the sea to put in and harm those who dwell there." (2.4–6; 11–13)

Thucydides admired sea power no less and depicted its importance more profoundly. His reconstruction of early Greek history, describing the ascent of civilization, makes naval power the dynamic, vital element. First comes a navy, then suppression of piracy and safety for commerce. The resulting security permits the accumulation of wealth, which allows the emergence of walled cities. This, in turn, allows acquisition of greater wealth and the growth of empire, as the weaker cities trade independence for security and prosperity. The wealth and power so obtained permits the expansion of the imperial city's power. This paradigm perfectly describes the rise of the Athenian Empire. Yet Thucydides presents it as a natural development, inherent in the character of naval power, and realized for the first time in the Athens of his day. (1.4–19)

Pericles himself fully understood the unique character of the naval empire as the instrument of Athenian greatness, and on the eve of the great Peloponnesian War, he encouraged the Athenians with an analysis of its advantages. The war would be won by reserves of money and control of the sea, where the empire gave Athens unquestioned superiority.

> If they march against our land with an army, we shall sail against theirs; and the damage we do to the Peloponnesus will be something very different from their devastation of Attica. For they can not get other land in its place without fighting, while we have plenty of land on the islands and the mainland; yes, command of the sea is a great thing. (1.143.4)

In the second year of the war, Pericles made the point even more strongly, as he tried to restore the fighting spirit of the discouraged Athenians:

> I want to explain this point to you, which I think you have never yet thought about; it is about the greatness of your empire. I have not mentioned it in my previous speeches, nor would I speak of it now, since it sounds rather like boasting, if I did not see that you are discouraged beyond reason. You think you rule only over your allies, but I assert that of the two spheres that are open to man's use, the land and the sea, you are the absolute master of all of one, not only of as much as you now control but of as much more as you like. And there is no one who can prevent you from sailing where you like with the naval force you now have, neither the Great King, nor any nation on earth. (2.62.1–2)

This unprecedented power, however, could be threatened by two weaknesses. The first resulted from an intractable geographical fact: The home of this great naval empire was a city located on the mainland and subject to attacks from land armies. Since they were not islanders, their location was a point of vulnerability, for the landed classes are reluctant to see their houses and estates destroyed.

Pericles made the same point: "Command of the sea is a great thing," he said. "Just think; if we were islanders, who could be less exposed to conquest?" (143.4–5) But Pericles was not one to allow problems presented by nature to stand in the way of his goals. Since the Athenians would be invulnerable as islanders, they must become islanders. Accordingly, he asked the Athenians to abandon their fields and homes in the country and move into the city. In the space between the long walls, they could be fed and supplied from the empire, and could deny a land battle to the enemy. In a particularly stirring speech, Pericles said, "We must not grieve for our homes and land, but for human lives, for they do not make men, but men make them. And if I thought I could persuade you I would ask you to go out and lay waste to them yourselves and show the Peloponnesians that you will not yield to them because of such things." (1.143.5)

But not even Pericles could persuade the Athenians to do that in midcentury. The employment of such a strategy based on cold intelligence and reason, flying in the face of tradition and the normal passions of human beings, would require the kind of extraordinary leadership that only he could hope to exercise, and even in the face of a Spartan invasion in 446/5, as we shall see, Pericles was not able to persuade the Athenians to abandon their farms. In 431, he imposed his strategy and held to it only with great difficulty. But by then he had become strong enough to make it the strategy of Athens.

The second major weakness was less tangible but no less serious, arising from the very dynamism that had brought the naval empire into being. Shrewd observers, both Athenians and foreigners, recognized this characteristic and the opportunities and dangers it presented. Many years after Pericles' death, his ward, Alcibiades, arguing for an imperial adventure against Sicily, painted the picture of an empire whose natural dynamism could only be tamed at the cost of its own destruction. Athens should respond to all opportunities for expanding its influence, he said, "for that is the way we obtained our empire, . . . eagerly coming to the aid of those who call on us, whether barbarians or Greeks; if, on the other hand, we keep our peace and draw fine distinctions as to whom we should help, we would add little to what we already have and run the risk of losing the empire itself." (Thucydides 6.18.2) Like Pericles, he warned that it was too late for Athens to change her policies; having launched upon the course of empire, she could not safely give it up: she must rule or be ruled. But Alcibiades went further, asserting that the Athenian Empire had acquired a character that did not permit it to stop expanding—an inner, dynamic force that did not allow for limits or stability: "A State that is naturally active will quickly be destroyed by changing to inactivity, and people live most safely when they accept the character and institutions they already have, even if they are not perfect, and try to differ from them as little as possible." (Thucydides 6.18.7)

In 432, when they tried to persuade the Spartans to declare war on Athens, the Corinthians made a similar point from a hostile perspective, connecting the dynamic nature of the empire with the similar nature of the Athenians themselves. They drew a sharp contrast between the placid, immobile, defensive character of the Spartans and the dangerous and aggressive character of the Athenians:

When they have thought of a plan and failed to carry it through to full success, they think they have been deprived of their own property; when they have acquired what they aimed at, they think it only a small thing compared with what they will acquire in the future. If it happens that an attempt fails, they form a new hope to compensate for the loss. For with them alone it is the same thing to hope and to have, when once they have invented a scheme, because of the swiftness with which they carry out what they have planned. And in this way they wear out their entire lives with labor and dangers, and they enjoy what they have least of all—men—because they are always engaged in acquisition and because they think their only holiday is to do what is their duty and also because they consider tranquil peace a greater disaster than painful activity. As a result, one would be correct in saying that it is their nature neither to enjoy peace themselves nor allow it to other men. (Thucydides 1.70)

Pericles emphatically disputed such analyses. He did not believe that the Athenian naval empire needed to expand without limit or that the democratic constitution and the empire together had shaped an Athenian citizen who could never be quiet and satisfied. This is not to say that he was blind to the dangers of excessive ambition. He knew there were Athenians who wanted to conquer new lands, especially in the western Mediterranean, Sicily, Italy, and even Carthage. But he was firmly against further expansion, as his future actions would clearly demonstrate. During the great Peloponnesian War, he repeatedly warned the Athenians against trying to increase the size of the empire. It is also revealing that he never spoke of the tremendous potential power of the naval empire until the year before his death, when the Athenians were despondent and needed extraordinary encouragement. He held back from this not merely, as he said, to avoid boastfulness, but chiefly to avoid fanning the flames of excessive ambition.

If Pericles ever had planned to expand the empire, the disastrous result of the Egyptian campaign seems to have convinced him otherwise. Its failure shook the foundations of the empire and threatened the safety of Athens itself. From that time forward, Pericles worked consistently to resist the desires of ambitious expansionists and avoid undue risks. He plainly believed that intelligence and reason could restrain unruly passions, maintain the empire at its current size, and use its revenues for a different, safer, but possibly even greater glory than the Greeks had yet known. As Bismarck believed and declared Germany to be a "saturated" power after its unification in 1871 and

Balkan quarrels "not worth the bones of a healthy Pomeranian grenadier," so Pericles considered the Athenian Empire large enough and its expansion both unnecessary and dangerous. The war against Persia was over; now the success of Pericles' plans and policies depended on his ability to make and sustain peace with the Spartans.

# 6

# PEACEMAKER

Pericles' grand strategy for Athens was to consolidate the empire by limiting it to a defensible size and by maintaining peace with its two powerful rivals, Sparta and Persia. The naval empire was secure because the Athenian fleet was strong enough to put down any rebellion by an island or coastal state. The treaty with Persia realistically reflected the Great King's reluctance to continue fighting Athens. The peace with Sparta, however, rested on unstable foundations, and the recently acquired land empire on the Greek mainland was vulnerable. It had been gained by a single victory at Oenophyta when the Spartans were off in the Peloponnesus and could not return, and it depended on friendly democratic governments imposed by the Athenians on the normally oligarchic Boeotian states. The oligarchs—some in exile, others remaining in their towns—did not accept their defeat and plotted revenge. The prospect of renewed Spartan support or any sign of Athenian weakness could be the signal for a general uprising that could be put down only by infantry, an arm in which the Athenians were at a disadvantage.

The Spartans, for their part, continued to smart over the Athenians' growing power. They were especially vexed by the alliance with Megara, the control it gave over movement to and from the Peloponnesus, the damage this did to Spartan prestige, and the threat all this posed to the Spartan alliance. The restoration of Cimon to power in Athens had given promise of negotiations to resolve these problems, or at least diminish them by friendly and reliable behavior. But his death destroyed those hopes. Sparta's flat rejection of the invitation to a Panhellenic Congress suggests that the friends of peace had already lost out to those who wanted to challenge the Athenians.

The Phocians, allies of the Athenians, had taken command of the temple and oracle of Apollo at Delphi after the Athenian victory at Oenophyta, back in 457. Probably in the spring of 448, the Spartans sent an army to Delphi to return it to the priests. The Spartan attack did not formally break the Five Years' Peace, but it certainly violated its spirit. The Athenian peace with Persia, moreover, made it morally easier to contemplate a conflict with the Athenians, for in opposing the Athenians now it could no longer be said that Sparta was aiding the barbarian. Athens' abandonment of Argos relieved the Spartans of a more practical restraint, for their recent treaty with the Argives defended their exposed flank in the Peloponnesus. Their forcible restoration of the Delphic priests won for Sparta the honor of the *promanteia*, the right to priority in consulting Apollo's oracle. It also helped restore their prestige, so badly damaged by Athenian victories and expansion, at Athenian expense.

Sparta's action was an open challenge to Athenian power and influence in central Greece; a failure to respond could be taken as a sign of weakness and encourage the enemies of Athens. Pericles, now in his prime at about forty-five years of age, marched an army to Delphi, restored its control to the Phocians, and regained the *promanteia* for Athens. Whatever he might have thought of the land empire, Pericles needed to answer the Spartan challenge.

The Athenian response, however, was not enough to prevent the trouble that had been brewing in Boeotia. Heartened by Sparta's action at Delphi, oligarchs in many of the cities launched a general uprising. In the spring of 446, exiled oligarchs seized two cities in western Boeotia, and oligarchs from other Boeotian cities, and from neighboring territories as well, quickly joined them in a movement to drive out the democratic puppets of Athens and to restore autonomy and oligarchy in their cities. The daring and aggressive Athenian general Tolmides wanted to take an army to Boeotia at once, but Pericles sought to prevent it. Plutarch says that Pericles "tried to restrain and persuade him in the assembly, making his famous remark, that if he would not be persuaded by Pericles, he would not go wrong in waiting for time, the wisest of counselors." (*Pericles* 18.2–3)

This well-remembered Periclean intervention provides a valuable clue to the situation. It shows that he was unwilling to risk a major land battle to preserve the empire in central Greece. If it could be held through surrogate regimes supported by occasional demonstrations of force, like the recovery of Delphi, well and good. But if a costly and dangerous campaign on land against an aroused and unusually unified Boeotia were required, the price was too high. Pericles, among other prudent Athenians, was prepared to abandon central Greece rather than put Attica and the naval empire at risk. The tenor of his argument, however, advising delay instead of complete restraint, suggests that the general mood in Athens was different. The majority must have thought that the rebellion could be readily suppressed, and they supported Tolmides in his determination to put it down. They voted him an army of a thousand infantry, which was joined by an unspecified number of allies, presumably whatever number the general thought necessary.

At first his confidence seemed justified, for he quickly captured one of the rebel cities. But the Athenians had badly underestimated the power of the Boeotians. On the march home the army walked into an enemy ambush and was destroyed. Many were taken prisoner, and among the large number killed were such eminent Athenians as Tolmides himself and Cleinias, father of Alcibiades. The Athenians at once entered into a treaty, agreeing to evacuate Boeotia in return for the captured Athenians. The fall of Boeotia made the alliances with Phocis and Locris beyond it untenable, and the Athenian land empire in central Greece was gone at a stroke.

Pericles may have been right in thinking that central Greece was not worth fighting for. But there were also risks in not fighting. In a divided world, the enemies of a great power are always alert for signs of fatigue or weakness on its part. If the Athenians had followed Pericles' advice and abandoned central Greece without a blow, they would not have lost the many men who fell in that campaign, and their dissatisfied subjects and allies would not have been encouraged to think that rebellion was safe. To be sure, sending an inadequate force and suffering defeat was worse than no action at all. But what if the Athenians had sent an army five times the size of Tolmides' corps, something easily within their power? It seems likely that such a force would have crushed the rebellion and returned unharmed, and such a show of strength might well have discouraged further trouble. If Pericles and the Athenians then thought it wise to withdraw from central Greece they could do so at leisure, with dignity and safety.

Pericles appears to have behaved with characteristic rationality. He judged the land empire untenable and unnecessary, so he accepted Athens' expulsion from central Greece. No doubt he was aware of the dangers of retreat, but he knew that Athens' new position was really stronger and more secure than before. It now rested firmly on an unbeatable fleet rather than on an inadequate army, a fact that should have been obvious to all. Rebellions by allies accessible by sea would be easier to put down now that the Athenians' responsibilities were fewer and their resources stretched less thin. But angry men resentful of past defeats do not always think clearly. They are often swayed by passion and are more likely to be deterred by fear and the appearance of power than by more accurate assessments.

Defeat in Boeotia, therefore, sparked new troubles. Athens' many enemies had been watching and waiting for a chance to strike, and this proof that Athens was not invincible gave them courage. The Spartans, also heartened by Athenian failure, appear to have concerted their actions with others. In the summer of 446, Euboea revolted—for Pericles a very different and far more serious danger than the loss of Boetia. Euboea, an island just off Attica's east coast, was a rich and important part of the naval empire containing several considerable cities that paid a large tribute. It was located directly on the vital route through the Dardanelles to the Black Sea. Pericles took personal command of the army sent to put down the rebellion; but he had scarcely arrived when he learned of an even more dangerous threat. The Megarians too had rebelled in collusion with the Spartans and, aided by their Peloponnesian neighbors Corinth, Sicyon, and Epidaurus, had destroyed the Athenian garrisons except for those who could escape to the fort at Nisaea. The Five Years' Peace had expired, the Megarian barrier blocking the road into Attica had been removed, and the Spartans were marching toward Athens at the head of a Peloponnesian army.

Almost overnight, Athens' security had evaporated. There was rebellion in the empire, and the homeland was threatened. Pericles quickly marched his men home to defend the city. The invading army was too strong for the Athenians, but the people still insisted on meeting the enemy in battle. The Peloponnesians, led by the young Spartan king Pleistoanax and his more experienced adviser Cleandridas, entered Attica and began to ravage the territory near the border. A decisive battle seemed imminent when the Peloponnesians inexplicably turned around and went home.

Ancient writers explain the withdrawal in a simple and obvious way: Pericles bribed the king and his adviser to give up the invasion. Plutarch reports that the Spartans were so angry that they punished King Pleistoanax with a fine he could not pay and thereby forced him into exile. Cleandridas also went into exile rather than face a trial and was condemned to death in absentia. Meanwhile, in his accounts for the year's campaign, Pericles listed an item of 10 talents "for necessary expenses." The normally suspicious Athenians accepted the accounts without investigating further. (*Pericles* 22–23)

Aspects of these stories may be true. We cannot be sure that Pericles did not bribe the Spartan leaders; it would be worth a lot more to Athens than 10 talents to get the Peloponnesian army out of Attica. But more probably, these tales are inventions to give plausible accounts for mysterious events. The two Spartans knew that to recall the army without accomplishing their mission would require a valid explanation, and to do so without one would result in punishment. Whether or not he offered them money, Pericles must also have proposed peace terms too good to reject in return for the withdrawal. Probably they were very similar, if not identical, to the terms he negotiated with the Spartans later that year in the Thirty Years' Peace. Central Greece was gone for good; Megara supported by a Peloponnesian army and ruled by a hostile government could not be recovered, nor was any attempt possible while Euboea was still in rebellion. Athens had everything to gain by accepting the new realities and nothing to lose.

Yet the Spartans, too, had good reasons to avoid a battle. Even if the Athenian army stood and fought and the Peloponnesians won, the battle at Tanagara had shown that the Athenians could inflict heavy casualties on the victors. The defeated army could then escape to within Athens' walls, leaving the enemy to ravage the countryside. In this way, with the city, its port, the fleet, and the reserve fund still intact, the Athenians could restore control of their Aegean empire. By fighting, the Spartans would gain nothing that Pericles was not already willing to give up to them. No reasonable Spartan could ask for more. In fact, Pleistoanax would show himself to prefer friendship with Athens throughout his life, and Cleandridas evidently shared his views.

Not all Spartans, of course, were equally reasonable. The more aggressive among them shared a hatred of Athens going back to the Athenian challenge to Spartan leadership in 478. They wanted nothing less than the destruction of the Athenian Empire and thought that a marvelous chance to achieve it had been allowed to slip away. They refused to consider the limited advantages offered by battle and probably believed that only corruption and treason could explain a decision not to fight. Their success in winning a condemnation of the generals shows that this faction could gain the upper hand. When passions cooled, however, the Spartans did not undo the arrangements negotiated by their exiled officials. Having come to their senses, they saw the advantages offered by a peace on the proposed terms and did not renew the war.

Sparta's withdrawal and continued restraint gave Pericles the respite he needed. He returned to Euboea with fifty warships and five thousand infantrymen and easily restored order. The people of Hestiaea, accused of atrocities, were entirely expelled, and their land given to Athenians. Athenians were also settled in cleruchies in the territory of other rebellious cities, garrisons were established, hostages taken, and harsh oaths imposed on the defeated rebels. If there had been any inclination on the part of other subjects to rebel, Pericles' swift and firm actions undoubtedly put an end to it.

In the second half of 446, the Spartans and the Athenians formally negotiated a peace treaty, and in the winter of 446/5 they swore the oaths that ratified it. We do not have a report of the entire agreement and must put its provisions together from scattered references, but the essential elements are clear. In the only territorial provisions, the Athenians agreed to give up all they held in the Peloponnesus, abandoning the continental empire they so briefly possessed. Naupactus on the north shore of the Gulf of Corinth is not mentioned, so the Athenians were allowed to keep that very valuable port. In return, the Spartans granted what amounted to official recognition of what was left of the Athenian Empire, for Sparta and Athens each swore oaths on behalf of their allies. The other provisions of the treaty assumed the division of Greece into two blocs, and members of each alliance were forbidden to change sides. This was an important, if obvious, attempt to prevent a repetition of the late war, which began when Megara moved from one alliance to the other. A more forward-looking clause permitted neutrals to join either alliance, an apparently innocent and sensible item that would cause a surprising amount of trouble. A special arrangement was also made for Argos, which had been allied to Sparta since 451. Argos was excluded from the Thirty Years' Peace and permitted to treat with Athens if it chose; but the resulting alliance could not be directed against Sparta until the expiration of the Argive-Spartan treaty in 421. In any event, the Argives did not take advantage of this permission.

The most novel and interesting clause required both sides to submit any future grievances to binding arbitration. This seems to be the first appearance in history of an attempt to maintain perpetual peace through such a device. We are not told who proposed the idea, but it is tempting to attribute it to Pericles, the originator of many other political and diplomatic innovations.

Not all treaties are the same. Some end a war in which one side has been completely destroyed, like the treaty concluding the last war between Rome and Carthage. This is less a treaty of peace than a statement to the relatives regarding disposal of the body. A second kind comes after a war in which one side imposes harsh terms on an enemy who has been defeated but not destroyed. Such was the peace that Rome imposed on Carthage after the Second Punic War, or that Prussia imposed on France in 1870, and, as the usual view has it, that was imposed on Germany at Versailles. Such a treaty often contains the seeds of another war, because it humiliates the loser without destroying the capacity for revenge. A third kind ends a conflict in which both sides have been made aware of the dangers of war and the virtues of peace, whether or not there has been a winner on the battlefield. The Peace of Westphalia in 1648 and the settlement with which the Congress of Vienna ended the Napoleonic Wars are good examples. Such a treaty aims not at destruction or punishment but at a guarantee of stability against the renewal of war. For this kind of treaty to succeed, it must accurately reflect the military and political situation, and must rest on a sincere desire to make it work. All must see it as a lasting peace, not merely a truce between battles.

The Thirty Years' Peace of 446/5 was closest to treaties of the third category. In many years of war, both sides had suffered losses and dangers. Neither had won a notably decisive victory, and each had been unsuccessful in the other's favored element. Each had reason to doubt that it could win a war and impose its will. The peace they made, therefore, was a compromise, and one that seems to have contained the basic elements for success. Most important was its realism. The Thirty Years' Peace realistically reflected the balance of power between the two alliances; by recognizing Spartan hegemony on the mainland and Athenian control of the Aegean, it took a long step toward eliminating a major cause of unrest in the Greek world since the Persian War.

The events of 479–477 had split the leadership of Greece. The fiction of unity under Spartan leadership had been maintained with increasing strain and difficulty until Cimon's expulsion from the Peloponnesus in 462. The First Peloponnesian War was a chance to restore unity under one leader or the other. Since neither side proved strong enough to defeat the other in its own element, a peace that recognized this dualism in the Greek world promised future stability.

But like any settlement, this one also contained elements of possible instability. Mutual distrust had by no means disappeared. Some Athenians had not given up their dreams of further expansion, and some Spartans resented sharing hegemony with Athens. Others and some of their allies feared Athenian ambition, and some believed that the very existence of a powerful Athens ruling over a vast naval empire threatened the safety and independence of the other Greeks. Athenians knew these suspicions and hostilities existed, and some of them were afraid that the Spartans and their allies were merely waiting for a favorable opportunity. Some Spartans must have been frustrated by Pleistoanax' withdrawal from Attica without a battle, convinced that a fight would have brought total victory, and were eager to resume hostilities when the chance came. Corinth was annoyed that the Athenians had been allowed to keep Naupactus; Megara was controlled by a government that had just massacred Athenian garrisons. Boeotia, and especially Thebes, had similar regimes and similar feelings. There was potential trouble in the fact that the Athenian Empire included states with special claims on the friendship of Sparta, like Aegina, and on Corinth, like Potidaea. The right of neutrals to join either side might, in some circumstances, produce conflict.

All these were possible sources of danger and instability. But we need not doubt that the men who made the peace intended to keep it. The arbitration clause, by no means conventional and easily rejected, suggests that both sides truly wanted peace and were ready to seek any means to avoid wars in the future. The important questions were: Could each side conduct itself so as to allay the suspicions of the other and build mutual confidence? Could the friends of peace in each state retain power, instead of more bellicose opponents? Could the leader of each side control its allies if they threatened to create instability? When Pericles concluded the Thirty Years' Peace in 446/5, he had good reason to believe that the answers to these questions would be affirmative.

The first test of the peace came from a surprising source: the distant land of southern Italy, near the limits of the Greek world. Nothing that took place there was important to the great powers, but Pericles found a way to use those events to communicate his peaceable intentions to the Spartans and their allies.

At the Gulf of Taranto lay the Greek city of Sybaris, whose citizens' taste for luxurious living has provided a synonym for voluptuaries. They were said to honor cooks with golden crowns and give them the same honors for preparing a fine meal that they gave the *choregoi* for staging winning tragedies. They taught their horses to dance and were once defeated in a battle when their opponents played tunes on the flute that lured their cavalry away. They went to parties at night and slept all day, imposing the first anti-noise legislation; even roosters were barred from the town.

Founded about 720, Sybaris was repeatedly destroyed in wars with its neighbors. Shortly after the Thirty Years' Peace in 445, the Sybarites, again defeated and homeless, tried to rebuild their city. This time they sought assistance from each of the leading cities in Greece, inviting both the Spartans and the Athenians to join in the new foundation. Most Greek colonies were sent off by the mother city as a way of easing population pressure on a home territory short of good farmland. Some were located with an eye to establishing a profitable trading post. The Spartans, of course, had no population to spare and no interest in trade, so they refused. The Athenians, on the other hand, had been sending out colonists and cleruchs for some time and were particularly active that year. Most of these settlements were in strategic locations in the Aegean, especially cities that had recently rebelled, and were aimed at making the empire more secure. They also show that Athens still had an excess population that was glad to trade a hand-to-mouth existence in the city for a good piece of farmland overseas.

The colonists sent to found the new settlement in Italy, in one of the most fertile areas inhabited by Greeks, must have gone primarily in search of land, for they did not go to form an Athenian colony but as individual settlers, citizens of the new Sybaris. The Sybarites, however, who had long had trouble with neighboring cities, now

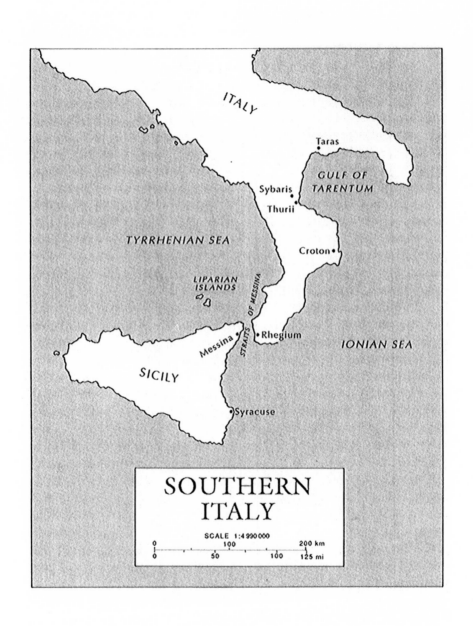

ITALY

Taras

GULF OF
TARENTUM

Sybaris

Thurii

TYRRHENIAN SEA

Croton

LIPARIAN
ISLANDS

STRAITS OF MESSINA

Rhegium

IONIAN SEA

Messina

SICILY

Syracuse

# SOUTHERN
# ITALY

SCALE 1:4 990 000

| 0 | 100 | 200 km |
|---|-----|--------|
| 0 | 50 | 100 | 125 mi |

quarreled with their new fellow-citizens. They claimed superior rights and provoked the new settlers to the point of civil war. The obnoxious and isolated Sybarites so enraged the others that they "were destroyed by the Athenians and other Greeks, who, although they had come to live with them, despised them so much that they not only killed them but moved the city to another place and called it Thurii." (Strabo, p. 263, 6.1.13)

The remaining citizen body sent to the Greek homeland for more settlers, and the Athenians again responded, but in a very different way. In 444/3, they organized a colonizing expedition to re-found Thurii on a new basis. Thurii was not to be an Athenian colony but a Panhellenic one, and the Athenians sent messengers all over Greece to recruit colonists. The chief founder was Lampon, and the settlers included the historian Herodotus and the orator Lysias—all friends of Pericles. The idea of Panhellenism is unprecedented in the foundation of Greek colonies but consistent with the Congress Decree, which Pericles himself had proposed a few years earlier. Why did he conceive this novel idea?

Some modern scholars believe that Pericles was an expansionist who did not even try to rein in Athenian imperial ambitions, and despite its Panhellenic facade, they see the foundation of Thurii as part of a continuing Athenian imperial growth, in the west no less than in the east. If they are right, Pericles must have pursued very different aims and policies from the ones we have described. But the evidence shows otherwise. The Athenians, in fact, showed no other interest in the west in the decade between the Thirty Years' Peace and the ultimate crisis that brought on the Peloponnesian War, so the test of the theory must be Thurii itself. In the new city only one of the ten tribes was made up of Athenians and the single largest group consisted of Peloponnesians, so Pericles could not have expected to control its behavior, much less use it for Athenian purposes. The colony's history, moreover, indicates that he had no such intentions.

Not long after its new foundation, Thurii fought a war against the Spartan colony of Taras and was defeated. The victorious Tarantines set up a trophy and an inscription at Olympia for all to see: "The Tarantines offered a tenth of the spoils they took from the Thurians to Olympian Zeus." At this point, those who believe that Thurii was intended as an outpost of Athenian imperialism have to contend with the curious behavior of the Athenians, who took no action. If Pericles meant for Thurii to be the center of an Athenian Empire in the west, he should have urged the Athenians or their western allies to inter-

vene. Instead, he stood by and allowed the victorious Spartan colony
to flaunt its success in the most public of Greek gathering places.

The Athenian attitude toward Thurii met a sharper test in 434/3,
in the midst of the crisis that would result in the Peloponnesian War.
Growing tension between Athens and Sparta in that year must have
provoked a quarrel among the Thurians as to whose colony it was.
The Athenians claimed Athens as the founding city since the greatest
number of settlers from a single city came from there. The others
argued that since there were more settlers from the combined cities
of the Peloponnesus than from Athens, the colony was Peloponnesian. The very argument shows that the city had never been regarded
as an Athenian colony but as Panhellenic. But the newly tense international situation created the desire for a different definition. Unable
to settle the matter, the Thurians sent to Delphi to ask, "Who shall be
called the founder of the city?" The god replied that he himself should
be considered the founder. Thus peace was restored. The Panhellenic
character of the colony was reaffirmed, and a connection with Athens
firmly denied.

Once again the Athenians did nothing, but this time their inaction is even more surprising. With a war against the Peloponnesians
a real possibility, Thurii took on new importance. In Athenian hands
it could be helpful as an outpost and a source of grain; in Peloponnesian hands it could serve the enemy in the same ways. Yet Pericles
did not urge intervention, even though Delphic Apollo was friendly
to Sparta,[1] and his acceptance as founder of Thurii made it more
likely that the colony would side with Sparta in case of war. Thurii
was plainly a Panhellenic colony and Pericles consistently treated it
that way.

Why did Pericles pursue these policies? It seems he simply
seized the opportunity to make a positive statement. An Athenian
refusal would have avoided provocation but would soon be forgotten.
By inventing the idea of a Panhellenic colony and planting it in an
area outside Athens' sphere of influence, Pericles was sending a diplomatic signal. Thurii would stand as visible evidence that Athens,
rejecting the opportunity to establish its own colony, had no imperial
ambitions in the west and wished to pursue a policy of peaceful
Panhellenism. We shall see that his message was received and understood.

The foundation of Thurii had attractions for Pericles apart from
foreign policy. In 444/3 he faced an unusually strong political challenge from Thucydides, son of Melesias, who opposed the use of

imperial funds for nonmilitary purposes, and whose rhetoric appealed to a combination of anti-imperialism and Panhellenism. Pericles accordingly seems to have used the request from the Thurians as a weapon in this domestic political struggle. At some point during that year, but certainly before the showdown that reslted in Thucydides' ostracism, Pericles announced his plan to found the new Thurian colony. In one stroke this would have taken the wind out of his opponent's sails, demonstrating his moderation, his adherence to the spirit of the Thirty Years' Peace, and his own Panhellenic sentiments.

Pericles may have had still another reason for taking an interest in the proposed colony, quite apart from politics and diplomacy. His adult life was dedicated to the development, glorification, and defense of a great city and a brilliant civic life on a grand and original plan. His native city was his workshop and the Athenian imperial democracy his masterpiece; but his achievement came in a framework created by others over many generations. The invitation to found an entirely new city at Thurii must have presented an irresistible opportunity to design the new colony de novo, employing the best minds of the day to create a city unlike all those produced by trial and error and unplanned by a ruling intelligence.

The choice of Lampon as chief founder may seem surprising, for although he was a friend and supporter of Pericles, he was also an important figure in the traditional religious life of Athens, a way of life not much favored by the rational and worldly Athenian statesman. Plutarch tells us that a unicorn was brought to Pericles in the company of both Lampon and the natural philosopher Anaxagoras. Lampon, a seer and interpreter of signs and oracles, interpreted the aberration as a cosmic message referring to the struggle between Pericles and Thucydides and predicting its resolution by a victory for Pericles and the reunification of the state. Anaxagoras, on the other hand, dissected the animal's skull and explained the phenomenon rationally and naturally as a malformation of the brain cavity. Pericles, no doubt, preferred the explanation of Anaxagoras; however, the leader of the Athenian contingent in the new colony had to be an Athenian. And since most Athenians, and especially the poorer people who were making the journey, firmly believed in supernatural signs and portents, Lampon was the prudent choice. For them, Lampon was not only a respected public figure but a reassuring symbol of divine approval and guidance.

The site of the new settlement was also chosen in the traditional way, according to the advice of the Delphic oracle. But the new city was laid out in the most up-to-date manner by the pioneer of Greek town planning, Hippodamus of Miletus, who not long before had laid out Athens' bustling and expanding port city of Piraeus.

Ancient cities were normally unplanned, growing out as the need arose. Their streets followed cow paths, winding and meandering about. A modern visitor can easily grasp their character by walking in the old section, the Plaka, north of the Acropolis in Athens today. If Hippodamus did not invent the urban grid, with the city divided into blocks by a pattern of parallel streets, he at least became the acknowledged master of the art of city planning. (A century later, Aristotle would recommend that the ideal city be laid out in the "modern" style of Hippodamus.) Hippodamus regarded himself as one of the group of natural philosophers who came from his native city—the home and center of the Greek Enlightenment—and he was, according to Aristotle, "the first man who was not engaged in politics who attempted to say something about the best constitution." (*Politics* 1267b).

The man assigned to draft the new city's constitution was Protagoras of Abdera, the leading political theorist of his day. We know that the Thurian constitution was democratic and that, like Athens, its citizenry was divided into ten tribes. But that is all we know. Still another founding settler was Herodotus of Halicarnassus, the inventor of a new genre of prose composition, historical investigation. Perhaps it was expected that he would write a history of this extraordinary foundation. It is tempting to think that Pericles, having made the necessary bow to tradition by appointing Lampon as founder, had urged his innovative friends, each at the forefront of his discipline, to lend their talents to the construction of a new city on rational principles. If so, he must have been disappointed with the results, for Thurii lost its first war, soon fell into civil discord, and joined the enemy side in the last phase of the Peloponnesian War. Although it continued to exist under the Roman Empire, it seems to have achieved nothing remarkable.

However, in respect to his foreign policy, the foundation of Thurii appears to have achieved its goal, as the outcome of a serious crisis would soon reveal. In the summer of 440, a war broke out between Samos and Miletus over control of a town that lay between them. The island of Samos was a completely autonomous ally of Athens, a charter member of the Delian League, and one of only three states that still paid no tribute and possessed its own navy. Miletus had also been a league member from the beginning; but it had twice revolted and had been punished accordingly. It was a subject ally, had no fleet, paid tribute, and it had a democratic constitution imposed upon it. Having deprived Miletus of the means of self-defense, the Athenians could not stand idly by while it was crushed by a powerful neighbor. Thus, when a Milesian delegation asked them to intervene they could not refuse.

The Athenians asked the Samians to submit the dispute to arbitration, but their request was rejected. This presented Pericles with a crisis of the first order. The rebuff was an act of defiance that could not be ignored, for if Athens could not defend the weak members of the alliance from the strong, its claim to leadership was a sham. Pericles therefore took personal charge, acting promptly and decisively. With forty ships he sailed to Samos and put down the rebellion. He replaced the ruling oligarchy with a democratic government, imposed a sizable indemnity, took fifty men and fifty boys as hostages to the island of Lemnos, and withdrew as swiftly as he had come, leaving a garrison behind.

The swiftness of Pericles' response had obviously taken the Samians by surprise. When they had recovered their composure and the Athenian fleet was gone, they began to plot a more effective rebellion. Until then their quarrel with Miletus and their defiance of Athens had limited goals. After Pericles' attack, the leaders of the Samian uprising were furious and turned their rebellion into a major revolution in which they "contested the supremacy of the sea" (Plutarch, *Pericles* 25.3) with Athens. Some fled to the continent and inland to the Persian satrap Pissuthnes, who allowed them to raise a mercenary army in his territory. He also stole the hostages from Lemnos, thereby freeing the Samian rebels to go forward. The conspirators and their hired army returned to Samos by night, catching the democrats and the Athenian garrison unaware. They imprisoned some democrats and sent others into exile. As a final act of defiance, the victorious Samian oligarchs sent the captured Athenian garrison and imperial officials off to the Persian satrap in Asia Minor.

News of the Samian rebellion raced through the empire, sparking emulation in many places, most dangerously at Byzantium, astride the vital Athenian grain route through the Bosporus. Mytilene, the major city of Lesbos, which had a navy of its own, awaited only a word of support from Sparta before joining the rebellion. Two elements of the coalition that would ultimately defeat Athens were now in place: revolt in the empire and support from Persia. Everything depended on Sparta's decision, for the rebellions would subside and the Persians would draw back if the Spartans stayed out of the dispute. Sparta's decision, in turn, was strongly influenced by Corinth, for the Corinthians alone among the Peloponnesians could produce the fleet needed to challenge Athens.

The test of Pericles' policy of peaceful coexistence with the Peloponnesians was at hand. If the Spartans and their allies, especially the Corinthians, regarded the foundation of Thurii as a prelude to the expansion of the Athenian Empire into the west, they might be expected to take advantage of the marvelous strategic opportunity offered by the rebellion in the Aegean.

The Spartans called a meeting of the Peloponnesian League to respond to the Samian request. Opinion was divided when a Corinthian intervention decided the issue. As a Corinthian spokesman later put it to the Athenian assembly, "We did not vote against you when the other Peloponnesians were divided in their voting as to whether they should aid the Samians," flatly taking credit for preventing Spartan aid to Samos. (Thucydides 1.40.5–6, 41.2) The congress departed without taking action, sealing the fate of Samos and ending the prospect of both a general rebellion and of further Persian intervention.

The Corinthians' hatred of Athens went back two decades and they would be the main advocates of war against them in the final crisis only a few years later. Why then did they act as peacemakers in 440? The most plausible explanation is that they then believed in the sincerity of Pericles' claim that the Athenians were not trying to expand their empire in the west and regarded the foundation of a colony at Thurii as innocuous. Pericles' insistence on making it a Panhellenic settlement was plainly understood in this way, and we may believe that it helped resolve a dangerous crisis without war.

Pericles was now free to put down the Samian rebellion, which remained a serious challenge despite the Peloponnesian refusal to intervene. The Samian fleet was strong enough to "contest the supremacy of the sea"; before the war was over they had come "within a very little of taking control of the sea away from Athens." (Plutarch, *Pericles* 25.3; Thucydides 8.76.4) Once again Pericles himself took command of the fleet that sailed to Samos. The military threat was serious, for the Samian navy gave a good account of itself. At one point the Samians cleared Athenian ships from the waters around the island for a period of two weeks, and their navy was not beaten until a squadron of reinforcements arrived from Athens. Even then, the stubborn Samians refused to surrender, holding out under siege into the ninth month. Pericles conducted the siege, and his problem was complicated by a rumor that the Phoenician contingent of the Persian navy was on its way to help the Samians. Although the Phoenicians never came, the rumor of their approach and the determination of the Samian defense created the risk that the rebellion would spread in spite of Sparta's unwillingness to help.

The danger of rebellion in the empire, whether in an oligarchic or democratic state, was always greatest among the rich and noble. Instead of leaving his fleet to assure the reliability of these men himself, Pericles took advantage of an inadvertent opportunity. One of the generals for that year was the tragic poet Sophocles. The Chian poet Ion, his contemporary, rightly described him as having no relevant credentials for the assignment; he was "just like anyone among the upper classes of Athens." (Athenaeus 603d) Sophocles appears to have been part of Cimon's circle of friends, who joined in the general union with the Pericleans after Cimon's return from exile and remained friendly with Pericles thereafter. Rich, noble, and distinguished, he was the perfect ambassador to the nobles of the empire, whose loyalty Pericles so desperately needed at that moment.

While Pericles awaited reinforcements for the assault on Samos, he sent Sophocles to Chios and Lesbos, the only remaining allies who retained autonomy and a fleet. No doubt the islanders had more than one reason for remaining loyal to Athens. But Pericles had reason to be pleased with the poet-diplomat. His mission was entirely successful, for not only did the two key islands not rebel, they both sent fleets to help the Athenians in their siege.

In 439, Samos surrendered, after holding out for nine months, and Byzantium followed soon after. The Samians were required to pull down their walls, give up their fleet, accept a democratic constitution, and pay a war indemnity of 1,300 talents in twenty-six annual installments. At fifty talents a year this was a considerable burden. On the other hand, they paid no tribute and were not compelled to receive garrisons or cleruchies. Byzantium, whose resistance had been mild, was allowed to return to the empire under the same conditions as before. There were no exiles, executions, or confiscations of land.

The defiance by the Samians, the fierceness of their resistance, their collaboration with the Persians, the danger of general rebellion in the empire, and war against the Peloponnesians that they had provoked must have frightened and angered the Athenians. There must have been some sentiment in Athens for a harsher punishment,[2] but Pericles was able to convince the Athenians to restrain their anger. This moderation was characteristic of Pericles' management of the empire in the remaining years before the Peloponnesian War. By the standards of the time, and sharply in contrast with Athenian practice after Pericles' death, his was a firm but reasonable policy. In this way, Pericles hoped to secure the safety of the empire and to avoid wasting money on the suppression of rebellions.

So ended the rebellion that had threatened to become a great war and to dismember the Athenian Empire. Pericles came out of the affair with his personal prestige at its peak. He had won a military victory that could be compared with Cimon's achievements. The diplomatic support afforded him by the Peloponnesians—active on the part of the Corinthians, passive as befit the Spartans—completely vindicated his policy toward them. The moderation of his treatment of the rebels and his employment of such orthodox and respected men as Sophocles and Lampon must have gone a long way toward dispelling the picture of Pericles as the immoral, aggressive radical that the son of Melesias had tried to paint.

Pericles was chosen to give the funeral oration over the men who had fallen at Samos, and it was greatly admired. Plutarch says that when he came down from the speaker's platform the "women clasped his hand and fastened fillets and wreaths on his head, as though he were some victorious athlete." (*Pericles* 28.4) But not everyone had been converted. Some spread the libel that Pericles had made war on the Samians at the urging of his mistress Aspasia on behalf of her native city, Miletus. Plutarch reports a negative reaction from a more interesting quarter. As the other women were adorning Pericles after his speech, Cimon's sister Elpinice drew near and said: "These are wonderful deeds you have done, Pericles, destroying so many of our good citizens, not fighting Phoenicians and Persians, as my brother Cimon did, but subjugating an ally and a city of our own blood." (*Pericles* 28.4) This kind of talk must have been widespread among the hard-liners who remained loyal to their exiled leader, Thucydides. Yet Pericles was content to reply mildly, for not many Athenians shared their views and no one had emerged to take the place of his latest challenger. Thus, in 439, Pericles not only stood without an effective rival, he had also gone far toward creating a consensus the like of which Athens had not seen for a long time.

The affair at Samos also strengthened the empire, for it showed the Athenian capacity to suppress rebellion and the great risk inherent in depending on support from Sparta or Persia. Peloponnesian restraint served to confirm a situation that had already been accepted by the Spartans and their allies in 446/5. There was every reason to think that peace was more likely after the Samian rebellion than before, and Pericles now had the financial and political resources to pursue his vision for the glorification of his native city.

# 7

# VISIONARY

ericles' long tenure as a political leader permitted him to aim at goals that went far beyond the immediate concerns that fully occupy most politicians and statesmen. Both his words and deeds reveal that he was one of those rare individuals who do not merely accept the conditions of the world they find but try to shape it to an image in their own minds. The evidence is unmistakable that Pericles had such a vision for his city and that he tried to bring it into being. He saw the opportunity to create the greatest political community the world had ever known, one that would fulfill man's strongest and deepest passions—glory and immortality. The satisfaction of these passions normally implies extraordinary inequality; yet Pericles believed they could be achieved by the citizens of a democracy based on legal and political equality. At the same time, he intended to create a quality of life never before known, one that would allow men to pursue their private interests but also enable them to seek the highest goals by placing their interests at the service of a city that fostered and relied upon reason for its greatness.

To shape that vision and persuade others of its virtues, Pericles needed to overcome the attractive force of two earlier views of the best human life. The older was the aristocratic image that emerged from the epic poems of Homer; it dominated Greek society for hundreds of years and always exerted a strong attraction. The newer image, provided by Sparta, took shape no earlier than the seventh century but immediately captured the imagination of many and continued to fascinate Greek thinkers for centuries. Both were serious challenges to the new conception proposed by Pericles. He met them by adapting the former to his own purposes and by rejecting the latter as inferior to the new society he had introduced in Athens.

Pericles' vision was the culmination of a long process whereby the polis had tried to impose its communal, civic values on a society that had always been organized by family, clan, and tribe. The older ethical tradition came chiefly from the Homeric epic, where the esteemed values were those of heroic individuals. Achilles came to fight at Troy not for any national, ethnic, or communal cause but for his own purposes: to obtain booty seized from captured cities and to display the heroic excellence that Homer called *arete*. Through such a display he hoped to win the kind of fame that would gain him immortality as the memory of his great deeds passed on through the generations, sung and embellished by bards like Homer. When, in the opening scene of the *Iliad*, Achilles' honor and reputation are diminished by Agamemnon's arrogance, he retires from the battle and sulks in his tent while the Greeks suffer a series of costly defeats. He even asks the gods to aid the enemy so that he may gain vengeance against Agamemnon because, as Achilles himself says, "he did no honor to the best of the Achaeans."

From the first, the Greeks faced the great truth of man's mortality squarely. They lived without the comfort of the two major devices that other cultures used to evade that terrible truth. They did not believe that man was entirely trivial, a mere bit of dust in the vast cosmic order, such that his passing was a thing of no account. Instead, they thought man was of the same race as the gods, a creature capable of extraordinary achievements. Nor did they believe in personal immortality, in which death is a blessing, a release from a painful and wretched life and admission to paradise. Death is the end; beyond it is silence and darkness. Homeric virtues and values, therefore, were worldly and personal. Courage, strength, military prowess, persuasiveness, cunning, beauty, wealth; these were examples of *arete*, the excellent qualities of the good, the fortunate, the happy man. Some were acquired by effort; others were simply a gift of irrational fate. But the reward of these virtues was *kleos*, the fame and glory that alone held out the hope of victory over death.

When some time in the eighth century the polis emerged, its needs at once came into conflict with the old heroic ethos. The polis was a political community and a sovereign entity competing in a world of similar communities. Wars were frequent; and in order to survive and flourish each polis required devotion and sacrifice from its citizens. One way that it gained the needed commitment was by creating, for the first time in history, a true political life which allowed its active citizens to exercise human capacity previously employed by very few.

Most poleis had aristocratic or oligarchic governments, but they were ruled by laws arrived at in discussions in the sovereign assemblies, and they were executed by councils and magistrates selected by the citizens from among themselves. Judgment was rendered according to their laws, once again, by courts made up of citizens. In early Athens, as in most of the Greek cities, political participation came to represent a crucial distinction between a free man and gentleman on the one hand, and a slave or churl on the other. Greeks deprived of the political life felt the loss keenly. When the Mytilenean poet Alcaeus was sent into exile the loss he complained of was not his house and fields but the scenes of political life: "I yearn, Agesilaidas, to hear the herald summon the assembly and the council." (Alcaeus, fragment 130) The chance to speak brilliantly and with results in the public meeting was a gift given only by the polis, a way of winning *kleos* by the arts of speech.

Beyond those advantages, its early champions tried to show that the polis was necessary for civilized life, and therefore deserved the highest sacrifice. Solon, an Athenian lawmaker of the early sixth century, went further, arguing that a well-governed polis was the best defense against injustice, faction, and turmoil: "It makes all things wise and perfect in the world of men."

But these benefits, important as they were, did not appeal to the most basic spiritual need of all, the need for *kleos* and immortality. When wealthy aristocrats won victories in athletic contests, they could pay poets like Pindar to preserve their memories in verse; they could sponsor public monuments by great architects and sculptors; the richest of them could even erect temples to the gods, dedicated in their own names. But most of the citizens, even in undemocratic states, had no such opportunities.

How could the ordinary man achieve *kleos*? Herodotus tells a story, metaphorically true even if historically dubious, in which Solon gave some answers. The Lydian ruler Croesus, the richest man in the world, expecting to hear his own name, asked the Athenian sage, Who was the happiest of mortals? Solon responded, "Tellus of Athens," a name neither Croesus nor anyone else outside of Athens had ever heard. Croesus asked why, and this was Solon's response:

> "Tellus' polis was prosperous, and he was the father of noble sons, and he saw children born to all of them, and they all grew up. And after a life spent in what among our people passes for comfort, he died most gloriously. In a battle between the Athenians and their neighbors near Eleusis, he came to the aid of his fellow-citizens, turned the enemy to rout, and died most nobly. The Athenians gave him a public burial on the spot where he fell [only the men who died at Marathon received the same extraordinary honor] had honored him greatly. (1:30)

The tale tells us much about Greek values. In what does happiness lie? In moderate material comfort, good health, long life, virtuous offspring, and an opportunity for *kleos*—the last two representing man's hopes for immortality preserved in the memory of his family and his polis. But even in Herodotus' tale such glory is for the rare individual who had both the ability and the opportunity to perform a great deed. The average citizen could not look even to his polis for the satisfaction of his greatest spiritual needs. It was still open to each man to seek satisfaction in the pursuit of his own interests and those of his family, if necessary at the expense of the polis.

The Spartans faced this fundamental problem of the polis in its sharpest form. They ruled over the regions of Laconia and Messenia in the Peloponnesus, where they were a very small minority of the total population. At an early date they had abandoned the normal means whereby men provide for themselves and their families, including all economic activity: farming, pasturing, trade, craft, and industry. For trade and the manufacture of whatever they needed, the Spartans relied on the *perioikoi*—people who lived in free communities in Laconia, gave control of foreign policy to the Spartans, and served under Spartan command in the army. For their food, the Spartans relied on the helots—slaves of the Spartan state who out-numbered the Spartans by at least seven to one, bitterly hated their masters, and, in the words of the fourth-century writer Xenophon, "would gladly eat them raw." (*Hellenica* 3.3.6) From time to time the helots would break out in revolt, threatening the very existence of Sparta.

To cope with this threat the Spartans turned their polis into a military academy and an armed camp, giving up the normal pleasures of life and devoting themselves entirely to the state. For them, noth-ing could interfere with the claims of the polis to their loyalty and devotion, so they rejected privacy, imposed a rigid economic equality on the members of the Spartiate class, attenuated the independence of the family and its control of its offspring, and made individual goals entirely subordinate to those of the state. They excluded money, the arts and sciences, philosophy, aesthetic pleasures, and the life of the mind in general, for all these things might foster individualism and detract from devotion to the polis. Their national poet, Tyrtaeus, specifically rejected the Homeric values and replaced them with a single definition of *arete*: the courage to stand bravely in the ranks of a hoplite phalanx fighting for Sparta.

The Spartan way of life inspired admiration in many other Greeks, though none went so far as to adopt the Spartan system. Cimon had praised the Spartan polis throughout his life and held it up for emulation to the extent that was possible in Athens. In the con-troversy attending the expansion of Athenian democracy under Ephi-altes and Pericles, we can be sure that his supporters regularly contrasted the Spartan way with the new democratic regime to the latter's disadvantage. Sparta's system appealed especially to aristo-crats, such as the young men "with the battered ears" who conversed with Socrates in the gymnasia. And when such philosophers as Plato modeled their utopian regimes on Sparta, they were building on a tradition that viewed its constitution as a standing rebuke to Athenian democracy.

In the real world, however, no one would adopt that demanding and perverse way of life except in the unique circumstances that brought it to Sparta. Least of all did it suit the open, democratic society that Athens had already become by the time Pericles was born. For Athenians, the individual and familial values sung by Homer remained vital and attractive; yet their polis needed a Spartan commitment and devotion to meet the challenge of the Persian invasions, of the acquisition of the empire, and of the jealousy of Sparta and her allies. But a free and democratic people, one not constantly fearful of deadly rebellions by furious helots, cannot simply be told permanently to subordinate their personal pursuits to the needs of society. To win the necessary devotion, the city—or rather its leaders, poets, and teachers—must show that its demands are compatible with the needs of the citizen, and even better, that the city is needed to achieve his own goals. Perhaps the most striking proof of Pericles' greatness lay in his ability to explain how the interests of the city and its citizens depended on each other for fulfillment.

The citizen of a free society has the right to ask, Why should I risk my life for my city? The willingness to perform military service for his homeland is the most fundamental and demanding duty of the citizen. Yet an Athenian reared in the Homeric tradition could also ask, "How can I achieve *kleos* and thereby a chance at immortality? Most of Pericles' answers to these questions can be found in the Funeral Oration that he delivered in the winter of 431/30, less than two years before his death, at the end of the first year of the Peloponnesian War. These solemn commemorations, apparently unique to the Athenian democracy, had a political dimension, for the speaker was someone "chosen by the polis as the man who seemed wisest in judgment and foremost in reputation." (Thucydides 2.34.6) Pericles had delivered the funeral speech during the Samian War, in which he had also commanded the campaign. In the first year of the Peloponnesian War, however, he had taken no part in any fighting. His selection as public orator was thus a tribute to his stature, reputation, and political power.

Pericles' Funeral Oration was delivered during a war that was clearly going to continue for some time. Thus its chief purpose, even more important than praising the dead, was to explain why they had been right to risk their lives and why the living should be willing to do likewise. In this respect it was very much like Abraham Lincoln's funeral oration at Gettysburg in 1863. With brilliant brevity Lincoln answered some questions by pointing to the greatness of the cause at issue. America was "a new nation, conceived in Liberty, and dedicated to the proposition that all men are created equal." Victory would mean "a new birth of freedom," and would ensure that "government of the people, by the people, and for the people, shall not perish from the earth." The fallen soldiers' purpose was to preserve a constitution and a way of life that was unique and worthy of sacrifice. More fully, and therefore at greater length, Pericles did the same thing. In the process, he presented his vision for Athens and the kind of citizen its unique constitution and way of life would produce. It contained a clear, if often implicit, contrast with the Spartan way of life, which so many Greeks admired but which Pericles regarded as inferior to the Athens he portrayed.

"First," he said, "I shall make clear through what practices we have come to our present position and with what political constitution and way of life our city has become great." The institutions responsible are original in Athens and have become the model for other states. They are, of course, democratic, but Pericles' explanation of what that means is a refutation of the attacks made by the enemies of democracy. The hostile descriptions emphasize its excessive commitment to equality, complaining of the absurdity of distributing offices by lot and the evils of payment for public service, but even more of the flaws in the democratic principle itself.

Plato asserted that democracy unjustly "distributes a sort of equality to equal and unequal alike" (*Republic* 55C), and Aristotle later claimed that in democracies justice "is the enjoyment of arithmetical equality, and not the enjoyment of proportionate equality on the basis of merit." (*Politics* 1317b) Democracy's critics also pointed to a perverted individualism that was called liberty but was really license and lawlessness. They also complained of the lack of uniform good character in the citizens, who were unpredictably involved in various activities and masters of none, with negative consequences for their military ability. Critics saw it as a special failure of the Athenian constitution that it did not put a common stamp on all the citizens, as the Spartan constitution did, and as many Greeks thought proper. Plato recognized that the freedom afforded by the Athenian democracy seemed pleasant to many people, but his own judgment was less friendly: Democracy is "an agreeable, anarchic form of society, with plenty of variety, which treats all men as equal, whether they are equal or not." (*Republic* 558C) The kind of man formed by such a constitution reflects its shortcomings:

> He lives from day to day indulging the appetite of the hour; and sometimes he is lapped in drink and strains of the flute; then he becomes a water-drinker, and tries to get thin; then he takes a turn at gymnastics; sometimes idling and neglecting everything, then once more living the life of a philosopher; often he is busy with politics, and starts to his feet and says and does whatever comes into his head; and, if he is emulous of anyone who is a warrior, off he is in that direction, or men of business, once more in that. His life has neither law nor order; and this

distracted existence he terms joy and bliss and freedom; and so he goes on. (*Republic* 561C)

Plato and Aristotle wrote long after the death of Pericles, and it is by no means clear that these descriptions fit the real Athenian democracy at any time. But they surely reflected contemporary criticisms. Pericles made use of this occasion to respond in detail and to show how the city he had in mind met their complaints. The Athenians depicted in his Funeral Oration are idealized images, and events would soon show the darker, less admirable side of Athenian society. But the Funeral Oration was intended to inspire the Athenians with a vision of excellence that justified their current efforts. It also had the practical purpose of justifying the war at a time when both the decision to fight and the strategy Pericles had chosen were under severe political attack.

Part of the speech met the challenge posed by the heroic tradition that emphasized competition, excellence, or merit and the undying glory that rewarded it. These aristocratic values never lost their powerful attraction to all Greeks, and Pericles claimed them for the Athenian democracy. He rejected the notion that democracy turned its back on excellence, reducing all to equality at a low level. Instead, it opened the competition for excellence and honor to all, removing the accidental barriers imposed in other constitutions and societies.

Pericles made no direct mention of the use of allotment and payment for public service, the chief targets of contemporary critics. These are only means to the end of liberating the talents of all to take part in the political life and serve the polis.

> Our city is called a democracy because it is governed by the many, not the few. In the realm of private disputes everyone is equal before the law, but when it is a matter of public honors each man is preferred not on the basis of his class but of his good reputation and his merit [*arete*]. No one, moreover, if he has it in him to do some good for the city, is barred because of poverty or humble origins. (Thucydides 2.37.1)

The aristocrat believed that the poor were not free, because their poverty deprived them of leisure and, therefore, of the opportunity to take part in public life. In the Athens of Pericles, however, the general prosperity and payment for public service gave the average man a degree of leisure unknown in other states. Pericles therefore asserts that "we conduct our public life as free men [*eleutheroi*]." (2.37.2)

Neither rich man nor poor is prevented from taking part in politics by the pursuit of his economic interests,

> and the same people are concerned both with their own private business and with political matters; even those who turn their attention chiefly to their own affairs do not lack judgment about politics. We alone regard the man who takes no part in politics not as someone who minds his own business but as useless. And we decide public questions ourselves, or at least come to a sound understanding of them. (2.40.2)

Thus the Athenian democracy, Pericles asserts, raises all its citizens to the level of noblemen by asking them to take part in political life and so to control their own destiny.

Pericles further claims for the men of his city an aristocratic character that we may call a kind of noblesse oblige: "We are also different from most people in our nobility of spirit [*arete*], for we gain our friends not by receiving favors but by doing them. . . . Finally, Pericles revels in the variety available to the citizens of Athens—an object of scorn to Plato, but another quality, we must remember, normally associated with aristocracy. Greek noblemen lived by the ideal of the accomplished amateur: good at a variety of skills—music, athletics, warfare, among others—but professionally devoted to none. They would have been appalled by Plato's notion that each man should do the one thing for which he was best suited, and so would the Athenians described by Pericles.

The rewards conferred by these aristocratic virtues are precisely those sought by the epic heroes: greatness, power, honor, fame. For Pericles, Athens itself was a competitor for these prizes in the *agon* among polis, past and present. But they are won by and for all the citizens of democratic Athens, and Pericles does not hesitate to assert the superiority of this collective achievement, going so far as to reject the need for an epic poet to guarantee its renown:

> We have provided great evidences of our power, and it is not without witnesses; we are the objects of wonder today and will be in the future. We have no need of a Homer to praise us or of anyone else whose words will delight us for the moment but whose account of the facts will be discredited by the truth. On the contrary, we have forced every sea and land to become an entrance for our daring, and we have everywhere established permanent monuments of the harm we have done our enemies and the good we have done for our friends. (2.41.4)

☐   *Pericles held the elected office of general for most of his adult life, so it was most appropriate to depict him in the typical pose shown above. The ancient comic poets used to joke about the elongated shape of his head, leading Plutarch to suggest that Pericles preferred helmeted portraits to conceal it. This marble bust is copied from the bronze statue made by Pericles' contemporary, Cresilas.*

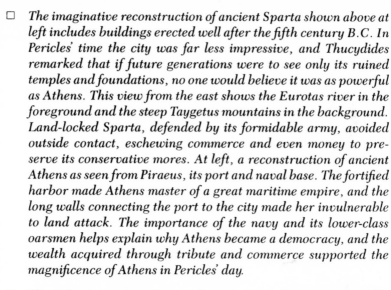

□ *The imaginative reconstruction of ancient Sparta shown above at left includes buildings erected well after the fifth century B.C. In Pericles' time the city was far less impressive, and Thucydides remarked that if future generations were to see only its ruined temples and foundations, no one would believe it was as powerful as Athens. This view from the east shows the Eurotas river in the foreground and the steep Taygetus mountains in the background. Land-locked Sparta, defended by its formidable army, avoided outside contact, eschewing commerce and even money to preserve its conservative mores. At left, a reconstruction of ancient Athens as seen from Piraeus, its port and naval base. The fortified harbor made Athens master of a great maritime empire, and the long walls connecting the port to the city made her invulnerable to land attack. The importance of the navy and its lower-class oarsmen helps explain why Athens became a democracy, and the wealth acquired through tribute and commerce supported the magnificence of Athens in Pericles' day.*

□ *The Athenian agora, shown above in a reconstruction, was the city's central marketplace. Here the wealth and variety of the whole eastern Aegean and beyond poured in at the height of Athenian imperial power, creating an unprecedented choice of goods. But the agora was much more than a market for spices, honey, olives, oil, and slaves from all over the world. It was also the center of Athenian civic life and contained temples, courts, the council house, and other public buidings. The agora's centrality in Athens explains why Plato often depicts Socrates engaging the citizens there in philosophical dialogues about the best way of life and the possibility of an ideal political order.*

□ *The theater of Dionysus, carved into the south slope of the Acropolis, is shown at left in a considerably embellished reconstruction. Here Sophocles, Aeschylus, Euripides, and Aristophanes presented their plays to the public. Large numbers of Athenians from all classes attended these performances at state religious festivals, and the plays often raised serious political questions. It was also the scene of Pericles' first public act as sponsor of Aeschylus' tragedy,* Persians. *Below, a fresco from Paestum (the ancient Greek colony of Poseidonia in southern Italy) depicting a symposium of the sort that typically formed the center of aristocratic social life. Only men took part, and after dinner the guests drank, sang, played games, recited poetry, or listened to the music of flute girls. In the right hand panel, the two men facing left are playing* kottabos, *whose object was to flick wine from one cup into another. The austere Pericles avoided such parties.*

ART RESOURCE    ART RESOURCE

☐ *Pictured here (clockwise) are some of the leading figures of the Greek Enlightenment of Pericles' time. Thucydides son of Olorus (circa 460–400) was the historian of the Peloponnesian War and the father of modern historiography. Plato (circa 429–347) may have been born in the year of Pericles' death, and his philosophical dialogues portray many of the statesman's friends and contemporaries. Aeschylus (525–456) was the first of the great tragedians, and Pericles produced his play, Persians, which describes the Athenian victory at Salamis. Socrates (469–399), the most important thinker of his time, powerfully influenced Plato and many others, including Alcibiades, before being put to death by the Athenian democracy. Aristotle (384–322) came from Stagira in northern Greece to study at Plato's Academy and later established his own school at Athens, the Lyceum.*

☐ *Aspasia, a professional courtesan from the city of Miletus, became Pericles'*
*intimate companion sometime in the 440s. He took her into his house when he*
*was already middle aged and treated her as his beloved wife for the rest of his*
*life. Aspasia was a woman of extraordinary intelligence and wide-ranging*
*interests, and she conversed with the leading men of Pericles' circle as no*
*ordinary Athenian wife was permitted to do. Aspasia came under attack by*
*his political opponents and was lampooned by comic poets, but Pericles*
*remained devoted to her.*

THE BETTMANN ARCHIVE

☐ *The word acropolis means "high city," and almost all Greek cities began as fortified settlements on or near a defensible hill. Over time the Athenians erected their most important temples on their acropolis, and later housed the vast imperial treasury within them. Among Pericles' most lasting achievements are the magnificent buildings with which he crowned the acropolis, seen below in its modern condition. The drawing above depicts the acropolis as it looked in Pericles' time.*

ART RESOURCE

□ *The Parthenon (left) was the jewel in the crown of the ambitious Periclean building program. Dedicated to the city's patron goddess, it carried architecture to new heights of refinement. Phidias, the architect—and Pericles' friend—skillfully employed proportion and variation in unusual ways to achieve a harmonious impression, and designed a complex sculptural plan for the external metopes and pediments, the interior frieze, and even the statue of the goddess within to communicate symbolic messages. The drawing below shows the pediment from the slightly older temple of Aphaia at Aegina, and its more standard features allow us to appreciate the novelty of Pericles' Parthenon, as well as the care and expense he devoted to it. The floral patterns on the metopes here, beneath the pediment, are replaced at Athens by a series of narrative sculptures. Furthermore, figures on the Aeginetan pediment, like most Greek temples, are left unfinished at the rear, while those of the Parthenon are fully rounded.*

☐ *The decorative frieze around the Parthenon's internal chamber, of which only fragments remain, was the most revolutionary element in this unusual structure. For the first time in Greek history, human beings are presented on a temple in place of gods and heroes. The scene is the annual Panathenaic procession, attended by representatives of the whole Athenian empire, in which the people of Athens carried a new garment, specially woven by a group of virgin girls, to clothe the statue of Athena. The presentation of this human scene was a daring statement of pride and patriotism that may have shocked pious traditionalists.*

☐ *The great statue of Athena that stood in the main chamber of the Parthenon was more than forty feet high, much larger than the Roman marble copy shown at left, and was covered with gold and ivory to represent the goddess' garments and skin. At Pericles' instruction, Phidias attached them to the core as removable plates so that the gold could be taken down in an emergency and melted into coin. When Phidias was later accused by Pericles' political enemies of thieving and fraud, he took down the plates and weighed them to prove that none of the allotted gold was missing.*

☐ *The Parthenon stood essentially intact until the seventeenth century, when its roof was blown off by a gunner in Venetian service. The Turks were using the temple to store ammunition, which exploded when struck by the cannon ball. To some, the resulting ruin is more romantic and evocative than the untouched original might have been. On the following page, the Parthenon is seen through the columns of the ruined Propylaea.*

The highest reward is the kind of immortality that was once reserved for epic heroes but which now has come to the Athenian soldiers who have died in the service of their city, and which Pericles urges the living to earn for themselves:

> They gave their lives for the common good and thereby won for themselves the praise that never grows old and the most distinguished of all graves, not those in which they lie, but where their glory remains in eternal memory, always there at the right time to inspire speech and action. For the whole world is the burial place for famous men; not only does the epitaph inscribed on monuments in their native country commemorate them, but in lands not their own the unwritten memory, more of their spirit even than of what they have done, lives on within each person. Now it is for you to emulate them; knowing that happiness requires freedom and freedom requires courage, do not shrink from the dangers of war. (2.43.2–4)

Pericles thus met the challenge of the heroic tradition by showing that democracy would bring to all the citizens of Athens the advantages heretofore reserved for the well-born few. The Athenian democracy would encourage merit in its traditional form and reward it with victory, glory, and immortality.

The more immediate challenge to the democratic vision came from Sparta. Its military power and tradition of leadership among the Greeks, the discipline and devotion to the public good displayed by its citizens, had already created an aura of virtue and excellence that a modern scholar has called "the Spartan mirage." Pericles needed to confront this challenge, and much of the Funeral Oration is therefore a direct comparison with Sparta. Athens is called a democracy because the many rule, not the few; everyone knew that in Sparta a small minority dominated the vast majority. Although all the men of the Spartiate class were called *homoioi* (peers), the kings had special privileges, and there was a class of noblemen distinct from the others. In Athens, all citizens were equal before the law. The Spartan imposed a property qualification for participation in public life; any Athenian citizen could sit on juries or the council and vote and speak in the assembly.

The Athenians prized thought, deliberation, and discussion. The Spartans were famous for their brevity and distrust of subtle reasoning, but Pericles praises the democracy's fondness for debate and discussion. Freedom of speech, extended to each and every citizen, was its hallmark and this freedom was the target of ridicule, not only by aristocrats who thought only those bred in political tradition or formally educated should speak, but also by the admirers of Sparta, where decisions were made by acclamation without debate. The Spartans believed in deeds, not words. Pericles took a different view: "We believe," he said,

> that words are no barrier to deeds, but rather that harm comes from not taking instruction from discussion before the time has come for action. We are superior in this way, too, that we are the most daring in what we undertake at the same time as we are the most thoughtful before going about it, while with others it is ignorance that brings boldness and thought that makes them hesitate. And it is right to judge those most courageous who understand both the pleasures and the terrors involved most clearly and yet do not turn away from dangers as a result. (2.40.3)

Here Pericles has identified a critical element of his vision for Athens: its commitment to reason and intelligence. Thought is not a barrier to the achievement of heroic goals. In fact, it is a prerequisite for them, for the brave deeds performed by enraged heroes who give no thought to danger are, by his definition, not brave at all. Only facing dangers that the mind can comprehend deserves to be called bravery, and that is what is expected of the men in his polis.

Sparta's great reputation, of course, depended on its extraordinary military achievements, and these were attributed in turn to its religious piety, single-minded severe system of training, the tight discipline imposed on all aspects of life, and the ascetic Spartan mores. Xenophon gives a good example of the absence of any privacy in Sparta:

> In other cities whenever a man shows himself to be a coward his only punishment is that he is called a coward. . . . But in Sparta anyone would be ashamed to dine or to wrestle with a coward. . . . In the streets he must get out of the way . . . he must support his unmarried sisters at home and explain to them why they are still spinsters, he must live without a wife at his fireside . . . he may not wander about comfortably acting like someone with a clean reputation or else he is beaten by his betters. I don't wonder that where such a load of dishonor burdens the coward death seems preferable instead of a dishonored and shameful life. (*Constitution of the Spartans* 9.4–6)

In contrast, Pericles points to the limited jurisdiction of the Athenian regime, which leaves a considerable space for individualism and privacy, free from public scrutiny. "Not only do we conduct our public life as free men but we are also free of suspicion of one another as we go about our every-day lives. We are not angry with our neighbor if he does what pleases him, and we don't glare at him which, even if it is harmless, is a painful sight." (2.37.2)

Yet this tolerant, easygoing way of life does not entail a disrespect for law or an invitation to licentious behavior. The Spartans were famous for their piety and reverence for law, and their blind obedience to it was thought to be the source of their great military prowess. In the face of this reputation, and in the teeth of its critics, who charged democracy especially with indiscipline and lawlessness, Pericles makes the claim for a higher obedience to law than was characteristic of the Spartans. They followed a written code that was exclusively in the interest of the ruling class. The Athenians, on the other hand, respected a broader and fairer concept of the law, with no less reverence:

> While we are tolerant in our private lives, in public affairs we do not break the law chiefly because of our respect for it. We obey those who hold office and the laws themselves, especially those enacted for the protection of the oppressed and those which, although unwritten, it is acknowledged shame to violate. (2.37.3)

Nor does Pericles concede that the strict discipline of Spartan training and the secrecy of its closed society produce better soldiers than the Athenian democracy.

> There is a difference between us and our opponents in how we prepare for our military responsibilities in the following ways: we open our city for everyone and do not exclude anyone for fear that he might learn or see something that would be useful to an enemy if it were not concealed. Instead, we put our trust not in secret weapons, but in our own courage when we are called upon to act. Our educations are different, too. The Spartans, from their earliest childhood, seek to acquire courage by painfully harsh training, but we, living our unrestricted life, are no less ready to meet the same dangers they do. . . . If, therefore, we are prepared to meet danger after leading a relaxed life instead of one filled with burdensome training, with our courage emerging naturally from our way of life instead of imposed by law, the advantage is ours. We do not wear ourselves out in advance of future troubles, and when they come we show ourselves no less bold than those who are always in training. In these ways our city deserves to be admired. (2.39)

Many of the qualities and characteristics envisioned by Pericles are related to military excellence, as is natural in a speech delivered in wartime to encourage the struggle for victory. But the most original aspect of Pericles' vision for Athens was its expectation of an enduring peace. He had made the strategic judgment that the empire as it stood was large enough to meet all the city's needs. Attempts to expand it would not only be unnecessary but endanger what already existed. And in his last recorded speech in 430, although its intention was to persuade the Athenians to keep fighting, he said: "For those who are prospering and who have a choice, going to war is folly." (2.61.1)

There is no reason to doubt his sincerity, for his actions were entirely consistent with that sentiment. The peace with Persia, the peace with Sparta—especially its arbitration clause—the Panhellenic colony in Italy, and the firm but moderate policy of imperial administration all point in that direction. The ambitious building program Pericles was about to undertake, meant to crown the Athenian achievement with visible evidence of its greatness, provides still more evidence. That program was far from completed when war finally did come, and as might be expected, it brought construction to a halt. There can be little doubt that Pericles' vision was of an imperial, democratic city at peace.

That conception ran counter to Greek experience, which had always been full of turbulence and warfare. Why did Pericles think Athens could live in peace after so many years of continuous fighting? The answer was to be found in the power of Athens, although less in its extent than its character. With a fleet that commanded the seas, the guaranteed revenues needed to support its navy and provide supplies against any siege, a city and port defended by impregnable walls, Athens had achieved unprecedented security. Repeated failures had taught the Persians they could not challenge Athenian naval power, while adherence to the right strategy—a refusal to fight a large land battle—deprived Sparta and its allies of any hope for victory. These facts were obvious to all and might be expected to deter aggression. For the first time in history a Greek state could conduct its life and plan for the future in the expectation of a lasting peace.

Welcome as this prospect was, it nonetheless presented a problem. Since the time of Homer the Greek, thirst for glory had centered on brave deeds in war: What would replace these in a world at peace? Part of the answer lay in a quality of life unknown elsewhere, a range of activities that brought the pleasures of prosperity to the appetite, joy and wonder to the spirit, stimulation to the intellect, and pride to the soul. Another substitution for the glories of war could be found in the exercise by each Athenian of his political duties. These were evidence of his freedom and importance, and so a source of pride. The poorest Athenian serving on a jury, voting in the assembly, or allotted to an office was thereby called upon to use his intelligence and experience on behalf of his polis. By sharing in the common responsibility he was able to develop powers and aspects of himself that allowed him to become more fully human than he could have on his own.

In war and in peace, the Athenian people showed themselves eager to accept the responsibilities that allowed them to share in their city's glory. That is why Pericles could make this extraordinary demand on them when the great war came:

> You must every day look upon the power of your city and become her lovers [erastai] and when you have understood her greatness consider that the men who achieved it were brave and honorable and knew what was necessary when the time came for action. If they ever failed in some attempt, they were determined that, at least, their city should not be deprived of their courage [arete] and gave her the most beautiful of all offerings. For they gave their lives for the common good. . . . (2.43.1–2)

During the war, even in its darkest moments, Pericles could count on a strong response when he reminded the people that they were right to love their city and even to risk their lives for it, because it was uniquely great, and because only by preserving and enhancing it could the ordinary man share in its glory and so achieve a degree of fame and immortality.

In the few of his speeches we have, Pericles spoke chiefly of the empire and military glory, and these were certainly important values to him and the Athenians. But we have these speeches because Thucydides reported them, and his subject was war. If we had access to Pericles' inner thoughts and to the many other speeches he delivered in his long career, we would possibly discover that he took no less pride in Athenians' peaceful achievements of mind and spirit. His political program allowed all Athenian citizens to take part in government, to help guide their own destinies and those of their polis, as befits free men. He believed that man's capacities and desires could be fulfilled at the highest level only through participation in the life of a community governed by reasoned discussion and guided by intelligence. Twenty-five hundred years later we remember him and his fellow-Athenians precisely because of their devotion to this great civic endeavor.

# 8

# EDUCATOR

A democratic leader, to be great, must be a teacher. For whatever the nobility of his vision and the excellence of his goals, they cannot be achieved in a free society unless the people truly share and are inspired to accomplish them.

The laws and customs of Athens contributed to this necessary education, but it was the special talent of Pericles to be able to formulate the democratic ideal nobly and clearly, to impress it on the minds of the Athenians, and to inspire them with the desire to achieve it. His speeches were a powerful medium of education, but the most striking and tangible embodiment of his vision for Athenians was the great building program he undertook at midcentury.

In the few years before the Peloponnesian War, Athens experi-

151 □

enced an unprecedented burst of artistic activity whose quality was
even more astonishing than its quantity. The speed with which these
masterworks were completed is no less amazing. Plutarch himself saw
them still intact five hundred years after their construction:

> For this reason are the works of Pericles all the more to be wondered
> at; they were created in a short time for all time. Each one of them, in
> its beauty, was even then and at once antique; but in the freshness of
> its vigor it is, even to the present day, recent and newly wrought. Such
> is the bloom of perpetual newness, as it were, upon these works of his,
> which makes them ever to look untouched by time, as though the
> unfaltering breath of an ageless spirit had been infused into them.
> (*Pericles* 13.3)

The scope of the program itself is impressive, involving all of Attica.
Temples were built to Poseidon at Sunium at the southern tip of the
peninsula, to Ares at Acharnae in the northwest, and to Nemesis at
Rhamnous in the northeast. But the focus was on Athens, where a
temple to Hephaestus and Athena was built on Colonus, a hill overlooking the Agora, and especially on the Acropolis. On its southern
slope Pericles constructed the Odeum, and on top of the great rocky
citadel he placed the Parthenon and the gateway to the Acropolis
called the Propylaea. Plans were also made for a temple to Athena
Nike (Victory) at the southwest corner of the Acropolis and probably
for one to Athena Polias to the north of the Parthenon, but these were
built only after Pericles' death.

The ambition of this program is all the more striking in light of
the fact that almost no public construction had taken place in the
three decades since the Persian War. The Persian retreat from Athens in 479 left a city burned and leveled to the ground, with only a
few houses standing. On the Acropolis, temples, monuments, and
statues were thrown to the ground and smashed. A temple to Athena
had been under construction when the Persians came, and this too
they knocked down, leaving column drums and building blocks scattered around. When the Athenians returned from their flight, they
hastened to strengthen the walls around the Acropolis and to rebuild
the walls of their city against another attack by the barbarian. They
used the materials lying around for foundations and tossed them
helter-skelter into roughly constructed battlements, with one striking
exception:

> Looking up from the Agora to the north face of the Acropolis one sees
> a wall of strangely assorted stones irregularly packed together; but in

the irregularity the eye focuses on a stretch of deliberate order. Near the top, embedded in the wall, is a conspicuous line of thick column drums. These are not packed together at random; they are deliberately placed in line to catch the eye. The Athenians knew that these were to have been the columns of their new temple of Athena. This was their war memorial, and on the top the ruined temple remained in ruins.[1]

And so it remained, along with Attica's other ruined temples and sanctuaries, for three decades until the commencement of Pericles' building program. Why the delay?

Lycurgus, an Athenian orator of the fourth century, reports an oath taken by the Greeks before their decisive battle against the Persians at Plataea in 479:

> I will not prefer life to freedom, nor will I abandon my leaders alive or dead, but I will bury all the allies who died in the battle. After I have conquered the barbarians in the war I shall not destroy any of the cities that have fought on behalf of Greece, but I will take a tithe from those that have taken the side of the barbarians. And I will not rebuild any of the temples that have been burnt or thrown down by the barbarians, but I will allow them to remain as a memorial to future generations of the sacrilege of the barbarians. (*Against Leocrates* 81)

Although some ancient and modern critics have doubted the authenticity of this document, archaeological excavations confirm that religious sites remained in ruins in Attica between the Persian Wars and the middle of the century. Since Athenian finances were easily capable of restoring at least some of them within a decade, the oath of Plataea offers the most plausible reason for the hiatus.

The easiest explanation for the resumption of activity in the 440s, therefore, "is that peace had been made with Persia, the Peace of Callias, and that the Athenians considered that this peace freed them from their oath."[2] Certainly peace was necessary before the vast and expensive program could begin; but it was not sufficient to achieve the purpose. In a larger context, the successful negotiations of Callias may be seen as one of several steps taken to make the building program a reality. Next came the scheme for a Panhellenic Congress to provide a moral basis for the program and the imperial revenues that made it possible. After that came the Papyrus Decree, which permitted the use of the imperial reserve for buildings in Athens. Finally, there was the Thirty Years' Peace with Sparta, which provided security and stopped the drain on the treasury caused by war.

Some of these steps were desirable for other reasons, but all together they were needed to allow the building program to go forward. This project was at the center of Pericles' policies. He was personally involved in the planning and supervision of much, if not all, of the building, and when professional involvement was needed, he, directly or indirectly, chose the experts. The undertaking created the most dangerous political challenge to his leadership before the outbreak of the war, and he was willing to risk ostracism to defend it. Nothing in his magnificent career matched its importance to him, for it opened the way for essential achievements in the realms of politics, economics, empire, education, and religion, and it presented a way to make the greatness of Athens tangible and visible to all.

The most obvious purpose of the building program was to celebrate the victorious conclusion of the war against the Persians. The Parthenon, in particular, with its sculptured scenes of battle between Athenians and Amazons, human beings and wild beasts, Greeks and Trojans, was a war memorial celebrating the triumph of Athens over its enemies, civilization over barbarism, and Greeks over Asiatics. Such a message had considerable political value for Pericles, for the peace he had concluded with Persia had not been universally popular. Some old Cimonians were unhappy at abandoning the aggressive campaigns against the Persians that had brought Athens wealth and Panhellenic glory. But the great buildings made possible by the end of that war, and the resulting new use of league funds made possible by the peace, overwhelmed such criticisms. They proclaimed and celebrated victory: What more could anyone ask?

The building program also helped Pericles strengthen his political influence through the economic opportunities it provided for the people. For almost two decades the works created a continuing demand for materials and labor, skilled and unskilled, that brought prosperity and rewarding activity to all elements of the population. It was one of those public works programs that helped create political support by creating jobs and profits for many citizens. Pericles appealed with success to the continuation of this general prosperity in his debate over the use of imperial revenue for the building program.

But it was more than material advantage that won the support and devotion of the Athenian people. They too were caught up in the magnificence of the structures they were building: "As the works went up, towering over others in their greatness and inimitable in their beauty and grace, the workmen contended with one another to surpass themselves in the beauty of their craftsmanship." (Plutarch,

*Pericles* 13.1) They understood that the buildings would be a memorial to their democracy and their empire, and they were captured by the prospect. When the great buildings on the Acropolis were completed, Athenians found it considerably easier "every day to look upon the power of [their] city and become her lovers" and to see in its success their own immortality. More than a century later, the Athenian orator Demosthenes confirmed this function of the building program and also its success. The Athenian democracy in the Periclean age

> was more avid for glory than for anything else, and here is the proof: after they had acquired more wealth than any other Greeks they spent it all for the sake of honor. . . . As a result they bequeathed immortal possessions, the memory of their deeds and the beauty of the memorials set up in their honor—the Propylaea over there, the Parthenon, the stoas, the docks. . . . They conquered their enemies, answered the prayers of every right-thinking man by establishing concord in the city, and left behind their immortal glory [*kleos*] as a legacy. (*Against Androtion* 76)

Apart from these purposes, the buildings on and about the Acropolis, and chief among these the Parthenon, were part of an effort at civic education that, along with the laws and institutions of Athens, would create the democratic state envisioned by Pericles. The revolution of 461 that took power from the Areopagus and distributed it among the democratic council, assembly, and law courts had been the first step. The democratic legislation of the 450s had been a second. The artistic and educational program begun in the 440s was to be the final and crowning aspect of the Periclean edifice.

The Acropolis was the place most sacred to Athena, the tutelary goddess of the city. Like the other Greek divinities, she was worshiped and celebrated in many guises. The oldest and most venerable, the focus of formal religious worship, was that of Athena Polias, goddess of the city. She took the form of a statue made of olive wood which according to legend had fallen from heaven, and it was worshiped as the "holiest of all things" even before the demes of Attica had been unified into a single polis. (Pausanias 1.26.6) She lived in "the old temple," probably the first one erected on the Acropolis, that had been destroyed by the Persians in 480. The wooden statue, not of colossal size, showed the goddess, probably seated, with a golden crown and jewelry, holding a libation-bowl in her hand. She was

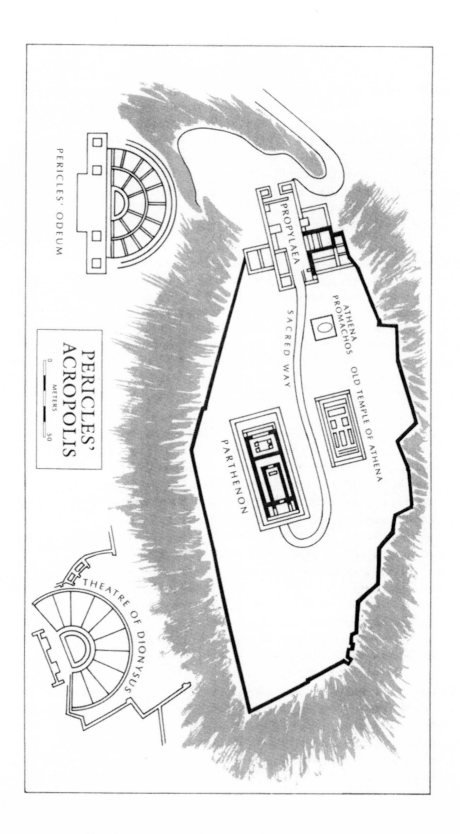

PERICLES' ODEUM

PROPYLAEA

ATHENA PROMACHOS

OLD TEMPLE OF ATHENA

SACRED WAY

PARTHENON

THEATRE OF DIONYSUS

PERICLES' ACROPOLIS

0  METERS  50

clothed in a peplos, a woolen robe in bright colors into which was woven a scene depicting the battle in which the Olympian gods defeated the giants. Each year the statue and the peplos were taken down to the sea and washed during the festival called Plynteria. Every fourth year, at the Great Panathenaic Festival, the goddess was presented with a new peplos woven by the Arrhephoroi (Carriers of the Unspoken Things), young girls between the ages of seven and eleven, chosen from aristocratic families and confirmed by a vote of the people to take part in mysterious nocturnal fertility rites. This Athena was a goddess of fertility, of agriculture, and of the household. To her were attached the priestesses of Athena, and the great sacrificial altar was dedicated to her worship.

But the goddess also appeared in a different guise, as Athena Parthenos (the Maiden), and like other unwed females such as the pugnacious Amazons, she is a warrior. Unlike Athena Polias, who brings fertility and prosperity in time of peace, Athena Parthenos brings protection and victory in time of war. Although Athena Polias remained the unique object of the state's worship, Athena Parthenos increasingly came to the fore in the public mind as Athens became less dependent on its own agriculture and more involved in foreign commerce and in warfare. Beginning in the sixth century, it was Athena Promachos (Forward Fighter, or Champion), a more militant version of the same aspect, who appeared on the large vases containing the sacred oil awarded to winners of the Great Panathenaic athletic contests and whose helmeted head appeared on the silver coins of Athens.

The Athenians were engaged in building a temple to the warrior goddess on the south side of the Acropolis, alongside the old temple to Athena Polias on the north, when the Persians came and leveled both. Phidias made a colossal bronze statute of the Promachos, probably in the 450s, and placed it in direct sight of anyone entering the Acropolis through the main gate. Pausanias says it was so tall that the tip of its spear and the crest of its helmet could be seen by a ship rounding Cape Sunium at the southern tip of Attica. Significantly, when Pericles undertook to restore the sacred buildings on the Acropolis, he did not begin with the shrine of the Polias, the traditional focus of the Athenian worship, but with the building dedicated to the Parthenos.

Work on the temple that would come to be called the Parthenon began in 447. Phidias' great gold and ivory statue within it was dedicated in 438, and the building was completed in 432. Pericles himself was on the commission of overseers (*epistatai*), and he discussed everything with Phidias, who was the general manager of the entire building program, creator of the design for the sculptures on the Parthenon, and sculptor of the mammoth statue in its eastern chamber. Ictinus was the head architect, assisted by Callicrates, among others.

Like all other temples built west of the Aegean, the Parthenon was a Doric temple. It was complicated, however, by the innovative inclusion of some Ionic elements and by an unusually complex plan and some novel features. The great size of Phidias' statue required a building larger, and especially wider, than usual. Earlier important temples had six columns across the front and twelve or thirteen down the sides, but Ictinus expanded the Parthenon to eight by seventeen, establishing a ratio of roughly four to nine, a proportion that characterizes spatial relationships throughout the structure and contributes to its remarkable harmony.

The builders introduced a number of very subtle refinements into its structure. These appear on other Doric temples, but they were carried to their highest perfection by Ictinus and his colleagues. Although the lines of the temple seem perfectly straight and square to the untutored eye, they deviate ever so slightly from the straight, the vertical, and the horizontal. The floor is not the level surface it seems but is slightly arched, the middle being four inches higher than the corners along the sides and two inches higher along the eastern and western ends, and its curves are picked up by the entablature on top of the columns above. The columns on each side, moreover, lean inward more than two inches, and the corner columns do so diagonally. The corner columns are thicker than the others and spaced more closely on each side. These refined details increased the time needed to complete the work and also its expense.

The interior of the temple consisted of a columned front porch on the east leading into the main room containing the great statue of Athena. Behind it was a smaller room, entered from the west through a columned back porch. This back room was the place properly called Parthenon, but its name came to be applied to the whole building no later than the fourth century. Its chief function was as a treasury to house the wealth belonging to Athena. Around these rooms and inside the outer colonnade ran a narrow walk at either end of which were the two porches, each of whose sets of six large Doric columns, almost thirty-three feet high, "must have seemed to stretch across the entire width of the temple creating the impression of a closely packed grove of columns similar to those in the great Ionic temples of Asia Minor."[3] The impression made by this Ionic effect in a Dorian temple would have been intensified by the four large Ionic columns that supported the ceiling of the treasury on the west and even more by the continuous, sculptured frieze that ran around the top of the interior building, a purely Ionic feature. Nor was the Ionic modulation of the basically Dorian temple confined to the inside. On the exterior, "the slender columns of the peristyle . . . seem to instill some of the elongated Ionic grace into the Doric order; and the octastyle facade calls to mind the wide fronts of the temples of the Ionian world in contrast to the compact hexastyle arrangements of most Doric temples."[4]

The sculptures of the Parthenon were an integral part of the total design. Many of them were badly damaged or destroyed by a great explosion in 1687, when a German gunner in Venetian service hit the Parthenon, which was serving as a Turkish powder magazine. From what is preserved, however, in ancient testimony and depictions, and from drawings made not long before the explosion, it is possible to reconstruct the subjects represented and a very good idea of how they were treated.

Greek temples sometimes contained sculptural references to the god they honored and, perhaps, to local legend. But most of their themes came from a traditional common repertory of subjects, such as the deeds of heroes, the wars between the Olympian gods and the giants, the human Lapiths against the half-beast Centaurs, and the Greeks against the Trojans. The Parthenon used most of these traditional subjects, but it was unique in devoting most of its decorative sculpture to the patron divinity. Even when it treated the traditional themes, episodes within them are made to coincide with similar subjects depicted on the great statue of Athena within the cella, the main chamber of the temple.

The exterior colonnade, holding ninety-two metopes, contained the more traditional subjects: gods against giants on the east. Greeks against Amazons on the west, Greeks against Trojans on the north, and Lapiths against Centaurs on the south. The central metopes on the south side appear to have represented scenes from early Athenian tradition, among them possibly the legendary King Erechtheus setting up the ancient statue of Athena. The sculpture on the pediments represented two miraculous moments in the career of Athena. The scene on the east depicted her birth, fully grown and armed, from the head of Zeus. The western pediment showed the contest between

Athena and Poseidon for the status of patron deity of Athens and Athena's magical gift of an olive tree that won it for her. Phidias' great standing statue of Athena in the cella was some forty feet high; over a wooden core were hung sheets of ivory representing the skin and removable golden plates the drapery. The expense was enormous, but the results magnificent. The statue of Athena wore a triple-crested helmet, and her left hand rested on a shield and held a spear. In her right palm stood a winged figure, Nike, the symbol of victory; this was very much the warrior-goddess. Her shield picked up the themes of the metopes on the temple, showing Athenians fighting Amazons on the outside and gods fighting giants on the inner surface, and her sandals repeated the battle between Lapiths and Centaurs.

The most original and surprising element in the sculpture of the Parthenon was the frieze around the cella. A continuous scene on a frieze, as opposed to separated scenes on metopes, was characteristically Ionic, and there is no certain evidence that it had ever before appeared on a Doric temple in mainland Greece. Even more shocking was its subject: For the first time in Greek history it shows mortal human beings.

Why was the Parthenon the first undertaking in Pericles' reconstruction of the Athenian Acropolis? What was the nature of this magnificent, innovative, and very expensive new building? What messages was it meant to convey and to whom?

To begin with, let there be no doubt that it was very expensive. The architectural refinements alone greatly increased the cost in time and money. The abundance of sculpture, with an Ionic internal frieze added to the Doric metopes and pediments, was greater than usual, and greater pains were taken with their detail. On other temples the backs of figures that could not be seen on the pediments were left rough. But the sculptors of the Parthenon finished them to perfection, as though they were intended to stand free and viewed from all sides, causing still greater expense. The gold and ivory on the colossal statue of Athena were, of course, immensely costly. Pericles might say in his Funeral Oration "we love beauty, with frugality," but he could not prove that by pointing to the Parthenon. It was magnificently opulent, sparing no expense, and it provided a natural target for the complaints of Thucydides, son of Melesias, and other critics of the building program. Yet Pericles was able to persuade the Athenian people gathered in deliberate assembly, which had to vote for every drachma and obol expended, to do so without interruption over a fifteen-year period.

It is all the more striking that they did so for a building on the southern part of the Acropolis, rather than the reconstruction of the temple on the northern part containing the holy places that were the focus of the state's worship. Work on that temple to Athena Polias (later called the Erechtheum) was not undertaken until 421, well after Pericles' death. Rather than undertake that project, moreover, Pericles turned to the construction of a grand entryway to the Acropolis, the Propylaea, which was not a religious structure at all.

Scholars have argued that, despite its dedication to Athena and her statue within, the Parthenon had little or nothing to do with religion and is not really a temple at all. One compared it to "a very superior ornament on a mantelpiece." Another regards its function as simply a treasury. These interpretations are too simple and severe, but it is true that there is no evidence connecting the building or its statue with cult or ritual. It is also striking that the Panathenaic procession pictured in such loving detail on the frieze along the cella shows the changing of Athena's robe, which took place not in the Parthenon but in "the old temple" where it was placed, and not on the mammoth gold and ivory statue made by Phidias but on the small "ancient statue" made of olive wood.

The Parthenon was certainly meant to be a temple and its construction was intended as an act of religious piety. But in a way that was typical of many Periclean endeavors, it had transforming new features. Perhaps it is best to think of it as "an *offering* consecrated within a place of worship,"[5] addressed not to the peaceful fertility deity—the patron goddess of the agricultural Athens confined to the land of Attica—but to the virgin warrior goddess that had come to be the symbol of the new Athens of crafts and commerce and naval empire. This Athena was also the goddess of the arts and sciences, of wisdom, of reason, intelligence, and humanity. All of these were the qualities and characteristics Pericles claimed for his Athens and its citizens. The Parthenon was an offering to Athena in gratitude for the victory over the Persians. It was also a tribute to Athena's people and a monument to the great city and empire they had created. But beyond all this, Pericles, as he often did, had an educational purpose in mind. The Parthenon was meant to achieve visually what the Funeral Oration aimed at orally: the depiction, explanation, and celebration of the Athenian imperial democracy. Phidias and his colleagues, in one way or another, addressed these concerns in the design of the building and the sculptures that adorned it.

To a modern reader it may seem implausible that the visual arts, unaccompanied by verbal explanation, could effectively communicate messages to a large portion of the comparatively uneducated Athenian people. But there is reason to believe that they did. We need to escape from the impressions of our own world, where verbal and written forms of expression have dominated since the invention of the printing press until the invention of motion pictures and television. We must imagine a world that is not constantly bombarded by visual images beyond the point of satiety until our senses and receptors are dulled in self-defense. In Pericles' day, most Athenians could read to some degree; but there was not much to read, and they did not read much. Most learning took place by listening to speeches, usually in poetic meter, or by seeing what there was to see. The Athenians heard rhapsodes sing Homer's epics, choruses and individuals sing lyric and elegiac poetry, and they saw and heard tragedies and comedies, which involved speech, song, and dance. There was also much to see: pottery painted with scenes from the myths treated by the poets; statues honoring the gods, sometimes illustrating the same myths; statues honoring heroes—the Athenian tyrannicides, for instance, who were credited with ending the rule of the Peisistratids and honored for bringing freedom to Athens.

These forms of communication and instruction, however, were comparatively rare. Poetic and musical performances were attached to religious festivals that occurred just once a year. They dealt with a relatively small body of Greek mythology well known to their audience or with recent historical events. As a result, the broad audience of citizens came to each event with sharply honed senses, keen attention, and a capacity to appreciate fine nuances of a very sophisticated art. In the same way, and perhaps even more intensely, they were remarkably open to impressions made by the visual arts. Public statues and carved monuments were few—and from 480 to about 450, few, if any temples stood in all of Attica. We may be sure, therefore, that when a new temple arose on the Acropolis, particularly the grandest and most lavish anyone had seen, it would be looked at with the greatest interest and intensity. Each Athenian would have gazed upon it thousands of times, and, since the commission of supervisors had to be elected by the people, their plans and choice of architects approved, and funds approved by the assembly over a period of fifteen years, there were countless opportunities for public discussion, which surely continued in private.

Different elements of the Parthenon focus on particular concerns. The introduction of Ionic features into a Doric temple can be explained, in part, by aesthetic considerations; they provided a sense of lightness, space, and variety not found in a typical Doric temple. At the same time, they carried a message that contemporaries were not likely to miss. Mainland temples up to the construction of the Parthenon, including all those in Attica, had been built in the Doric style. Athens, however, claimed and was recognized to be the mother of the Ionian cities on the Aegean islands and coasts that made up a large part of her empire. In reorganizing the empire, Pericles had emphasized this assertion of kinship by requiring the allies to bring a cow and panoply to the Great Panathenaic Festival, just as Athenian colonies did. The Ionians, therefore, would have marched in the procession bringing her peplos to Athena Polias, and as they paraded past the temple to the Parthenos they would not have failed to notice the Ionic elements blended into the great offering to the goddess, just as they themselves were blended into the procession of worshipers and their cities into the league under Athenian leadership. Less obvious, but understandable to alert viewers, was a message reflecting yet another theme in Pericles' Funeral Oration. As one perceptive scholar has put it, "The Ionic order called to mind the luxury, refinement, and intellectualism of Ionia; the Doric was associated with the sombre, stolid simplicity of the descendants of Herakles in the Peloponnesos. In a temple which embodied Athens, it was natural that Pericles should want the two to be harmonized."[6] That harmony was just what Pericles claimed for Athens when he said, "we love beauty, with frugality, and we love wisdom, without softness." (2.40.1)

The refinements of the Parthenon may have been intended to convey an even more subtle message. They can, of course, be explained on various grounds: in a less-developed form they were common to Doric temples of the time; from a functional point of view the domed floor provided excellent drainage, like the crown in the center of an athletic field; aesthetic considerations adjusting to the nature of human perception were also important. An ancient theory asserted that the refinements were meant to compensate for optical illusions that make long horizontal lines seem to sag in the middle, end columns seem thinner than they are, and so on; the refinements would make all lines appear straight and all columns of uniform size. A second interpretation is exactly the opposite. It observes that a horizontal line seen from below seems to bow up rather than sag. The curvatures, therefore, deliberately intensified the natural distortion to make the building seem taller and bigger than it was. Yet another opinion is that the refinements deliberately vary from what the eye is accustomed to see in order to create a tension between what is expected and what is seen. The mind of the viewer is therefore compelled to grapple with the discord between expectation and reality and to reconcile them; this sharpens the viewer's attention by requiring an active involvement and heightens the liveliness, vitality, and lasting interest of the building. There is something to be said for each of these views, but one scholar makes an arresting case for this last one, which, he says, "seems to reflect most naturally the intellectual experience of the age."

> It suggests that in the Parthenon things as they *appear* are harmonized with things as they are *known*. *Aletheia*, "reality" as known by abstraction (e.g., mathematical proportions), is presented as the basis of *phantasia*, experience of things through the medium of our senses and brain. The new world of Protagoras is brought into balance with the older world of Pythagoras—the foremost of several fusions of opposites which make the Parthenon the most vivid and comprehensive embodiment in the visual arts of Classical Greek thought and experience.[7]

Such rarified ideas would have been understood by only a few Athenians. The many sculptures that decorated the Parthenon, however, spoke more clearly and vividly to a much larger audience. The metopes and pediments and the statue of the goddess carried the traditional themes of Athenian and Greek mythology; celebrating the victory of Europe over Asia, with its obvious reference to the Persian Wars, of intelligence over brute force, of wisdom over arrogance. Olympian gods over giants, Greeks over Trojans, Lapiths over Centaurs, Athenians over Amazons—in each case we see the victory of the more intelligent, more thoughtful, more civilized force. Yet it is a victory in a battle, requiring courage, strength and fighting ability as well as intelligence. The idea is very much like the one expressed in the Funeral Oration, in which Pericles claims that "We are superior in this way, too, that we are the most daring in what we undertake at the same time as we are the most thoughtful before going about it, while with others it is ignorance that brings boldness and thought that makes them hesitate." (2.40.3)

On the eastern pediment, at the place of honor over the entrance to the temple, the scene of the birth of Athena from the head of Zeus symbolized her special place—and therefore her city's—as paradigm of intelligence and wisdom, and (being closest to Zeus) the source of justice. The battle of the gods and giants on the eastern metopes, memorialized regularly by a scene woven into the peplos of Athena, was of special importance because of her heroic role in the battle. Beyond that, the myth came to signify the destruction of hubris, represented by the giants. The moral law that hubris should be punished is the basis of tragedy, history, and religious thought in the fifth century. All the metopes, in fact, can be seen as illustrations of its suppression by nobler forces. "Implied throughout," in the words of a shrewd observer, is the idea "that Athena is the champion of the universally accepted moral law, that she is on the side of *sophrosyne* [moderation] against *hybris*."[8] Here again there is a parallel to the Funeral Oration, where Pericles asserts that the Athenians, especially, obey those laws "enacted for the protection of the oppressed and those which, although unwritten, it is acknowledged shame to violate." (2.37.3)

The sculpture on the continuous frieze within the Parthenon represents on a contemporary scene, the citizens of Athens moving forward in the great Panathenaic procession. On the eastern end, the ceremony involving the handing over of the peplos is observed by the Olympic gods and the ten legendary heroes whose names were given to the ten tribes of Athens. The living human beings depicted on the Parthenon are elevated by association with the immortal gods and heroes. Together with the scene on the west pediment of two gods vying for the honor of becoming patrons of Athens and the metopes showing Athenians defeating Amazons, it is a patriotic declaration that expresses the connection of the people of Athens with their tutelary goddess and heroic ancestors, making it easy for them to "look upon the power of [their] city and become her lovers." (2.43.1) It recalls the Funeral Oration in still another way, providing a tangible basis for Pericles' claim that "We have provided great evidences of our power, and it is not without witnesses; we are the objects of wonder today and will be in the future. We have no need of a Homer to praise us. . . ." (2.41)

Jerome Pollitt has suggested an even higher status for the Athenians shown on the frieze:

> Pericles' Funeral Oration depicted Athenian society with god-like qualities, and perhaps the Parthenon frieze, where the visible and spiritual gap between men and gods vanishes, was intended to convey the same vision. Perhaps we see the citizens of Periclean Athens apotheosized.[9]

Perhaps so, but possibly the Athenians on the frieze are depicted from a philosophical perspective that saw no advantage in deification, one that had no real place for the gods, regarding humanity as sufficiently elevated. Such seems to have been the outlook of Pericles' friend and associate, the Sophist Protagoras. His two most celebrated observations seem to support such a possibility. He is the first agnostic whose words have come down to us: "About the gods I cannot know whether they exist or not or what form they have; for there are many barriers to knowledge, among them the obscurity of the subject and the shortness of human life." Since no account can be taken of the divine, Protagoras' other famous assertion follows logically: *Man* [my emphasis] is the measure of all things: of those which are, that they are, and of those which are nót, that they are not." If Protagorean thought had an effect on the design of the Parthenon frieze, these passages would point to an emphasis on the humanity of the figures rather than their quasi-divinity.

Such an emphasis, in fact, may be a major part of the message. On the eastern end, where the procession reaches its climax, "The divinities appear physically and psychologically distant."[10] They are on the fringe of the action, taking no interest in ritual, talking to each other, absorbed in themselves and each other, turning their backs to the human beings and the ritual that culminates the procession and the entire festival. All this is critical to the artist's Protagorean intention: "It suggests that the gods are apparent rather than true objects of ritual. It makes a visual shift cardinal to the Sophist's thought, that at the center of religion is not the divine *per se* but the human act of piety."[11] Such an interpretation, if it is correct, would have been grasped only by a few. But the humanity of the depicted Athenians, their distance from rather than their proximity to divinity, would probably have been emphasized by the presence of the distracted and disinterested gods and heroes. From this point of view, the juxtaposition of human beings with divinities may be seen as part of the patriotic symbolism that dominates the temple, connecting all the people of the Athenian democracy to their heroic ancestors and the victorious goddess who is their patron and symbol of wisdom and intelligence.

The complexity and the carefully planned significance of the various elements of the Parthenon fit well with the thinking of Pericles and his friend Protagoras. Both understood the importance of civic education for the success of democracy. Protagoras, who has been called "the first democratic political theorist,"[12] certainly believed that education in the civic virtues was essential in a democracy, and in the Platonic dialogue that bears his name he urges the centrality of education for any civilized society. To justify the democratic practice of trusting ordinary citizens rather than specialists and experts, he employs a myth that amounts to a statement of fundamental democratic assumptions: Once only the gods existed. They then created the shapes of mortal creatures below the earth. Before these creatures were brought into the light, Epimetheus gave each species its own peculiar qualities on an equalizing principle, so that each might be protected against the other and against the elements. Man, however, had no such protection, so Prometheus stole fire and other technical skills for them so that they alone developed religion, speech, and material comforts. But they lived separately, without cities, a condition inadequate for defense against the beasts. For this purpose they founded poleis. But lacking the art of politics, they quarreled, were unable to live together, and were soon scattered again. Zeus, featuring the extinction of the race, sent Hermes to bring to men *aidos* (reverence) and *dike* (right), the components of political virtue, to make communal life possible. The crafts and skills had been distributed among men in the same way as the powers among animals, different crafts to different people. But Hermes put a question to Zeus: "Shall this be the way I should distribute right and reverence, or shall I give them to all?" "To all," said Zeus. "Let all have a share; for cities cannot exist if only a few share in the virtues, as in the arts. And also make a law, by my authority, that a man who is not capable of reverence and right shall be killed as a plague to the *polis*." (*Protagoras* 322 C–D)

Nevertheless, Protagoras believed that, although all normal human beings have some share in the political virtues, this capacity was distributed unequally. Some had more than others and were able to improve their fellowmen by instruction. Not only did he believe such education to be possible, he felt it was necessary for a healthy political society. In his discussion with Socrates he asks: "Is there or is there not one thing in which all citizens must share if there is to be a *polis* at all?" He concludes that there was such a thing and it was "justice, moderation and holiness, the excellence [*arete*] of a man." (325A) That was the justification for his own work as a teacher of young men. He claimed to teach them the art of politics and to make them good citizens, to improve their judgment in managing their private affairs and their ability to speak and act well in the business of the state. (*Protagoras* 318E–319A) But he understood that the democratic populace might get a civic education from other sources than Sophists like himself. This instruction was provided to the citizens beginning in infancy and continued throughout their lives.

Each Athenian baby was taught by his parents and, when he was able to understand, by tutors. All taught him "what is just and unjust, what is fine and what is shameful, what is holy and what is unholy, what to do and what not to do." (325D) And when he was ready he was sent to other teachers to learn reading and music, but they were even more concerned with teaching him good behavior. The next stage was to read the epic poets for the purpose of acquiring noble examples of action as both an individual and a citizen. Then he was taught to play the lyre and to sing the songs of the poets in order to become "more gentle and harmonious, and rhythmical, and so better suited for speech and action." Next, the young were sent to the gymnasium "to make their bodies better servants of their sound minds, so that they may not be compelled to be cowardly because of the weakness of their bodies, whether in war or elsewhere." (326B–C) Finally, they were educated by the laws of the state, which made them live according to the model they provided, not just in any way they liked.

To be sure, not all Athenians lived up to the high standards taught by this cradle-to-grave education, working on them from every direction. But without that education they would certainly have been worse, and civilized life would have been impossible. Protagoras tells Socrates that "the man who you think is the most unjust among those raised in laws and humanities would appear as just and as a master of justice if you had to compare him with men without an education [paideia], or law courts, or laws." (327D)

Pericles also understood the need for public education from as many sources as possible, and accordingly added to the devices enumerated by Protagoras the visual instruction provided by the buildings and sculptures on the Acropolis and elsewhere. Just as he called Athens "the education of Greece," so these monuments were meant to be part of the education of Athens.

The building that bears his most personal stamp rose on the south slope of the Acropolis. The music hall, or Odeum, had several purposes, one of which was to commemorate the victory over the Persians. The building had a sloping circular roof said to be an exact copy of the pavilion of the Great King of Persia, and Pericles decorated its interior with the spars and masts of captured Persian ships. The new musical contests provided the Athenians with pleasure and recreation, but the Odeum had an educational function as well. We should not be surprised that the pupil of Damon should take such an interest in music, for his master had taught that "when modes of music change the fundamental mores [nomoi] of the state always change with them." Anyone who has lived through the change in taste from the romantic ballads of the era before World War II to the popular music of our own time, and considered the accompanying change in mores, will have no trouble understanding Damon's point. The new Odeum housed the musical contests that became a part of the Panathenaic Festival by a bill Pericles introduced himself, and his involvement did not end there. He himself was elected manager of the contests and established the rules for the contestants in the flute, singing, and cithera competitions.

The entire artistic endeavor, then, must be seen as part of a broad educational program meant to instill in the Athenians the love for their city that Pericles required and to instruct them in the virtues they needed. For Pericles knew that any successful society must be an educational institution. However great its commitment to individual freedom and diversity, it needs a code of civic virtue and a general devotion to the common enterprises without which it cannot flourish or survive. It must transmit its understanding of good and bad and a sense of pride, admiration, and love for its institutions and values to its citizens, especially the young. Every leader who makes any impression at all acts as an educator for good or ill, knowingly or not. His people pay attention to his words and deeds as to few others, and he contributes to their vision of the world, their nation and themselves, and the relations among them.

The leader's vision may be confusing and chaotic, or it may be organic, clear, and orderly; it may encourage or discourage; it may degrade or elevate the people. As a leader of the Greek Enlightenment, Pericles was committed to the power of reason and persuasion. He understood better than perhaps any leader in history his higher tutelary function, and he pursued it consciously, thoughtfully, and vigorously in speech and action. He sought to be the "nous" that guided his fellow-citizens away from subjection to selfish passions and the chaos these engendered, toward civic virtue and the order and excellence it could bring. Since his vision was democratic and not authoritarian, he did not practice indoctrination by compulsion but through genius and inspiration. He did not appeal to the lowest in his people but to the highest, not to fear and greed, but to honor and greatness.

The buildings carrying this education, although innovative and unusual, were religious in character or connected with religious rituals. Yet they aroused some opposition that had a religious aspect. As the Parthenon rose, Thucydides, son of Melesias, and his fellow-conservatives focused their opposition on the building program. To be sure, they mainly complained of its great cost and decried the misuse of imperial funds. But their assault also contained a religious rebuke: "We are gilding and adorning our city like a wanton woman, dressing it with expensive stones and statues and temples worth millions. . . ." (Plutarch, *Pericles* 12.2) The implicit accusation is that such things are unseemly and verge on impiety. And some modern scholars have suggested that Pericles was irreligious, even an atheist, and that his buildings, including the temples, were purely secular.

Pericles certainly shared the secular views of his teachers and friends. He was free of the common superstitions of his time, and he sought natural, rational explanations for the phenomena he observed in the world around him. A passage in the Funeral Oration he delivered over the men who died in the Samian War in 440, moreover, is reminiscent of the agnostic views of Protagoras. He said: "They have become immortal like the gods. We cannot see the gods themselves, but from the honors they receive and the benefits they bestow we infer that they are immortal. It is the same with those who die fighting for their country." (Plutarch, *Pericles* 8.6)

And yet a more nuanced understanding of Pericles' religiosity is called for. Ancient religion was very different from such modern ones as Christianity and Judaism. There was no central religious creed in pagan Greece, no holy book of faith, no set of religious laws governing all of human life; the heart of Greek religion was cult and ritual, not doctrine or belief. A fervent patriotism, a strong commitment to Athens, was not necessarily separate from sincere devotion to its patron goddess.* Pericles' building program served traditional needs, although in a new way.

The Parthenon clearly tested even the loose ancient understanding of religious worship: "It was a proud piety by which a triumphant *demos* exalted itself as a half-century of democracy had fashioned it."[14] But this new sort of piety disquieted more traditional Athenians, including many among the masses.

Pericles' aristocratic opponents, on the one hand, and the superstitious masses, on the other, were not the only Athenians troubled by the fresh breeze of rationalism and enlightenment represented by

---

* A sensitive scholar has seen the point: "To the Pericleans . . . Athena is Athens; the best that Athens stands for. Athena's attributes, victorious prowess in war, intelligence, love of the arts, are precisely the attributes of the Athenian people as Pericles describes them in the Funeral Speech. In this sense, every thinking Athenian who had been fired by the Periclean ideal 'believed' in Athena."[13]

Pericles and his friends. The tragedian Sophocles, by no means a political opponent, though a pious traditionalist in religious matters, was at best of two minds about new ideas. His *Antigone*, performed in 441 on the south slope of the Acropolis, from where the Parthenon could be seen still under construction, reveals his doubts. Its plot centers on the conflict between the practical interests of the state as set forth by its intelligent, patriotic leader who is interested only in reason and power, and the demands of nonrational, traditional religion represented by a girl who insists on the formal burial of her brother, an enemy of the state. Sophocles presents and understands the case for the ruler Creon, but he clearly prefers the one for the girl Antigone. The old religion is not to be tampered with or cast aside.

Events would soon show that Pericles' rationalism and intellectualism, the novelty and daring of his apparently religious efforts, the untraditional and largely alien "brain trust" with which he surrounded himself, disturbed many Athenians who could cause trouble for him. Thucydides had failed in his attack on Pericles with its veiled reference to impiety. But in the next decade, new enemies and old would fix on religion and different aspects of the building program to attack Pericles, his associates, friends, and loved ones.

# 9

# PRIVATE MAN

By 440, Pericles had been Athens' leading politician for twenty years, longer than the dominant period of Cimon. In 443, he had rid himself of his chief opponent, Thucydides, son of Melesias, and attained a degree of power and influence unequaled in living memory. Malevolent people began to murmur about his alleged physical resemblance to the hated Peisistratus. Some comic poets were bold enough to call him and his companions the "new Peisistratids," demanding that "he swear an oath not to become a tyrant, on the grounds that his supremacy was not commensurate with a democracy and was too oppressive." (Plutarch, *Pericles* 16.1)

The son of Melesias and his partisans had been appalled by the growth of Pericles' power and professed to oppose him so that Athens "should not become a monarchy, pure and simple." (Plutarch, *Pericles* 11.1) Many Athenians must have shared that suspicion, and Pericles' opponents obviously thought he might be vulnerable to attack from that direction. Most Athenians were evidently satisfied with the state of their city and its empire and happy to have Pericles manage their affairs. Even so, a new set of opponents arose to challenge his leadership. So great was his influence and popular support that they could not immediately attack him and his policies. Political attacks would have to be cloaked in some other pretext; they would need to focus on his personality, his way of life, his friends.

Leadership takes different forms in different polities. In monarchies, dictatorships, or despotism of any kind the leader strives to seem greater than and far above ordinary people. Thus, Alexander the Great is said to have asked to be declared a god. In the last days of the Roman Republic, Julius Caesar was charged with seeking to become king; in Roman eyes that was a claim almost as bizarre. Caesar and many successors to the imperial throne were deified upon their deaths. The earthy Vespasian mocked this custom with his last words: "Oh, my; I think I am becoming a god." But his successors took the matter more seriously, understanding that in a monarchy it is useful for the people to hold the ruler in awe as a superior being.

In democracies, the situation is different. Although the people occasionally choose a man of extraordinary dignity and magnitude to lead them, like George Washington, they usually select someone more comfortable. It is an advantage to be born in a log cabin and grow up splitting rails like Abraham Lincoln. If the leader happens to be rich or well born, he is still expected to have the common touch. In the fifth century, most political leaders in Athens were aristocrats, but the most successful before Pericles was Cimon, who mingled easily with the ordinary man and spoke in his language. Pericles was very different.

The story is told of a vulgar and ill-mannered nuisance who followed Pericles all day as he went about his public duties, abusing and insulting him. All this was in the open marketplace, the most crowded spot in Athens. But Pericles took no notice and never said a word. When evening came he turned for home, showing no sign of annoyance, while the man followed him shouting vulgar abuse all the way. By the time he reached his door it was dark, so he ordered a servant to light a torch and see the man safely home. (Plutarch, *Pericles*, 5.2–3) It was a striking display of the restraint and good manners of a nobleman and the detachment of a philosopher. Admirers might applaud such behavior as evidence of lofty nobility, but others took a dimmer view. He was called presumptuous, arrogant, and haughty. His aloofness was seen as an expression of contempt for ordinary people, and his austerity was called conceit and an attempt to gain a grand reputation. His electoral and legislative success show that most Athenians took the kinder view, but to all but a few he remained a cold, remote, and lonely figure.

The public image of Pericles was of a powerful and solitary being who spoke with a force and eloquence not given to ordinary men, holding himself aloof from the social life of his class, a distant individual who well deserved the Olympian epithets fixed upon him by the comic poets. They apparently based this divine association chiefly on his rhetorical talents, showing him as "thundering," "lightning," and "carrying a terrible thunderbolt on his tongue." (Plutarch, *Pericles* 8.3) But the manner of his life, no less than his power and elevated language, shaped his austere public image.

The reserve admired by aristocrats, the frightening events of his childhood, and his philosophical education all produced a natural tendency toward a certain detachment. But Pericles chose a pattern of behavior that intensified rather than diminished his lofty remoteness. He rarely appeared in public except in the execution of his duties, and then only on the street connecting the places of public business. He avoided the dinner and drinking parties that were the chief form of sociability among men of the upper classes. On only one occasion do we hear of his going to such a party, and that was the wedding of a relative. Even then, he stayed only until the drinking began and then took his leave.

In fact, Pericles had many friends and associates, a surprising number of whose names we know. But his relationship with them was somewhat different from the ordinary practice of his contemporaries. Instead of joining them during leisure hours at the gymnasium, the dinner table, or over bowls of wine, some he met during business hours in connection with common activities, such as politics or architectural and artistic projects, and others he engaged in philosophical conversation, his favorite diversion.

His political friends and colleagues were many, for no one can function as the leading figure in a democracy for three decades without a great deal of help. Among these friends was Pyrilampes, a man who made several embassies to Persia. He also accompanied Callias to Persia in 449 and received the gift of a peacock from the

Great King, becoming famous as a breeder and displayer of those birds.[1] Menippus, another close associate, was a general alongside Pericles. Glaucon, a member of Pericles' tribe, repeatedly served with him on the board of generals, as did Hagnon, who also served as founder of the colony of Amphipolis. Cleinias, also a general and the mover of a decree tightening control of tribute payments, was close enough to Pericles to make him co-guardian of his orphaned sons. A fragment from a comic attack tells of another of Pericles' friends who seems to have been like Poo-Bah in Gilbert and Sullivan's *Mikado*, a kind of Lord High Everything Else:

> *Metiochus is a general, and Metiochus cleans the*
> *    streets;*
> *Metiochus bakes the bread, and Metiochus makes*
> *    the barley-cakes;*
> *Metiochus does everything; and Metiochus will be sorry.*

These men, and many others whose relationship with Pericles is not documented, worked with him in the military, diplomatic, and political service of Athens and became close enough to him to be publicly considered his friends. Another group comprised the better part of the intellectual and cultural elite of the fifth century, including his teachers and philosophical associates, Damon, Anaxagoras, and Protagoras. He is also associated with the philosopher Zeno of Elea, probably the inventor of dialectic and famous for his paradoxes that appear to show the impossibility of motion or change. Pericles also knew personally at least two of the great triad of Athenian tragedians: Aeschylus and Sophocles. Herodotus, the historian of the Persian Wars who, it is believed, read his work aloud in public at Athens, joined in Pericles' attempt to found an ideal city at Thurii. His sympathetic treatment of the Alcmaeonids in his *History* suggests that he was especially close to Pericles.

Lampon, the famous Athenian seer, was a very useful friend, whom Pericles entrusted with several political assignments, including the foundation of Thurii. Plutarch calls him one of Pericles' "trusted men." (*Moralia* 812) He was an interpreter of oracles and an *Exegetes*, an expounder of the unwritten sacred laws—the one, in fact, chosen for the post by the priests of Pythian Apollo at Delphi. One scholar goes so far as to call him "a veritable minister of religion."[2] In *Rhetoric*, Aristotle describes a conversation in which Pericles trips up the rather pompous man of religion. "Pericles asked Lampon about initiation into the sacred rites of the savior goddess. He answered that he who was not initiated was not permitted to hear about them. Pericles asked if Lampon himself knew what they were, and he said he did. 'How can that be,' asked Pericles, 'since you are not an initiate.' " (1419a) Aristotle uses the exchange to illustrate an opportune device in which an opponent has made such a statement that an additional question leads him to absurdity. But the story also suggests an easy relationship in which Pericles can twit the revered religious expert.

Pericles also had a close and easy friendship with Sophocles, stemming from the year of their common generalship in 441. One of many stories about them had the two generals off with the fleet when Sophocles praised the beauty of a boy who had caught his attention. Pericles rebuked him, suggesting that peculation was not the only form of corruption for a public official: "A general must not only have clean hands, Sophocles, but clean eyes, as well." (Plutarch, *Pericles* 8.5)

Sophocles, like many Athenians of the upper classes, took pleasure with lovers of both sexes—the great tragedian was reputedly notorious for his sexual appetites. Pericles, however, appears to have been strictly heterosexual, like his predecessor Cimon. Both were victims of merciless satirical attacks by the comic poets for many years, and homoerotic behavior was one of their favorite targets. Like Cimon, Pericles was frequently accused of sexual misdeeds, but always with women. The ancient evidence does not permit us to know whether Sophocles or Cimon and Pericles were more typical of the tastes of Athenian aristocrats, and it is even harder to know if they were the same as those of the ordinary man.

Pericles' conversations with Protagoras seem to have been more serious. One of them, repeated by Pericles' son Xanthippus, gives the impression of authenticity. The young man, angry with his father and wishing to make him seem ridiculous, went all over town telling this story. During an athletic contest, a javelin hurled by one of the competitors struck and killed a bystander. Pericles and Protagoras, according to Xanthippus, spent a whole day discussing the question of responsibility: Was it the javelin, the man who threw it, or the organizer of the games who bore the blame "according to the strictest reasoning?" (Plutarch, *Pericles* 36.2–3) This is just the kind of philosophical discussion we might expect from two friends highly trained in ethical and logical analysis. They would have been seriously interested in the deeper significance of the issues while also deriving the greatest pleasure from the matching of wits in conversation. To the man in the street, of course, they would have seemed heartless and absurd.

Far from the remote, aloof, solitary, dour figure we expect to find, the picture of Pericles that emerges from even this limited evidence is that of a man with a wide circle of friends and acquaintances. He was intimate to the point of easy jocularity with some, he derived the deepest intellectual pleasure from others, and he made use of the talents and friendship of all. Pericles made no distinction between Athenians and foreigners in this respect. In fact, some of the most visible of his companions—Anaxagoras, Hippodamus, Herodotus, Pythocleides, and Protagoras—were not Athenians. In a city that was becoming more and more aware of the distinction, this was not necessarily a benefit.

Athenian marriage, especially among the upper classes, was usually neither romantic nor emotionally satisfying. It was typically arranged to advance family standing or acquire property, and the bride's father provided a dowry to accompany her into her husband's house. Marriage within a circle of kinsmen were frequent. Men generally waited until they were past thirty before marrying, and their wives were usually about fifteen. It was not, therefore, a union of equals; such a disparity in age meant that the young girl passed from the authority of one fully grown man, her father, to that of another, her husband. From the modern point of view, such marriages could not have been emotionally or sexually satisfying, especially for the women, who were kept at home, their chastity carefully watched and guarded. Men were expected to seek the pleasures provided by women outside the household. As Demosthenes candidly put it: "We have courtesans [hetairai] for pleasure, concubines [pornai] to serve the daily needs of our bodies, and wives so that we may breed legitimate children and have a trusted person watching over what we have in the house." (Against Neaira 118–22)

By this criterion, if not by modern ones, Pericles' marriage was a great success. He married a woman of his own class, a relative of some kind, probably around the year 463,[3] and had two healthy sons, Xanthippus and Paralus, both probably born by 460. In other respects, however, the marriage did not succeed. Husband and wife did not get on well. Divorce in Athens was easily available either by mutual consent or on the initiative of either party, and about 455 the marriage came to an end. The dissolution of Pericles' marriage seems to have occurred by mutual consent, for he himself arranged his wife's second marriage, in accordance with her wishes, to Hipponicus, son of Callias, one of the richest men in Athens.

Their sons seem not to have turned out well, either. In response to a pointed question from Socrates as to whether Pericles had been able to make his sons wise, Plato reports Alcibiades as saying: "Well, if the two sons of Pericles are simpletons, what of it? (*Alcibiades I* 118E) Nothing is known about the career of Paralus, the younger son, but Xanthippus, the elder, was plainly on bad terms with his father. Xanthippus was a spendthrift, and he compounded the problem by marrying a woman of noble lineage and extravagant tastes. Since Pericles controlled the family property, his son depended on an allowance from his father, which he found inadequate. In fact, the support Pericles gave his sons was not copious and he doled it out at measured intervals. Pericles' own legendary incorruptibility seems to have been connected with a fundamental indifference to money. As we have seen, he led a modest social life, and we do not hear of any great personal expenditures. He did not build temples to honor his own achievements, as Themistocles had done, or make gifts to his friends and supporters in the manner of Cimon. The one exception was his expenditure as *choregus* for Aeschylus' *Persians*, and that must be understood as an investment in his political future.

The ordinary Athenian landowner lived on his country estate for some part of the year, used some of its products to sustain his household, and sold off any surplus. Once Pericles set out on the road to political leadership, affairs of state absorbed all his time and interests. He did not manage his own estate, as was normal even for active politicians. Instead, he put it into the hands of Evangelus, an excellent steward who managed it on the most economically sound principles. Pericles, who spent most of his time in the city, instructed his manager to sell all the products of the estate at the appropriate time and used the proceeds to buy what he needed. By treating his farm as a business venture run by an agent, he was free to think about affairs of state and the life of the mind.

His sons and their wives did not appreciate this plan, regarding him as stingy. Xanthippus dealt with the problem by going to one of Pericles' friends and asking for money on the pretense that it was for his father. When the friend asked to be repaid, Pericles not only refused but brought a suit against his son. But it seems unlikely that the bitterness of the quarrel can be explained solely by disagreements over money. The boys may have been distressed by their parents' divorce, and held Pericles responsible. At any rate, the family quarrel became public, as Xanthippus went around telling discreditable stories about his father. The breach was never healed.

Critics took note of Pericles' failure to make his sons men of outstanding virtue and achievement. Plato has Socrates use this failure as evidence that virtue cannot be taught, to which Protagoras responds that a teacher cannot succeed if his pupil lacks natural capacity. (*Protagoras* 327b) It must have been galling for this great educator and instructor of the Athenian people to acknowledge that he had not succeeded with his own sons. His disappointment might have been eased had he known that another son, also called Pericles—the product of his love match with Aspasia—would be elected general more than twenty years after his own death.

Perhaps he tried to compensate for his disappointment with his sons and his estrangement from them by accepting the guardianship of Alcibiades and the young Cleinias, the orphaned sons of his friend Cleinias. The elder Cleinias died at the battle of Coronea in 447/6, when Alcibiades was about five and his brother even younger. Normally, their custody would have fallen to the father's closest adult male relative, but the boys' mother was an Alcmaeonid, and their father apparently had greater trust in her relative and his friend, the foremost man in Athens.

Pericles got little joy from the young Cleinias. A modern scholar describes him as a "psychotic delinquent,"[4] perhaps a more clinically precise diagnosis than the evidence warrants, although Alcibiades himself referred to his brother as a madman. (Plato, *Alicibiades I* 118E) His testimony, to be sure, must be weighed against the fact that Pericles sent the young Cleinias to live with his own brother Ariphron, "fearing that he would be corrupted by Alcibiades." But Ariphron sent him back within six months, "not knowing what to do with him." (Plato, *Protagoras* 320 A–B)

Alcibiades himself presented different problems. He inherited his father's wealth, which was so enormous that, in 416, he could run seven chariots in the race at the Olympic games, more than any private citizen had entered before. He was very handsome, so much so that "he was hunted by many women of noble family." (Xenophon, *Memorabilia* 1.2.24) He was trained to be an outstanding speaker, and his intelligence led one philosopher to call him "the most capable of all men in discovering and understanding what was necessary." (Theophrastus in Plutarch, *Alcibiades* 10.2–3) Even his flaws helped him as much as they hurt him. He had a famous lisp, but people found it charming. He was willful, spoiled, unpredictable, and outrageous, but his boyish antics won him admiration and public attention.

Pericles was far too busy to have spent much time with either boy during their childhood, but the precocious Alcibiades appears to have been impressed and inspired by the greatness of his famous and powerful guardian. The talented boy, his ambition already whetted and his expectations raised by the tradition of his father's house, set his sights high, and he was encouraged by many sycophants. According to Plutarch, "His corrupters seized upon his ambition and love of fame and thrust him prematurely into great undertakings, persuading him that as soon as he began his public career he would not only eclipse the other generals and politicians at once but would surpass the power and reputation even of Pericles." (Alcibiades 6.3) That is precisely what he set out to do, and he achieved great things. But he lacked the experience, the wisdom, and especially the character of his guardian, and badly overreached himself. Xenophon's verdict is severe: He was "the most licentious, the most arrogant, and the most violent of all those who lived under the democracy." (*Memorabilia* 1.2.12.) Twice he was condemned and driven from Athens by his fellow-citizens, and he ended his days, disgraced, in exile.

All this, however, took place after Pericles' death. As an adolescent and young man, Alcibiades seems to have spent some time in conversation with his guardian, where he revealed both his cleverness and his contempt for conventional ideas of morality. There is a famous story of his going to see Pericles and being told that the great statesman was too busy, for he was seeing how to render his accounts to the Athenian people, as public officials were required to do. "Wouldn't it be better," said Alcibiades as he turned to go, "if he looked to see how *not* to render his accounts to the Athenians?" (Plutarch, *Alicbiades* 2.7.2)

Xenophon reports a conversation between Pericles and Alcibiades when the young man was still in his teens.

> "Tell me, Pericles," he said, "can you teach me what a law is?"
>
> "Certainly," said Pericles.
>
> "Then please teach me," said Alcibiades, "for whenever I hear men praised for abiding by the law, I realize that no one deserves to be praised for that unless he knows what a law is."
>
> "Well, Alcibiades, there is no difficulty about what you are eager to learn: what is a law? Laws are all those things considered and voted by the majority gathered in assembly saying what should be done and what should not."
>
> "Do they think it is right to do good or evil?"
>
> "Good, of course, my boy, not evil."

"But if it is not the majority, but rather, as happens in oligarchies, a minority that meets to write laws saying what should be done, what is that?"

"Whatever the sovereign power in a state enacts governing what should be done is called a law."

"And if a tyrant is the ruler of the state and enacts what the citizens must do, is that a law, too?"

"Even what a tyrant enacts as ruler, that also is a law."

"But what are force and lawlessness? Aren't they at work when the stronger compels the weaker to do as he wishes, not by persuasion but by force?"

"Yes, I agree with that."

"So whatever a tyrant compels the citizens to do by enactment, not by persuasion but by force, is lawlessness?"

"I believe so, and I retract my statement that whatever a tyrant enacts without persuasion is a law."

"And whenever a minority passes acts, not by persuading the majority but by using its power to compel them, shall we call that force, or not?"

"Everything, it seems to me, that does not persuade but compels people to do something, whether it is an enactment or not, is force, not law."

"Well, then, everything that the ruling majority enacts over those who have property, without persuading them, would be force, not law?"

"Alcibiades, at your age we were also clever at this sort of thing. For the puzzles we spent time over and split hairs about then were just the same as the ones you seem to think about now."

"O Pericles," he said, "how I wish I had known you then, when you were at the peak of your form in these matters." *Memorabilia* 1.2.40–46)

The young Alcibiades had obviously studied with a newer generation of sophists whose "enlightened" critique of the legal and political tradition had gone much further than that of men like Protagoras. To serve as his guardian must have been a stimulating, if somewhat disconcerting, responsibility.

For some six or seven years after his divorce, Pericles appears to have lived without a consort. But then he entered into a liaison that was unique in his time, one that brought him great happiness, a barrage of criticism, and considerable trouble. His companion was Aspasia, a young woman who had left her native Miletus, perhaps in the early 440s, and come to live in Athens. The ancient writers refer to her as a *hetaira*, a kind of high-class courtesan who provided men with erotic and other kinds of entertainment. She clearly had a keen and lively intellect and may well have been trained in the latest ideas and techniques of discussion in Miletus. In any case, Socrates himself thought it worth his time to talk with her in the company of his followers and friends, and in the dialogue *Menexenus*, Plato jokingly gives her credit for writing Pericles' speeches, including the Funeral Oration.

At the same time, she must have been a beautiful young woman who appealed to Pericles' strong erotic inclinations. Contemporaries accused him of using all sorts of dishonorable means to satisfy these appetites. They said that Phidias and Aspasia herself procured women for him; they charged him with seducing the wife of Menippus; they charged his friend Pyrilampes of using his famous peacocks to bribe women on Pericles' behalf and even went so far as to accuse him of sleeping with his own son's wife. So many slanders of the same kind are unlikely to be random inventions but, rather, exaggerations of real foibles. Plutarch is probably right in rejecting Aspasia's intellectual qualities as her main attraction and in declaring that Pericles' love for Aspasia "was more of the erotic kind." (*Pericles* 24.5)

In every way, Aspasia represented something wonderfully different from Athenian women. She was not a sheltered and repressed creature confined to the narrow world of slave women, children, and female relatives. She was a beautiful, independent, brilliantly witty young woman capable of holding her own in conversation with the best minds in Greece and of discussing and illuminating any kind of question with her husband. There can be no doubt that he loved her dearly and passionately, since he took her into his house and, whether or not they were legally married, treated her as his beloved wife. Each morning when he left home and every evening when he returned he embraced and kissed her tenderly, by no means the usual greeting between an Athenian man and his wife.

About 440, Aspasia bore him a son whom they named Pericles. As the offspring of a foreign mother, young Pericles was legally a bastard (*nothos*) in the sense that he was not a citizen eligible to inherit his father's property and carry on the family name. But Pericles already had two legitimate sons who would precede Aspasia's child as heirs in any case.

For an Athenian to consort with courtesans was normal; to take one into his house and treat her as a concubine, perhaps only a little less so. What was by no means normal, but shocking and offensive to many, was to treat such a woman, and a foreigner, too, as a wife: to lavish such affection on her as few Athenian wives enjoyed, involve her regularly in conversation with other men, and discuss important matters with her and treat her opinions with respect.

The personal behavior of leaders, especially in sexual matters, often has political significance. In democracies, especially, violations of public morality that provoke scandal can be terribly damaging. The scandal surrounding Pericles' liaison with Aspasia was immense, and the comic poets made the most of it. They called her a whore and her son a bastard; they called her Omphale, the legendary Lydian queen for whom the hero Heracles had worked as a slave, and Pericles' enemies carried this image even further by comparing her with Thargelia. This beautiful and clever Ionian courtesan had consorted with many important Greek men and used her influence to bring them over to the Persian cause. The implication was clear: Pericles was enslaved by the charms of this foreign woman and she was using her hold over him for her own political purposes. The Samian War, which arose over a quarrel between Aspasia's native Miletus and Samos, intensified these allegations, for the story spread that Pericles had launched the war at her bidding. After Pericles' death, Aristophanes picked up these old charges and comically worked them around to blame Aspasia for the Peloponnesian War as well.

The slanders swirling about Aspasia touched Pericles, too, and not merely because of his association with her. In the comedy *Cheirones*, performed in 440, Cratinus satirized them together: "In olden days Faction and Cronus married and she bore him the greatest tyrant of all, whom the gods call Head-collector. And on Lewdness he begot Aspasia as his Hera, a dog-eyed whore." (Plutarch, *Pericles* 3.3; 24.6) Here the jokes are thickly packed. The Titan Cronus, instead of being married to Rhea, as in the myths, is married to Faction [*Stasis*], a reference to Pericles' rise to power out of party conflict. Cronus' son was Zeus, whom Homer calls "Cloud-gatherer"; Cratinus' Zeus is Pericles, whom he calls "Head-gatherer," making a harmless but funny reference to the odd shape of his head, but also to his position of leadership. Homer admiringly called Zeus' wife Hera "the Ox-eyed lady," but Cratinus calls Pericles' consort "the dog-eyed whore."

Much of this is mere comic abuse. But the reference to tyranny had political significance. The movement of a popular leader rising to power out of factional strife and making himself tyrant was a common pattern in Greek history and had special meaning for the Athenians. The tyrant Peisistratus had come to power in just that way, and the behavior of his tyrant-sons, including their treasonous association with the Persians, left a bitter memory for all Athenians. Any linkage with that memory was bound to be damaging to an Athenian politician. The problem was compounded by the fact that Peisistratus, like Pericles, had been a great builder. When Cratinus joked about Pericles and his most recent construction project in the comedy *Thracian Women*, performed not long after the ostracism of Thucydides, he may have intended a subtle reminder: "Here comes squill-headed Zeus with the Odeum on his cranium, now that the ostracism is over." (Plutarch, *Pericles* 13.6) And when people pointed out that its roof was just like the one on the pavilion of the Great King of Persia, they may have been inferring monarchical pretensions.

In 438, Pericles' new political opponents found another way to get at him. They launched a series of attacks against his friends using the plausible and potent pretext of irreligion. Phidias had been working on the enormous and expensive gold and ivory statue of Athena to be placed in the cella of the Parthenon. Once it was completed and dedicated, the sculptor was accused of embezzlement and impiety. About the same time, Aspasia, too, was charged with impiety. Then a bill was introduced declaring atheism and "teaching about the heavens" public crimes: The obvious target was Anaxagoras. Finally, Pericles himself was accused of embezzlement and bribery. It is clear that political enemies had launched a concerted assault on Pericles and his friends with the intention of undermining his popular support and destroying his power.

Possibly his enemies had studied Pericles' own career and were taking a leaf from his book. Finding Cimon and the Areopagus politically unassailable, Ephialtes and Pericles had taken advantage of the unpopularity of a long war against a rebellious ally to accuse the individual Areopagites and Cimon himself of financial wrongdoing. Although the indictments failed to convict Cimon, they succeeded in removing some Areopagites, and they helped undermine support for Cimon's party. When his pro-Spartan policy later suffered a reversal, the ground had been prepared for bringing him down.

In 438, the rebellions at Samos and Byzantium were less than two years in the past. The siege of Samos had been long and costly, both in casualties and money. That it was unpopular in some quarters is shown by the critical remarks of Cimon's sister Elpinice and also by the allegations that Pericles had been led into it not by necessity but in behalf of Aspasia. The time was ripe, and the unveiling of Phidias' statue in the Parthenon provided the occasion.

The charge against Phidias was that he had stolen some of the gold consigned to him for the statue. The target was especially attractive, not only because Phidias was so close to Pericles but also because Pericles, as a member of the board of supervisors of the project, would share responsibility. According to Plutarch, some of the accusers were personal enemies of Phidias, but others "were testing out what sort of a judge the people would be in a case involving Pericles." (*Pericles* 31.2) One of the sculptor's assistants sat down in the suppliant's seat in the marketplace, asking immunity if he brought a charge against Phidias. We do not hear of this procedure on any other occasion; it may have been an act of political theater intended to dramatize the fearful power that his enemies alleged Pericles wielded. At any rate, when his request was granted by the people, he formally made the charge in the assembly. Pericles, however, had ordered Phidias to put the gold on the statue in such a way that it could easily be removed in an emergency, such as a protracted war in which the Athenians might be running short of money; the gold could then be taken down, melted, and used for public purposes. On this very different occasion, Pericles asked Phidias to take down the gold plates and have them weighed; the results showed that no gold was missing.

That was not the end of Phidias' troubles, however. He was next charged with impiety because, in the scene of the battle with the Amazons he had carved on Athena's shield, one of the figures "suggested himself as a bald old man lifting on high a stone with both hands," and another was an excellent likeness of Pericles fighting an Amazon. Plutarch, who had seen the sculptures himself, remarks: "The arrangement of the hand, holding out a spear in front of Pericles' face, is cleverly worked to hide the resemblance, but it is perfectly obvious when seen from either side." (*Pericles* 31.4) This is the sort of amusement engaged in by many artists of the Italian Renaissance, but it was a daring and dangerous joke to play in the fifth century. No living human being had ever been shown on a Greek temple before Phidias put a great number of anonymous Athenians on the frieze of the Parthenon. To carve recognizable people on the statue of the goddess was far too bold for the ordinary citizen, who was likely to consider it an act of *hubris* that could endanger the entire city.

In spite of the intellectualism and rationalism of their leader, most Athenians remained religious in the traditional way and, by our lights and those of the "enlightened" few contemporaries, very superstitious. When the Spartan army invaded Attica at the beginning of the Peloponnesian War, seven years after the trial of Phidias, the rational and skeptical Thucydides tells us that "oracle-mongers chanted oracles of every kind, according to the sort that each wanted to hear." (2.21.3) When a terrible plague broke out the next year, the Athenians remembered with terror that the Delphic oracle had promised the Spartans victory and its own assistance, and to it they attributed the plague which had fallen on them but not on the enemy. Such religious fears and superstitions always lay close to the surface, and the attack on Phidias brought them into the open. The sculptor was convicted and went off into exile.[5]

Their success encouraged the attackers to bring a charge of impiety against Aspasia. Hermippus the comic poet was the accuser, but the details are unclear. Plutarch says that in addition to this charge she was alleged to have procured free women for Pericles' enjoyment. Whether that act in itself could be considered one of impiety or whether it supplemented some other accusation is not known. Certainly something more substantial than this flimsy and improbable claim should have been necessary to secure a conviction. No doubt the plaintiff hoped that the general prejudice against Aspasia, amplified by the resentments raised against her by the Samian War, would weigh more heavily than specific details. Pericles, in any case, took the threat very seriously, for the proud, reserved "Olympian" came into court and broke down in tears as he successfully begged the jurors to acquit her.[6]

Now the frantic voices of the "old-time religion" came fully into play. In 438, a bill providing that "those who do not believe in the gods or who teach doctrines about the heavens should be impeached" (Plutarch, *Pericles* 32.1) was introduced by the oracle-monger (*chresmologos*) Diopeithes, a man "chock-full of ancient prophecies and reputed to be eminently wise in religious matters." (Plutarch, *Agesilaus* 3.3) Aristophanes refers to him as "the great Diopeithes, the man with the crippled hand," the very model of uncontrolled frenzy (*Birds* 988, *Knights* 1085, *Wasps* 380), and other comedians questioned his sanity. However, other people took him seriously, and the bill seems to have understood that Anaxagoras was the target. This was one challenge that Pericles did not dare meet head on. No trial appears to have taken place. As Frank Frost has remarked, "In this crisis, the spirit of Galileo rather than that of Socrates prevailed, and the scientist was sent out of town."[7]

Pericles' position had been weakened by these attacks, and his enemies now took aim at their real target. A certain Dracontides proposed a bill that required Pericles to place his public financial accounts in the hands of the Prytanies, the presidents of the council, and to answer a charge of stealing sacred property. An unusual, perhaps unique, proviso required the jurors to use "ballots that had lain at the altar of the goddess on the Acropolis." (Plutarch, *Pericles* 32.3) The sacred character of this procedure "would make superstitious jurymen almost duty-bound to find Pericles guilty."[8] Pericles had no reason to worry about a simple inquiry into his financial probity, but the extraordinary legal procedure suggests that his enemies meant to use the prejudices of religious orthodoxy aroused by the other trials and legislation to embarrass and, perhaps, convict him. At this point, his friend, the prestigious general Hagnon, came to the rescue. He amended the bill, requiring that the case be tried by a jury of fifteen hundred using ordinary procedures. That put an end to the entire plan, for nowhere in Athens could a jury of fifteen hundred men be found to convict Pericles of anything, much less a charge of stealing public property. There is no reason to believe that the case ever came to court.

Was there a discernible political group behind these attacks, as there had been behind those against the Areopagites and Cimon in the 460s? Certainly some Athenians had found Pericles' policies insufficiently aggressive during the First Peloponnesian War. After the ostracism of Thucydides in 443, they probably became more vocal and active, since they no longer needed to rally round the democratic and imperial cause. They may also have believed that the settlements with the rebellious Samians and Byzantines were too lenient. If the Euboeans, who rebelled in 446/5, had their lands confiscated with Athenians settled among them as cleruchs, why should the more recent rebels receive better treatment? At the very least their tribute should have been raised sharply. But it was not, and some Athenians must have argued that such moderate punishment would only encourage new defections. That certainly was Cleon's argument in the 420s when he urged the Athenians to put the rebellious men of Mytilene to death.

In the last years of Pericles' life, Cleon would become his chief critic and opponent, although in 438/7, Cleon had probably not yet become the recognized leader of the main competing faction. But by the first years of the Peloponnesian War he was already making demagogic attacks upon Pericles' lax conduct of the war. Cleon was one of a new class of Athenian politicians, not aristocrats but rich men of common ancestry whose wealth usually came from manufacturing and commerce rather than land. Such occupations were considered base and unworthy by the aristocratic code of the Greeks, and the license allowed to comic poets permitted Aristophanes to mock Cleon as a tanner and a leather-merchant, to call him a thief and brawler whose voice "roared like a torrent" and sounded like a scalded pig's. He is depicted as always angry, a lover of war who constantly stirs up hatred. These are the exaggerated epithets of Athenian comedy, but even the sober historian Thucydides called him "the most violent of the citizens," and portrayed his style of speech as harsh and bullying. Aristotle fills out the same negative picture: Cleon "seems to have corrupted the people more than anyone by his attacks; he was the first to shout while speaking in the assembly, first to use abusive language there, first to hitch up his skirts [and move about] while addressing the people, although the other speakers behaved properly." (*Constitution of Athens* 28.3) The contrast with "Olympian" Pericles could not have been greater.

It is interesting that the comic poet Hermippus, who wrote verses supporting Cleon's side of that argument, was the same man who brought charges against Aspasia. But Cleon was not the first demagogue to come before the people of Athens. In his comic play *Knights*, Aristophanes presents an oracle telling how Cleon (called Paphlagon in the play) will be destroyed: "The oracle says clearly that first will come an oakum-seller who will govern the affairs of the state. . . . Second, after him, comes a sheep-seller. . . . He will rule until a greater rascal than he appears; then he is destroyed. In his place will come a leather-seller, Paphlagon, the thief. . . ." (*Knights* lines 128–37) Ancient commentators identify Eucrates as the oakum-seller, and Lysicles, who was an orator and general in the time of Pericles, as the sheep-seller. These were probably the men who assailed Pericles in 438/7, helped by the up-and-coming dealer in hides, Cleon. Unlike Pericles and all previous Athenian political leaders, these men were not nobles but wealthy tradesmen. Closer to the average Athenian, they were more likely to understand and, perhaps, to share the resentment many felt against the sophists, philosophers, and artists—most of them foreigners—with whom Pericles consorted. They also distrusted the new rationalism and intellectualism the foreigners brought, and the neglect of traditional religion that resulted.

Pericles weathered this storm, although at considerable personal cost, and his political position remained fundamentally sound. In the years following these trials he would show that he could still count on majority support for his policies, even those that were novel and not inherently popular. Like all imaginative and thoughtful democratic leaders, he needed to maintain a delicate balance. The assignment of the leader is to go beyond the present in his thoughts and policies, while that of the people is to pursue immediate, practical goals and adhere to their traditions. The resulting tension is bound to involve some disagreement, even between a popular leader and the most devoted populace, and oppositional elements generally seize upon the opportunity thus created.

The charge of Periclean monarchy probably arose about this time. From a constitutional point of view it was absurd. The people in their assembly were sovereign. They could reject their leader's policies, remove him from office, and punish him as they would. Yet there is some truth in the claim, for Pericles exercised the kind of control that great intelligence imposes. A modern scholar makes the point well: "If there once was a 'Greek miracle' . . . it was really that this dialogue between intellectual sovereignty and legal sovereignty concluded in agreement, certainly not without dissonances, but durable enough that its echo and its fruit were perennial."[9]

The trials of 438 represented a turning point in Pericles' career. For more than two decades, he had achieved amazing things, going from success to success. Occasional reverses had not prevented a consistent progress toward the accomplishment of his vision. Heretofore his opponents had been the same that he had faced from the beginning—conservative aristocrats, friends of Sparta, enemies of democracy and of an empire under its control, "rightists," to use a helpful if anachronistic term, led by Thucydides, son of Melesias. These conservative elements feared the rapid growth of democracy supported by the wealth acquired from the empire, the increased power of the masses and the politicians dependent on them, and the loss of influence by men like themselves.

Now, for the first time, Pericles encountered opposition from the left, whose leaders came from a class of Athenians previously excluded from the highest positions in political life. They were men who gained influence through the money they had made in commerce and by their skills in rhetoric and political organization. In foreign affairs, they seem to have favored imperial expansion and harsh treatment of the allies. They were hostile to the Spartans and far more willing than Pericles to risk a fight against them. At home, their chief goal was to remove Pericles to make room for themselves, and they used popular religious fears and prejudices to attain their ends.

Their movement was unfamiliar and potentially dangerous, for it threatened to cut Pericles off from his main political base. His firm belief in reason and in his own rhetorical ability had led him to assume that he could educate Athenians to choose the best direction. Though he successfully passed through them, the events of 438 suggest that to some degree, at least, he had miscalculated.

# 10

## STATESMAN

n 437 Pericles could look at the world with
considerable satisfaction. The empire was once again peaceful and
prosperous. The accord with Sparta and the Peloponnesians had been
severely tested by the Samian crisis of 440–439, but it had held. In
Athens, Pericles had defeated one set of opponents and survived the
assaults of another. The Parthenon was finished, and work was going
forward on the great new gateway to the Acropolis, the Propylaea. His
private life was enriched by the beautiful Aspasia, who had increased
his happiness by presenting him, in his mid-fifties, with a new son. His
fame was at its height, and Thucydides rightly described him in the
year 433 as "the foremost man [*protos aner*] among the Athenians at
that time, the most potent in speech and action." (1.139.4)

All this success and good fortune would soon be undone by the outbreak of war. From the perspective of the Greeks of the fifth century, the conflict deserves to be thought of as a world war no less than that of 1914–1918 seemed to Europeans of the time. It was "the greatest upheaval that had ever shaken the Hellenes, extending also to some part of the barbarians, one might say even to a very large part of mankind." (Thucydides 1.1.2) It would cost the Athenians more than a third of their population; the loss of their fleet, walls, and empire; and, for a time, even their democracy and autonomy.

Like so many other great wars, the conflict that led to the Peloponnesian War arose in a remote area of no intrinsic importance. Thucydides begins his account of it by saying, "Epidamnus is a city on the right as you sail into the Ionian Gulf." (1.24.1) He needed to say that, because most of his contemporary readers had no idea where it was. Epidamnus was even more remote from the interests and knowledge of Athenians and Spartans than Sarajevo was from Europeans at the time of Archduke Ferdinand's assassination, which led to World War I. Called Dyrrachium by the ancient Romans and Durazzo by modern Italians, Epidamnus is now the town of Durres in Albania. Well to the north of the normal sailing route from Greece to Italy and Sicily, it was not especially rich or strategically placed, and it was not associated with either of the great alliances. No one could have predicted that a domestic quarrel in this remote and unimportant place would lead to so great a war.

Epidamnus was controlled by an aristocracy, but civil strife and a war against neighboring barbarian tribes had weakened the hold of the aristocrats. At last, the democrats joined forces with the barbarians and drove their enemies from the city. Epidamnus was a colony of Corcyra (modern Corfu), so the losing faction turned to the mother-city for help. The Corcyreans, however, content with their isolation, refused to become involved.

Rejected by their mother, the Epidamnian aristocrats turned to their grandmother—that is, to Corinth—the mother-city of Corcyra. Corinthian relations with Corcyra were peculiar to the point of perversity. Corinth had many colonies and enjoyed warm relations with all except Corcyra. For centuries the colony and its mother-city had been at odds, quarreling and fighting wars, often over the control of some other colony that both claimed as their own. The Epidamnian aristocrats now offered to make their city a Corinthian colony in return for assistance against their enemies. The Corinthians accepted at once and sent a force into the city, driving out the democrats and their barbarian allies and restoring the aristocrats. They did so in full expectation of Corcyrean opposition and were undeterred by the prospect. The Corinthians, in fact, were spoiling for a fight, not only because of their old competition with the wayward colony but from a deeper and less rational motive. They became involved, according to Thucydides,

> in part because they thought that the colony was no less theirs than the Corcyreans; at the same time also out of hatred for the Corcyreans, for they paid no attention to the Corinthians even though they were their colonists. In the common festivals they did not give them the customary privileges nor did they begin by having a Corinthian commence the initial sacrifices, as the other colonies did, but treated them contemptuously. (Thucydides 1.25.3–4)

Nothing compelled the Corinthians to intervene in Epidamnus. There was no threat to any of their interests or to their power or prestige. But they eagerly seized the opportunity to annoy and humiliate their insolent colony, knowing full well that war might result. They must have expected no interference, for Corcyra had no allies, and the Corinthians had many friends in the Peloponnesian League. If the Corcyreans chose to fight, Corinth was confident of victory.

The Corcyreans for their part did not care who won the civil war at Epidamnus. But they strongly objected to Corinthian involvement. They sent a fleet to Epidamnus to lay down the law: The Epidamnian democrats were to send away the colonists and garrison sent by Corinth and take back the exiled aristocrats. The ultimatum was obviously unacceptable. Thus, despite their isolation, the Corcyreans, too, were ready to fight, confident in the superiority of their fleet. Apart from Athens, Corcyra was the only Greek state to maintain a navy in peacetime, and it was a very impressive fleet of 120 warships. Corinth, on the other hand, though a major commercial power, had no warships to speak of. The haughty tone of the Corcyreans indicates that they expected to win easily.

In considering only the correlation of forces at the beginning of the quarrel, however, Corcyra made a great mistake. The Corinthians were rich, adaptable, angry, and determined. They were ready for a major commitment and a long struggle, for which their potential resources were far greater than Corcyra's. The Epidamnian democrats rejected the ultimatum, and forty Corcyrean ships, the aristocratic Epidamnian exiles, and the Illyrian barbarians laid siege to the city by land and sea. But the Corinthian response showed how short-sighted the Corcyreans had been. They announced the foundation of a new colony at Epidamnus and invited settlers from all over Greece to join it. The response was impressive. A large number of settlers sailed for Epidamnus accompanied by thirty Corinthian ships and three thousand soldiers. Additional help came from several cities asked by Corinth to supply ships and money—the most important of these being Athens' unfriendly neighbor, Megara—even little Tro-ezen and Hermione had been asked to make their tiny contributions of two and one ships, respectively, surely more for psychological than military purposes. Most of these cities were members of the Pelo-ponnesian League, but Sparta was not among them. A Spartan force at Epidamnus would have had an intimidating effect on Corcyra, but as far as we know the Spartans were not asked. Perhaps they had already expressed their disapproval of the Corinthian expedition.

Even without the Spartans, the coalition gathered by Corinth frightened the Corcyreans out of their confident arrogance. When they heard of the preparations they sent an embassy to Corinth to discuss the situation. The envoys began by repeating Corcyra's orig-inal demands but offered, at the same time, to submit the case to arbitration by any mutually acceptable Peloponnesian state or by the Delphic oracle if the Corinthians preferred. This appeal was followed by a threat: The Corinthians should not allow war to come; if they did, the Corcyreans would be forced to seek friends elsewhere, beyond those they had already turned to, in order to gain assistance. The reference to Athens was unmistakable.

The Corcyreans sincerely sought a peaceful settlement. Corin-thian zeal and diplomatic success proved they had miscalculated, and they were no longer eager to fight. The offer to seek a Peloponnesian arbitrator is further evidence of their good faith and willingness to accept a compromise solution or even a diplomatic defeat. They were not, however, prepared to accept the humiliation of surrender in the face of the Corinthian threat. If pushed to the extreme they would fight and go to Athens in search of help.

A minor incident in a remote corner of the Greek world had now developed into a threat to the general peace. The Spartans were alert to this threat, for the Corcyreans had not come to the negotiations in Corinth alone. They were accompanied by formal representatives of Sparta and Sicyon, who were there to lend weight to the Corcyrean request for a peaceful settlement. When the crisis began, the Spar-tans favored its peaceful resolution. They feared that if war came,

Corcyra would turn to Athens for help; if Athens agreed, Corinth would try to involve Sparta. The result might be a major war arising from a matter of no interest to the Spartans.

Despite Sparta's intervention, the Corinthians rejected a variety of Corcyrean proposals and declared war. Their decision reveals that they did not believe in the seriousness of Corcyra's threat to make an alliance with Athenians, for Athenian intervention in a naval war would guarantee the defeat of Corinth. The Corcyreans might seek such an alliance, but the Corinthians were confident that Athens would refuse. They rightly believed that Pericles would want no part of it, interpreting the Thirty Years' Peace and Athenian actions since its enactment to mean that Athens had conceded to Corinth a free hand in the west. That view, however, overlooked a feature of the quarrel that created special problems, namely the great Corcyrean navy. Corinthian anger thus led to a misunderstanding of the situation that would have deadly consequences.

Seventy-five ships under Corinthian command accordingly sailed north toward Epidamnus. On the way, they were intercepted by a Corcyrean force of eighty ships and defeated in the battle of Leucimne. On the same day, Epidamnus surrendered to the besieging Corcyreans. Corcyra held the disputed city and dominated the seas. To increase Corinth's humiliation, the Corcyreans ravaged and burned the territory of Corinth's allies in the west.

The Corinthians may have been defeated, but they were not deterred, and during the next two years they prepared for revenge. They built warships at an unprecedented pace and hired experienced crews from all over the Greek world, including the Athenian Empire. The Athenians made no attempt to interfere, showing that they were not yet involved or alarmed. The Corcyreans, on the other hand, were thoroughly frightened. They understood that, unassisted, they could not forever withstand an aroused Corinth, supported by many allies and mercenary oarsmen. The Corinthians, in short, had called their bluff. So the Corcyreans sent ambassadors to Athens. Learning of this, the Corinthians also sent an embassy, "to prevent the addition of the Athenian fleet to the Corcyrean, since that would be an impediment to the resolution of the war in the way they desired." (Thucydides 1.31.3)

It is hard for a modern reader to imagine the scene that took place in Athens in the summer of 433. In the United States, discussion of these matters would take place between the foreign envoys and the elected and appointed officials receiving them. These talks would be private and secret, and the major decisions would be taken even before any treaty was presented to the Senate for ratification. The ordinary citizen would be only an observer of what was made public. The Athenian procedure was far different. All discussion took place in the open on the hillside of the Pnyx from which the assembled citizens of Athens could see their own marketplace and the newly constructed Parthenon and Propylaea on the Acropolis. They heard every word spoken by the ambassadors from both delegations. Then they debated among themselves what action to take, each citizen, however, humble, hearing every argument and contributing the same single vote as the most experienced political leader. Everyone knew that the issues involved the security of the city and its empire, a question of war and peace; if the result should be war, the citizens themselves would do the fighting.

The Corcyrean spokesman faced a difficult task, for the Athenians had no obligation to them and no history of previous friendship. Athens under Pericles wanted to remain at peace, and none of its interests were directly involved in the quarrel between Corcyra and Corinth. After a preliminary assertion of the moral and legal rights of his cause, the speaker turned to the heart of the matter, appealing to the main Athenian interest. "We possess a navy that is the greatest except for your own," a force that would be added to the power of the Athenian alliance. "In the entire course of time few have received so many advantages all at once, and few when they come to ask for an alliance offer to those whom they ask as much security and honor as they expect to receive." (Thucydides 1.33.1–2)

Appealing next to fear, the Corcyreans claimed that the Athenians needed the alliance as much as they did. A war between Athens and the Peloponnesians is coming, they insisted.

> If any of you thinks it will not happen his judgment is in error, and he does not perceive that the Spartans are eager for war out of fear of you, and that the Corinthians have great influence with them and are your enemies; they are making an attempt on us now with the thought of attacking you in the future, in order that we may not stand together out of common hatred toward them and so they may not fail to accomplish two things before we do: either to harm us or strengthen themselves. (1.33.1–2)

Since war was inevitable, the argument ran, the Athenians must act to protect themselves. Corcyra, the speaker pointed out, was conveniently located for the coastal voyage to Italy and Sicily. Whichever side controlled it could prevent fleets from those places, populated chiefly by Dorian colonists friendly to Sparta, from coming to the aid of the Peloponnesians, and could send its own ships there in safety. Athens must accept the full offensive and defensive alliance they were offering, they concluded, because its own fate depended upon it. The proof was brutally clear and simple:

> There are three fleets worthy of mention in Greece, yours, ours, and the Corinthians'; if the Corinthians get control of us first, you will see two of them become one and you will have to fight against the Corcyrean and Peloponnesian fleets at once; if you accept us you will fight against them with our ships in addition to your own. (1.33.3)

The task of the Corinthian spokesmen was no easier. Their moral case was bad, for they were clearly the aggressors at Epidamnus and had rejected every proposal for a peaceful solution, even against the advice of their allies, Sicyon and Sparta. The best they could do was remind the Athenians of past favors and defame the character of the Corcyreans. They had a stronger argument, although still a problematic one, about the legality of a treaty with Corcyra. Technically, such a treaty would not violate the letter of the Thirty Years' Peace, but it would surely run counter to its spirit: "For although it says in the treaty that any of the unenrolled cities may join whichever side it likes, the clause is not meant for those who join one side with the intention of injuring the other." (1.40.2) That is, the clause was never intended to permit one side to make a treaty with a neutral that was already at war with the other side. The strictest interpretation of the treaty permitted Athens to accept Corcyra. But common sense argued that doing so would amount to an act of war against Corinth, and by extension, a breach of the Thirty Years' Peace. In any case, the Corinthians made it clear that if the Athenians made an alliance with Corcyra, they would have to fight Corinth, "for if you join with them it will be necessary for us to include you in our punishment of them." (1.40.3–4)

Finally, the Corinthians had to answer the most powerful Corcyrean argument: the assertion that war between Athens and the Peloponnesians was inevitable. Their response was simply to deny this inevitability and to place the burden of decision on the Athenians. If the Athenians joined Corcyra, there would be war; if they refused, there would be peace. The Corinthians also reminded the

Athenians of the service they had done them during the Samian rebellion by helping to dissuade Sparta and the Peloponnesians from attacking Athens at a moment of weakness. They believed that they had confirmed on that occasion the key principle governing relations between the alliances: noninterference by each side in the other's sphere of influence.

> Circumstances have brought us under the principle that we ourselves expressed at Sparta, that each side should punish its own allies. Now we come to you demanding the same thing: that you should not injure us with your vote, since we helped you with ours. Pay us back in equal measure, knowing that this is the crucial moment when assistance is the greatest friendship and hostility the greatest enmity. Do not accept the Corcyreans as allies against our wishes nor help them to do wrong. In doing what we ask you will be behaving properly and serving your own interests in the best way. (1.43)

The Athenians were then left to consider both arguments and to make their decision. The Corcyreans insisted that war was inevitable. The Athenians, therefore, could not let Corinth defeat them. For if the Corinthians won and absorbed the Corcyrean navy, it would lead to the immense and dangerous growth of the Peloponnesian fleet. Thus, the Athenians must make the alliance not to avert war but to guarantee victory when the unavoidable occurred.

Up to this point Pericles had by no means believed war to be inevitable, nor was it evident that a Corinthian victory over Corcyra would make it so. On the contrary, the Corinthians argued that Athenian abstention would avoid war and confirm the effectiveness of the Thirty Years' Peace, a very plausible prediction. At the same time, there could be no guarantee that there would not be another war against the Peloponnesians, for the years since the establishment of the Athenian Empire had shown the lasting presence of a Spartan faction jealous of and hostile to Athens. On several occasions this faction had gained the upper hand and might do so again. In that event, Athens could ill afford the risk of a powerful Peloponnesian navy. Whatever her desire to keep the peace and to avoid remote entanglements, Athens could not allow a major change in the balance of power.

The Athenian situation closely resembles that of Great Britain in the early years of the twentieth century. When Germany began to build a navy of a size and quality to challenge British supremacy, the British, who preferred to live in "splendid isolation" from the continent, reversed a century-old policy and aligned themselves with their traditional enemies France and Russia. They were ready to fight a great war to defend their naval supremacy. Such is likely to be the action of any state whose sustenance depends on control of the sea.

The Corinthians did not grasp this point, although their Spartan and Sicyonian allies did. They appear to have expected the Athenians to refuse alliance with Corcyra, possibly even to join with them against the Corcyreans. Why did they miscalculate so badly? For them, the quarrel with Corcyra was a purely local affair. They believed that Periclean Athens had no ambitions in the region and that Athens wanted peace. They also thought their friendliness during the Samian crisis would be reciprocated. The Corinthians themselves had no plans for a war against Athens, so they did not anticipate the Athenian alarm at the growth of their naval power, as they should have. Instead of making sure that the Athenians would stand aloof, they ignored the danger and plunged ahead, hoping and assuming that all would be well. In their anger and optimism they indulged in wishful thinking and forced the Athenians to make an unpleasant decision. Corinth would not be the last state in history to let its passion dominate more prudent calculation in this way.

Almost all debates in the assembly were decided in a single day. But the argument over the treaty with Corcyra so divided the Athenian people that it carried over to a second session. On the first day opinion leaned toward the Corinthian side and rejection of the treaty. But in the second debate Pericles "persuaded the people to send help to the Corcyreans who were fighting the Corinthians and to attach themselves to a vigorous island with naval power." (Plutarch, *Pericles* 29.1) Nevertheless, the Athenians did not accept the proposal for an offensive and defensive pact requested by Corcyra, the normal form of alliance in the Greek world. Instead, they made a purely defensive alliance, the first we know of in Greek history. This innovation, very likely the invention of Pericles, may have been conceived as a way of preventing the defeat of any alliance at all.

The opposition was probably led by Pericles' old competitor, Thucydides, son of Melesias. The ten years of his ostracism had come to an end in the spring of 433, several months before the debate, and his return apparently gave new life to his scattered and disheartened faction. What gave him such strong support was the general understanding that a Corcyrean alliance could lead to war with Sparta, and some of the moderates on whom Pericles relied must have been attracted by his arguments. The danger to Athens was remote and problematical, and she had no material interest in the quarrel itself. Why should Athens risk a war on behalf of Corcyra?

The historian Thucydides asserts that the Athenians voted for the treaty because they believed that war with the Peloponnesians was inevitable, and they wanted to gain a strategic advantage before it came. That the war was inevitable was the historian's own opinion, based on hindsight, and it is by no means clear that he was right. Certainly, the many who opposed the treaty did not share that view, and the evidence strongly indicates that neither did Pericles as early as 433. He supported the treaty because he was unwilling to tolerate a rapid and dangerous shift in the balance of naval power. He did not, however, intend the treaty with Corcyra to bring on war; rather it was meant to avoid war while preventing a Corinthian victory of Corcyra. He did not support the normal offensive and defensive alliance that would have made a war hard to avoid, for such a treaty could have encouraged the Corcyreans to take reckless actions that would embroil the Athenians with Corinth. Instead, he proposed the novel defensive alliance, a precisely crafted diplomatic device calculated to meet the special needs of the moment. Pericles could hope that this measure would bring Corinth to her senses and deter her from further adventures. Rather than fight the Athenians, the Corinthians could save face by accepting arbitration or a negotiated settlement. If the Corinthians were reasonable, in other words, there would be no war, no shift in the correlation of forces, and no new danger to Athens.

The choice presented by the Corcyreans was between a very active policy that ran a high risk of conflict quite soon and an entirely passive one with a high risk of Athenian disadvantage in a possible future war. Pericles invented a middle way that tried to avoid both possibilities. A moderate diplomatic approach, active rather than passive, aimed at deterrence without provocation characterized Pericles' statesmanship throughout the crisis. Its success would require the Athenians' actions be governed by intelligence and reason and that Athenian policy persuade the other states also to act on the basis of reason instead of passion.

As tangible evidence of their commitment, the Athenians sent a fleet to Corcyra. Its numbers, leadership, and instructions neatly illustrate the Periclean policy. There were only ten ships, a force that was obviously more symbolic than militarily significant. If Pericles seriously intended to fight the Corinthians, in preparation for a war against the Peloponnesians or not, he should have sent some two hundred warships. If a battle ensued, such a force, combined with the Corcyrean fleet, would have guaranteed a smashing victory and possibly the obliteration of the enemy's navy. The smaller force would make little difference in a battle if their presence failed to deter the Corinthians. Among the three commanders was Lacedaemonius, son of Cimon. Although he was an experienced commander of cavalry, we know nothing of his naval experience. But the choice cannot have been a coincidence. His family's close friendship with the Spartans made it clear that his selection for this assignment was meant to disarm Spartan suspicion.

The generals were ordered not to engage the Corinthians unless they attacked Corcyra itself. Only then should the Athenians intervene, and only to prevent a landing on Corcyrean territory. "These orders were given in order not to break the treaty," says Thucydides. (1.45.3) As any field commander knows, such instructions are a nightmare. How, in the midst of a naval battle, can a man be certain of the intentions of the participants? The Corinthians might approach Corcyra as part of a tactical maneuver, with no intention of landing, but this might not be clear until the last moment. By hanging back, however, it might be too late to prevent a landing if that was what the Corinthians intended. Then the commanders could be blamed for failing to carry out their assignment. On the other hand, if they attacked a Corinthian ship that seemed to be heading for land, they could be blamed for an unnecessary action. In that case it would be especially helpful if the crucial decisions were made by Lacedaemonius, a well-known friend of the Spartans.

Pericles' decision was an effort at what is called in current jargon "minimal deterrence." There need be no war, the Athenians indicated by their action, if Corinth would refrain from attacking Corcyra and seizing her fleet. The presence of an Athenian force was proof that Athens was determined to prevent a shift in the balance of naval power; but its small size showed that the Athenians would not seize the opportunity to diminish or destroy Corinthian power. If the ploy worked, the Corinthians would sail home without a fight and the crisis would pass. That should not disturb the Spartans, who, still earlier, had themselves tried to restrain the Corinthians.

Even if the Corinthians chose to fight, Pericles seems to have hoped that the Athenian fleet could stay out of the battle. The Corcyreans might win, as they had done at Leucimne, without Athenian intervention. Even better, from the standpoint of some Athenians, the two fleets might do great damage to each other, and the battle end in stalemate, with their naval power shattered. Thucydides tells us that the Athenians had just such a thought in mind when they made the defensive alliance with Corcyra. They hoped "to wear the two sides out as much as possible against each other so that they might find Corinth and the other naval powers weaker in case it should be necessary to go to war with them." (1.44.2) Only in the worst case and at the last moment might the Athenians need to fight.

This, too, was the moderate position among those available, and it is clear that the extremes had some support. Those Athenians who had opposed the alliance also opposed the expedition. No doubt they were the ones who impugned Pericles' motives in sending Lacedaemonius, claiming that he had taken the command "against his will" and that Pericles had chosen him so that "if he should accomplish no great or outstanding deed, he might be blamed for his Laconism." (Plutarch, *Pericles* 29.2–3) On the other hand, many others thought the fleet was too small, and complained that Pericles "had offered small assistance to those who needed it but a great pretext for those who accused Athens." (Plutarch, *Pericles* 29.3) Despite these criticisms, Pericles held to his rational and moderate policy, hoping that the Corinthians would act on the same basis, but prepared to respond in kind if passion prevailed.

The arrival of the small Athenian squadron at Corcyra did not deter the Corinthians, as a larger force might have done. They sailed toward their hated colony with the largest fleet they had yet amassed: 90 ships of their own and 60 from their colonies and allies for a total of 150 warships. It is noteworthy that only two allied cities took part in this campaign, compared with the eight who had contributed at the battle of Leucimne. These were Elis and Megara. The remaining six may have been restrained by the involvement of Athens, but it also seems likely that the Spartans had applied pressure on their allies to stay out of the conflict. Against this powerful armada the Corcyreans put to sea with 110 ships accompanied by the 10 from Athens. In the battle that followed, which takes its name from a nearby group of islands called Sybota, the Athenians found themselves on the right wing of the line, directly facing the Corinthians. The engagement was fought in the clumsy, archaic way long since abandoned by the Athenians. The ships on both sides, their decks full of infantry and bowmen, grappled one another and fought what amounted to a land war on stationary ships.

The Greek ship of the line, the trireme, was a torpedo-shaped vessel some 120 feet from stem to stern and only 16 feet wide. Although it had a mast and sail that moved it when there was a favoring wind, these were removed when the battle began. In combat, the trireme was propelled by the power of 170 rowers superimposed one over the other and staggered from outboard to inboard. These ships were not very seaworthy and sometimes foundered in rough waters; but in a quiet sea, with a well-trained crew, experienced steersmen, and skillful captains, they could do amazing things. They could start fast, maintain high speeds for short bursts, and make very sharp turns. This agility allowed them to use their hard-wood, metal-sheathed prows to ram the enemy ships from the side or rear. Once its hull was breached, a trireme was swiftly swamped and left to founder and slowly sink.

In the fifty years they ruled the seas, Athenians had mastered the skills of naval warfare as no other state had. Their wealth made it possible for them to keep their ships and crews at sea for many months each year, giving them the time to acquire needed discipline and to practice maneuvers. In a fight in open water, even if outnumbered, the Athenians were likely to win.

At Sybota, however, the Athenians were handicapped by their orders. It did not take long for the Corinthians to gain the upper hand, and the Athenians were gradually forced to take part.

> When the Athenians saw the Corcyreans pressed, they began to help them without reservation. At first they held back from making an actual attack on the enemy ship, but when it became plain that a rout was taking place and that the Corinthians were in hot pursuit, then at last each man took part in the work and fine distinctions were no longer made; the situation had developed to the point where the Corinthians and Athenians had necessarily to fight one another. (Thucydides 1.49.7)

Nevertheless, the Corinthians drove their opponents back toward their island. The Corcyreans, now reinforced by the Athenian contingent, reorganized their forces and prepared to defend their city from invasion. The scene that followed would be implausible even in an old Hollywood movie, but we must believe it because the story is told by the most sober and austere of historians. Suddenly the Corinthians, who had sounded the signal to attack, began to back water. Why had they pulled back from the coup de grace? The answer became apparent when twenty Athenian warships appeared on the horizon. They had been sent twenty-three days after the first ten, when the Athenians decided that a larger force would be needed. Pericles had evidently been compelled to yield to the more hawkish element who had no faith in the delicacy of his policy. It was thus becoming increasingly difficult to hold to a thoroughly reasoned and carefully measured policy once the commitment had been made and passions began to rise.

The Corinthians could not know how large the reinforcement coming from Athens was going to be. The twenty ships they had seen might very well be only the first squadron of many to arrive, so they withdrew to avoid being caught between the two fleets. Night fell without further fighting and the next day found the shoe on the other foot. The Corcyreans, strengthened by thirty undamaged Athenian ships, came out to fight, but the Corinthians would have none of it. Not only had the balance of forces changed to their disadvantage, but they were also afraid that the Athenians might regard the previous day's skirmish as the beginning of a war against Corinth and an excuse to destroy the Corinthian fleet on the spot.

In fact, both sides moved cautiously to avoid an irrevocable conflict. Neither party wanted to be blamed for a formal breach of the peace. The Corinthians sent some men to talk to the Athenians without the herald's wand—the Greek equivalent to a flag of truce—for carrying that stick would be a formal admission that a state of war existed. They accused the Athenians of breaking the treaty by preventing the Corinthians from punishing their enemies. "If you intend to prevent us from sailing to Corcyra or anywhere else we like," they said, "and in this way to break the treaty, first seize us and treat us as enemies." The Corcyreans were enthusiastic about this suggestion and urged the Athenians to kill the envoys. Instead, the Athenians returned a very careful answer in perfect accord with their strict orders and limited objectives:

> We are not beginning a war, O Peloponnesians, nor are we breaking the treaty, but we have come to bring help to our Corcyrean allies. If you want to sail anywhere else we will not hinder you, but if you mean to sail against Corcyra or some part of her territory, we will not permit it, insofar as it is in our power. (Thucydides 1.53.4)

Each side, for its own reasons, was meticulous in trying to avoid responsibility for breaking the treaty. The Corinthians knew that any chance they might have of winning a war against Athens depended on embroiling the Spartans and the Peloponnesian League. But the Spartans had already indicated their disapproval of Corinthian policy; and if the Corinthians were shown to have broken their oaths, the chance of involving Sparta would be even slimmer. The Athenians were also concerned not to give the Spartans reason to enter in the quarrel. The policy was to avoid war altogether, and they could only hope that the evidence of Athenian commitment and seriousness demonstrated at Sybota might deter Corinth from continuing the contest.

The Athenians had succeeded in saving Corcyra and her fleet without going to war. But that success cannot be attributed to Pericles' policy. His symbolic dispatch of ten ships had failed to deter the angry and overconfident Corinthians, nor would they have been sufficient to defend Corcyra. It was the policy imposed on Pericles by the more militant Athenians who put their faith in superior force rather than diplomacy that saved the day. Where the will for victory obscured the risk involved, his opponents apparently understood the situation better than he. As the international crisis deepened, passion would prevail over reason more and more.

# CRISIS MANAGER

ericles' statesmanship during the growing crisis appears to have been an attempt to extend to the international scene the techniques that had worked so well for him in Athenian politics. In both spheres, his goal was persuasion—through reasoned discourse when possible, by symbolic gesture when needed. But persuasion and diplomatic gesture failed to solve the problem at Corcyra. Blood had been spilled, and a general conflict threatened the Thirty Years' Peace.

Pericles was soon faced with a series of crises that required swift responses to unforeseen and uncontrollable events. Accordingly, the principles that governed his conception of relations among the Greek states had to be adapted to fast-paced actions and the dangers they presented. The rational calculations, and the assumption that others would act rationally, on which his policies rested, were more and more confounded by the powerful emotions that inspired the behavior of all parties to the conflict. In these circumstances Periclean statesmanship gave way to crisis management.

Any hopes he may have had that the Corinthians would subside were quickly shattered. On their way home from Sybota, they seized Anactorium, a colony disputed with Corcyra, making it clear that they intended to continue the struggle even at the cost of provoking Athens. Pericles, therefore, had to prepare for a war against Corinth. But he hoped and expected to contain it as a limited conflict that would not involve the Peloponnesian League. He first interrupted his building program in order to preserve and safeguard the money that would be needed for war and solidified Athenian alliances in the west.

But his most striking, and in some ways most puzzling, measure was the Megarian Decree. Passed some time after Sybota (between September of 433 and the summer of 432), it barred the Megarians from the harbors of the Athenian Empire and from the marketplace in Athens. The use of economic embargoes as a diplomatic weapon is common in the modern world and has been employed as a means of coercion short of war. However, it has rarely succeeded and often served merely as a prelude to armed conflict. In the ancient world, we hear of no previous embargo imposed in peacetime.[1]

There can be no doubt that it was another Periclean innovation, for he defended it stubbornly to the end, even when it became the sole issue on which peace or war depended, and contemporaries blamed the decree for the coming of the war and Pericles for the decree. The comic hero of Aristophanes' *Acharnians*, produced in 425, six years into the war, explains the war as the result of the theft by some drunken Athenians of a Megarian whore and the countertheft of two prostitutes from the house kept by Aspasia. Pericles, in his fury,

> enacted laws which sounded like drinking songs, "That the Megarians must leave our land, our market, our sea and our continent." Then, when the Megarians were slowly starving, they begged the Spartans to get the law of the three harlots withdrawn. We refused, though they asked us often. And from this came the clash of shields. (*Acharnians* 532–39)

None of this is to be taken literally, of course, for the main aim of the poet is to inspire a good laugh. The story is a parody of the rape of

Helen that was the cause of the legendary Trojan War and possibly also of the reciprocal rapes reported by Herodotus as the ultimate cause of the Persian Wars. The terms of the decree and the severity of its results are comically exaggerated, and the portrayal of Aspasia as a madam and the cause of Pericles' support of the decree are malign jokes; but at its core is the malicious charge that Pericles was responsible for the war because of his insistence on the Megarian Decree. That view certainly reflected a significant segment of public opinion both during the crisis and after the outbreak of the war.

Why, then, did Pericles support and hold fast to the Megarian Decree? Scholars have seen it variously as an act of economic imperialism, a device deliberately intended to bring on the war, an act of defiance to the Peloponnesian League, an attempt to enrage the Spartans into breaking the peace and bearing the blame for the violation of the oaths, and even as the first act of war itself. The official version held that the decree was provoked by the Megarians' cultivation of sacred land claimed by the Athenians, their illegal encroachment upon borderlands, and their harboring of fugitive slaves. The modern theories do not bear close scrutiny, and the ancient complaints clearly form a mere pretext. Rather, the Megarian Decree must be understood as a moderate intensification of diplomatic pressure to help prevent the spread of the war to Corinth's allies. Pericles knew that the Corinthian strategy could only succeed if the other Peloponnesians, and especially Sparta, could be made to join the fight. If Megara's defiance went unpunished, other states might join the Corinthians in the next encounter; if enough of their allies took that step, Sparta could not remain aloof.

The Megarians were ancient enemies of the Athenians and were especially hated since their murderous treachery at the end of the First Peloponnesian War. Thus it was relatively easy for Pericles to persuade the Athenians to take some action against them. Some Athenians must have wanted to go further and attack Megara, while at the other extreme, some wanted to take no action at all. Pericles again took the middle path. The embargo would not bring the Megarians to their knees or even do unbearable economic damage. The starving Megarians lampooned by Aristophanes were brought to that condition not by the embargo but by regular invasions that destroyed their crops. The decree would only cause general discomfort to most Megarians and do significant harm to the men who prospered from trade with Athens and her empire; some of these, no doubt, will have been members of the oligarchic council that ruled Megara. This punishment might persuade Megara to stay out of trouble in the future; it might also dissuade other Peloponnesian states, especially the mercantile cities on the coast, from becoming involved in Corinth's quarrel with Athens.

Some Athenians may have pointed out the danger inherent in the decree: The Megarians would surely complain to their powerful allies, who might then feel the need to come to their aid. Pericles, however, had reason to believe they would not. The decree was not technically a breach of the Thirty Years' Peace, which contained no clause governing trade or economic relations. The Spartans were always reluctant to break their oaths. Beside, Pericles was a close friend of the only king in Sparta, Archidamus. He knew that Archidamus favored peace, and he must have believed that his royal friend would understand his own peaceful intentions and the limited purposes of the Megarian Decree. He was right about Archidamus, but events would show that here, too, he placed a heavy burden on the strength of reason when confronted by the power of emotion.

During the same winter of 433, the Athenians took another action prompted by the quarrel with Corinth, this time against Potidaea, a city in the northern Aegean, on the Chalcidic Peninsula bordering on Thrace and Macedonia. The Potidaeans were tribute-paying allies of Athens while at the same time being loyal colonists of Corinth, receiving annual magistrates from the mother-city. The Athenians knew that the Corinthians were planning revenge, and feared that they might join with the hostile king of Macedon to provoke a rebellion in Potidaea which could spread to other states. The Athenians therefore ordered the Potidaeans to pull down the city walls that protected them on the seaward side, to give hostages, and to send away their Corinthian magistrates. This action would separate Potidaea from Corinth and put the city entirely at the mercy of Athens.

Like the Megarian Decree, this ultimatum was a measure meant to deal with the growing threat of war against Corinth. If successful, it would deter a rebellion in Potidaea and the entire Thracian district of the Athenian Empire. Like the decree, it attempted to prevent Corinth from extending the area of conflict and from gaining allies. Neither step, if properly understood, need alarm Sparta. Once again, the tactic represented the moderate choice between extremes. Inaction might encourage a successful rebellion; sending a force to gain physical control of the city might be provocative. But issuing these orders was an act of imperial regulation that should avoid the rebellion without impropriety.

The Potidaeans must have been shocked and angered by the Athenian instructions. We do not know whether they were yet disaffected, but their tribute had recently been sharply increased, so they may already have been restive. Outwardly, the Potidaeans acted appropriately, sending an embassy to Athens to argue against the ultimatum. The negotiations went on all winter, until the Athenians became suspicious and prepared to impose their will. Meanwhile, however, the Potidaeans had also sent an embassy to Sparta, accompanied by the Corinthians, and obtained a promise to invade Attica if the Athenians attacked Potidaea.

This remarkable reversal of policy shows how seriously the recent events had affected Spartan opinion. The battle of Sybota, the Megarian Decree, and the ultimatum to Potidaea, coming in swift succession, had alarmed the Spartan ephors to the point of making war. That does not mean, however, that they could persuade their countrymen when the time came. The great debate on war or peace the next summer, in fact, shows that the decision was not a foregone conclusion. Even when the Spartans voted for war, they did not at once carry out their promise to invade Attica, although the Athenians were already besieging Potidaea.

In the spring of 432, the Athenians, exasperated by the fruitless negotiations, sent a force of warships and infantry to settle with the king of Macedonia. Along the way, the commander was ordered to "take hostages from Potidaea, take down their wall, and keep watch over the neighboring towns so that they should not revolt." (Thucydides 1.57.6) But the force was too little and arrived too late. Encouraged by the promise of Spartan support, the Potidaeans rebelled and succeeded in raising revolts in neighboring cities. The Athenian commander, his force too small to attack the walled city, concentrated on Macedonia. As before, the moderate policy proved inadequate. As with the Megarian Decree, Pericles did not expect the ultimatum to cause trouble, so he sent a force unable to impose its will. He expected the Potidaeans to act reasonably, since reason showed their cause to be hopeless; he had not counted on the reckless courage of angry and desperate men.

The Potidaean rebellion was a great opportunity for the Corinthians. But they dared not send an official expedition, which would have been a formal breach of the peace. Instead, they organized a corps of "volunteers" commanded by a Corinthian general, who led a force of Corinthians and Peloponnesian mercenaries to the aid of Potidaea. It was a very thin deception, but it shows how careful the

Corinthians were to avoid the charge of breaking the treaty. The political situation in Sparta was closely balanced, and the advocates of war needed every advantage to win over their reluctant fellow-citizens. Faced by this serious challenge, Pericles patched up a treaty with the Macedonians to free his forces for the siege of Potidaea. He also dispatched reinforcements, and by the summer of 432 a large force of men and ships surrounded Potidaea. The siege lasted more than two years and cost a vast sum of money.

Pericles' attempt to avoid extremes had produced an outcome that could hardly be worse. If he had taken no action at all, Potidaea might not have rebelled. Had he sent a large force at once, the Athenians might quickly have taken the city. Instead, he chose to take a less provocative action. In its first conception, the Potidaean ultimatum was nothing to alarm the Spartans, only the exercise of discipline within the Athenian Empire. Yet it developed into a ponderous military and naval action that could be seen as an unprovoked assault on a small state asking only to maintain its autonomy. Joined with the Megarian Decree, the ultimatum seemed to cast a different light on the Athenian alliance with Corcyra. It could now appear as an unwarranted interference in a quarrel that had nothing to do with Athens. A clever enemy could string these incidents together to paint a picture of the Athenians as a people who had become arrogant, aggressive, and a threat to the liberty of all Greeks. Perhaps the main cost of the affair at Potidaea was neither military nor financial, but psychological. It may have enabled the friends of war at Sparta to gain control of Spartan policy.

The siege of Potidaea infuriated the Corinthians and intensified their eagerness to bring Sparta and the Peloponnesian League into the war. They encouraged their Peloponnesian allies and other states who had grievances against Athens to put pressure on the Spartans. Finally, in July of 432, the ephors called a meeting of the Spartan assembly and invited anyone with a complaint against the Athenians to come to Sparta and speak his piece.

This was not a meeting of the Peloponnesian League, which would normally require a previous decision by the Spartan assembly. The bellicose ephors plainly did not believe the Spartans wanted war, so they invited the angry foreigners to help them change their minds. The Megarians were the loudest complainers, especially since the decree. But the most effective advocates of war were the Corinthians. There was reason to distrust them, for they were pleading their own cause after pursuing a dangerous policy against the Spartans' advice.

212 PERICLES OF ATHENS

They clearly meant to use the Spartan alliance for their own purposes, as they had done in the past, and Spartan advocates of peace would be suspicious. Also, their legal and moral position was weak, since the Athenians had committed no formal violation of the Thirty Years' Peace.

The Corinthian strategy was to persuade Sparta that its traditional policy of caution and reluctance to fight was disastrous in the face of the greatness and dynamism of Athenian power. Since the facts of Athenian behavior did not support their case, they resorted to generalities. Spartan lethargy had allowed the Persians to reach the Peloponnesus before they were stopped; the same qualities had also allowed Athenian power to grow dangerously strong. The chief argument lay in the comparison between the characters of the two peoples.

> You have never considered what sort of men you are going to fight and how totally different they are from you. They are revolutionary and quick to formulate plans and put them into action, while you preserve what you have, invent nothing new, and when you act do not even complete what is necessary. Again, they are daring beyond their power, run risks beyond wisdom, and are hopeful amidst dangers, while it is your way to do less than your power permits, to distrust your surest judgments, and to think that you will be destroyed by any dangers. Besides, they are unhesitating while you delay, they are always abroad, while you stay at home, for they think that by their absence from home they may gain something while you will lose what you already have. When they have conquered their enemies they pursue them as far as possible, and if beaten they yield as little ground as they can. In addition to that they use their bodies in the service of the city as though they belonged to someone else, at the same time as they keep their judgment solely their own as to use it for the city. And when they have thought of a plan and failed to carry it through to full success, they think they have been deprived of their own property; when they have acquired what they aimed at, they will think it only a small thing compared with what they will acquire in the future. If it happens that an attempt fails, they form a new hope to compensate for the loss. For with them alone it is the same thing to hope and to have, when once they have invented a scheme, because of the swiftness with which they carry out what they have planned. And in this way they wear out their entire lives with labor and dangers, and they enjoy what they have the least of all men because they are always engaged in acquisition and because they think their only holiday is to do what is their duty and also because they consider tranquil peace a greater disaster than painful activity. As

a result, one would be correct in saying that it is their nature neither to enjoy peace themselves nor to allow it to other men. (Thucydides 1.70)

This picture is not very different from the one painted by Pericles in his Funeral Oration, but it is the mirror image in its evaluation of the Athenian character. Both halves of the comparison are exaggerated, however. The Spartans surely could not be so sluggish and still have become the leaders of the Peloponnesian League. But the speech was not meant to describe the whole Spartan people. It was an indictment of the peace faction and their policy, and it was intended to gain support for their opponents.

Whatever the truth there may have been in the Corinthians' depiction of the Athenian character, it had little relation to Athenian behavior since Pericles had adopted his policy of peace. Athens had made no significant territorial acquisitions since the 450s, and since 445 the Athenians had acted fully in accordance with the letter and spirit of the Thirty Years' Peace, as the Corinthians themselves acknowledged when they restrained their allies during the Samian rebellion. Only within the last year had the Athenians taken actions that even remotely fit the charges of the Corinthians, and these had been brought on by Corinth's quarrel with Corcyra—just the sort of private involvement that made Sparta suspicious of Corinthian motives.

Since references to these recent events were embarrassing, the Corinthians quickly turned away from them, falsely implying that they were part of a well-established policy that arouse inevitably from the institutions and character of the Athenian people. The Corinthians described the Athenian character so as to show that peaceful coexistence with such a people was impossible even if the current crisis could be resolved. Prejudice, suspicion, and fear were called in to overshadow the facts of recent history and to drive the Spartans toward war. Finally, the Corinthians moved from the realm of rhetoric and threatened practical consequences if the Spartans failed to carry out the promise made by their ephors to invade Attica at once: They must launch the invasion "lest you betray your friends and kinsmen to their worst enemies and turn the rest of us to some other alliance." (Thucydides 1.71.4) The threat, in fact, was empty, for there was no other alliance to which they could turn, and no new one would have a chance against the Athenians without Spartan participation. To the Spartans, however, the very suggestion of defections from their league was a frightening prospect.

With these thoughts in mind, the Spartans listened to the next speaker, one of the envoys from Athens. Thucydides tells us he was part of an embassy that "happened to be present beforehand on other business." (1.72.1) We never learned what their official cover story was, but it is hard to think of what other business they might have had. Pericles must have heard about the Corinthians' efforts and of the ephors' invitation for any aggrieved parties to bring their complaints to Sparta. It was an important part of Pericles' understanding of the relationship between Athens and Sparta, established by the peace, that the Athenians should not send an official spokesman to answer these complaints. That would be inappropriate, for the Athenians did not accept the Spartans as their judges any more than the Spartans would accept the Athenians if the situation were reversed. On the other hand, the envoys must have been instructed to intervene in the discussion at the appropriate time and to deliver a message that would convey Pericles' policy.

The Athenians described their purpose in speaking as follows: to prevent the Spartans from yielding to the arguments of their allies, thereby making a bad decision on important matters; to show that Athens had come into possession of her empire justly; and to demonstrate that the power of their city was far from contemptible. The Athenians depicted the rise of their empire not as an example of ceaseless and insatiable ambition but as a response to a series of necessities imposed by the needs of fear, honor, and a reasonable self-interest. These were forces they fully expected the Spartans, themselves the leaders of a powerful alliance and a comparable superpower, to understand. But their tone was factual and not especially conciliatory, and their conclusion insisted on the strict letter of the treaty: the resolution of all disputes by arbitration. If the Spartans should refuse, however, "calling on the gods by whom we have sworn as witnesses, we shall try to take vengeance on those who have started the war when you have led the way." (Thucydides 1.78.5)

Some modern scholars have seen this speech as deliberately provocative, meant to anger the Spartans and bring on the war. Such an interpretation rests on a naive understanding of international relations not uncommon in our century. It assumes that attempts to appease anger, to explain differences charitably, to make concessions are the only ways to seek peace. Experience suggests that such an approach may even help bring war on, as evidenced by World War II. Sometimes the best way to deter war is to convey a message of strength, confidence, and determination. That interpretation, in any case, directly contradicts the judgment of the best contemporary witness. Thucydides believed that the Athenians wanted to persuade the Spartans not to decide hastily. "At the same time they wanted to make clear the power of their city, to offer a reminder to the older men of what they already knew and to the younger men of the things of which they were ignorant, thinking that because of their arguments the Spartans would incline to peace instead of war." (1.72.1)

Pericles' policy here, as throughout the crisis, was to pursue the middle path between fighting a war and making unilateral concessions under the pressure of explicit or implicit threats (i.e., deterrence). Now, however, confronted by Sparta herself, he coupled determination with a willingness to resort to arbitration as provided by the treaty. The Athenian spokesman must have hoped that his speech would calm the fear and cool the anger engendered by the speeches of Sparta's allies by reminding the Spartans of Athens' power. At the same time, he offered an honorable device for achieving a peaceful solution to a crisis in which no direct Spartan interest was involved. Pericles and his agents had good reason to believe that their plan would work, especially since Sparta's only active king was Archidamus—the leader of the faction favoring peace, a personal friend of Pericles, and "a man with a reputation for wisdom and prudence." (Thucydides 1.79.2)

After the speech of the Athenians, the Spartans sent the foreigners away and discussed the matter among themselves. Archidamus behaved as Pericles would have expected. He expanded on and documented the portion of the Athenian speech aimed at deterring rash Spartan action. The Athenian power was not only great but of a kind most difficult for the Spartans to overcome. The Spartan hotheads expected a short and easy war, but Archidamus told them, "I fear, rather, that we shall pass this war on to our children." (Thucydides 1.81.6) He next turned with contempt to the arguments of the Corinthians, whom he saw as the originators of the trouble. They had gone to war too lightly, underestimating their opponents' strength and misjudging the diplomatic situation. Now they sought to embroil Sparta in a dangerous war to serve their own selfish interests.

It is clear that Archidamus wanted peace. But the mood of the assembly was still angry, so it would have been unwise for him simply to support the Athenian proposal. Instead, he offered a practical and realistic alternative. First, the Spartans should send ambassadors to Athens to make official complaints without making clear their own intentions. At the same time, the Spartans should prepare for the kind of war they must face if negotiations failed. They should seek ships and money from barbarians (undoubtedly the Persians) as well as Greeks. If the Athenians yielded to the Spartan complaints, there need be no war. If not, there would be plenty of time to fight when the Spartans were better prepared, *in two or three years*.

These proposals would have suited Pericles perfectly, but they did not suit the Corinthians and their aggrieved allies. If Potidaea could be saved at all, the attempt must be made immediately; every day that passed brought capitulation closer. Nor would arbitration help the Corinthians. They did not want a settlement of grievances; they wanted a free hand against Corcyra; they wanted revenge on Athens to restore their prestige; and now they wanted nothing less than the destruction of the Athenian Empire. The war faction in Sparta felt the same way, and most Spartans had come to their view. The king's speech did not change their minds. It was not the troubles of Corinth, Potidaea, or Megara that moved them, but what seemed to them the arrogant and dangerous power of Athens. About this there could be no negotiations or compromise: Athens must be humbled.

The response of the war faction's spokesman, the ephor Sthenelaidas, was short and blunt:

> I don't understand the lengthy arguments of the Athenians. They praise themselves highly, but they don't deny that they are doing wrong to our allies and to the Peloponnesus. If they behaved well against the Persians and are now behaving badly towards us, they deserve a double punishment because they have become bad after having been good. But we are the same now as we were then, and, if we are wise, we will not look on while they wrong our allies, nor will we delay in seeking vengeance; for our allies are already suffering. Others may have much money, ships, and horses, but we have good allies whom we must not betray to the Athenians. Nor should we submit to judgments by courts or words, for we have not been injured by words. Instead we must take swift vengeance with all our forces. And let no one tell us that we must take time to consider when we have been wronged; rather let those who contemplate doing a wrong reflect for a long time. So vote for war, Spartans, in a manner worthy of Sparta. Do not allow the Athenians to grow stronger and do not betray your allies, but let us, with the help of the gods, march out against the wrongdoers. (Thucydides 1.87)

The ephor called for a decision on whether the Athenians had broken the peace treaty. The vote was taken in the usual form, by acclamation, but Sthenelaidas could not tell which roar was the louder, or claimed that he could not. He then resorted to a division in which a large majority voted that the Athenians had violated the treaty; it was a vote for war.

Why did the Spartans decide to fight what might be a long and difficult war against a uniquely powerful opponent for no tangible benefit, at the instigation and in the interest of a manipulative, willful, and selfish ally? What had undone the normally conservative Spartan majority favoring peace, led by the prudent and respected King Archidamus? Thucydides tells us that the Spartans voted for war not because of anything their allies said "but because they were afraid that the Athenians might become more powerful, seeing that the greater part of Greece was already in their hands." (1.88) He is right to emphasize the role played by the old fear and suspicion of Athens in bringing about the Spartan decision; but that fear had been insufficient to get the Spartans to favor war until the very day of the vote. Until then they had worked for a settlement, holding back their allies from the quarrel between Corinth and Athens, trying to restrain Corinth, and taking no action themselves. Even after the ephors had promised to invade Attica in the spring of 432, they had been unable to make the Spartans fulfill the promise.

Allied complaints, especially the frightening speech of the Corinthians at the assembly, helped change the mood. But none of this would have been enough without the unintentional help of Pericles' own policy. After Sybota, he meant to prepare for the threatened conflict with Corinth while avoiding a clash with Sparta; but his action did not have that result. The Megarian Decree caused the greatest difficulty. Here the Athenians were not moving against Corinth directly but against an ally of Sparta strategically located at the gateway to the Peloponnesus. Archidamus and his friends might know that the novel device of a trade embargo, far from being an act of aggression, was really a compromise measure to limit the scope of a possible war with Corinth by warning off potential allies. To the ordinary Spartan, however, frightened and inflamed by Corinthian rhetoric, it was an arrogant and aggressive action.

The ultimatum to Potidaea could only contribute to the cause of the Spartan war faction. The Athenians were right to think that Potidaea was the place most vulnerable to Corinthian agitation, but at the time the ultimatum was delivered the Potidaeans had done nothing to justify its harsh demands. To the Spartans, the affair at Potidaea must have seemed another instance of Athenian aggression against an innocent bystander. The Corinthian speech played on the emotions stirred by the decree and the ultimatum to change the mood and hence the balance of political power in Sparta.

In such a climate, the tone and character of the Athenian reply seem ill chosen. Pericles had no doubt instructed the ambassadors in what line to take before they left Athens. A firm, unyielding posture backed by a show of strength is a fine tactic of diplomacy if the adversary is calm, thinking clearly, and persuaded of its employer's basically unaggressive intentions. That was Sparta's attitude most of the time, under the influence of Archidamus and the peace faction, and that was the Sparta Pericles must have expected his envoys to address. But the same approach can be dangerous with a people who have come to fear the power and ambition of its user, and in the Spartan assembly of July 432 this hard-line tactic helped convince the uncommitted Spartans, and some who had favored peace, to vote for war.

In August, the Peloponnesian League met to ratify the Spartan decision. The majority wanted to fight, but not all the league's members were present and in any case the majority was not so large as it had been among the Spartans themselves. Not everyone was convinced that war was inevitable; not everyone believed that it was a just war; not everyone thought it would be easy and successful; not everyone thought it was necessary.

The vote of the league's congress opened the way for an invasion of Attica that would have redeemed the promise to the Potidaeans only a few months late. It would take only a few weeks for the Spartans and their allies to make the simple preparations needed for the invasion, and they would have plenty of good weather in September and October to do their damage. Although the Athenians' crop of grain had long been harvested and the favorite season for an invasion had passed, there was still time to do significant harm to grape vines and olive trees and to the houses outside the walls. If the Athenians were going to come out and fight, as the Spartans expected, they had plenty of reason to do so. In fact, the Spartans and Peloponnesians took no military action for almost a year, and even then the war began with a Theban attack on Plataea that forced the Spartans' hand. In the interim, moreover, the Spartans sent no fewer than three missions to Athens, ostensibly to preserve the peace—at least one of them clearly appears to have been sincere. The delays shows that after the excitement of the debate, the rhetoric of the Corinthians and the annoying response of the Athenians had faded from memory; the cautious and sober words of Archidamus began to have their effect. The war might yet be averted.

The first Spartan embassy demanded that the Athenians "drive out the curse of the goddess." (Thucydides 1.126.2–3) This was a reference to the conspiracy of Cylon two centuries earlier that had given rise to the famous "curse of the Alcmaeonids." This mission surely had cynical motives. The Spartans were aiming at Pericles, widely identified with his mother's illustrious family. They believed it would be easier to win concessions on the disputed points if Pericles were banished, but they had no real hope of bringing about his exile. Instead, they hoped he would be discredited and blamed for Athens' troubles because, Thucydides tells us, "as the most powerful man of his time and the leader of his state, he opposed the Spartans in everything and did not allow the Athenians to yield but kept driving them toward war." (1.126.3) The embassy, therefore, was more an act of psychological warfare than an attempt to keep the peace. Pericles had always opposed concessions without arbitration; now that the Spartans and their allies had voted for war, he believed that further negotiations offering no Spartan concessions and refusing to submit disputes to arbitration were merely tactical maneuvers in a war already declared. By the autumn of 432, Pericles had become unyielding, and the Spartans' stratagem, obvious as it was, shows that they thought there might be enough opposition in Athens to undermine him.

While Pericles had survived the attacks on him and his friends in 438, his troubles were not over. Thucydides, son of Melesias, was back in Athens and probably at the head of at least part of his former faction. It seems likely that this was the group that had opposed any alliance with Corcyra, and it probably resisted the Megarian Decree and the ultimatum to Potidaea. They passionately opposed war and would insist on the repeal of the Megarian Decree when the crisis reached its climax. At the other extreme was the group that would not yield an inch to the Spartans. They must have been the ones who had favored a full offensive and defensive alliance with Corcyra and demanded the sending of reinforcements to the battle of Sybota. Cleon had probably already become their leading spokesman and was a rival to Pericles, however unequal, for influence with the masses. Opposition had been effective during and after the Corcyrean debate in 433. All the prejudices that the average Athenian felt toward their aloof and unusually intellectual leader must have come to the fore in these difficult and dangerous times, and his political enemies might be expected to reap whatever advantages they could.

The trials of Phidias, Anaxagoras, and Aspasia had involved impiety, so it was no accident that the Spartans revived an old charge that also dealt with a branch of religious practice. We may be sure that both the aristocratic friends of Thucydides and the democratic supporters of Cleon, for different purposes, made much of the air of impiety surrounding Pericles. Their attacks, however, failed. "Instead of suspicion and slander, Pericles achieved a still greater confidence and honor among the citizens as a man who was most hated and feared by the enemy." (Plutarch, *Pericles* 33.1) All the evidence testifies to Pericles' unshaken position on the eve of the war. When he was making the crucial decisions he made them because he thought them right, not because his hand was forced by domestic politics.

Pericles was not unaccomplished in the art of political propaganda, as the Athenians' response to the Spartan demand makes clear. In reply to the suggestion that the curse of the Alcmaeonids be expelled, they answered that the Spartans should drive out the curse of Taenarus, and doubled the bid by insisting that they expel the curse of Athena of the Brazen House as well. The Spartans had once put to death some helots who had taken sanctuary in the temple of Poseidon at Taenarus, and it was the common belief that this sacrilege had caused the great earthquake of 464. This obvious parallel was convenient for embarrassing the Spartans. The curse of the Brazen House referred to another breach of sanctuary, when Pausanias—the notorious victor at Plataea who tyrannized over the Greek allies, committed treason with the Persians, and plotted with the helots—had been shut up in the temple of Athena and allowed to starve to death. This was also a religious violation and was recognized as such by the priests at Delphi, who insisted on a complicated and expensive act of atonement.

By invoking this second scandal Pericles subtly reminded the Greeks of how objectionable Spartan hegemony had been when unchecked by Athenian power. Considering the Spartan record in the years after the Persian Wars might lead them to regard the impending conflict as something other than a simple struggle for freedom against tyranny. At the same time, the reference to Pausanias may also have been aimed at internal Spartan politics. The aggressive policy of Pausanias and King Leotychidas during those years had brought Sparta loss of popularity and respect, treason in high places, and rebellion within the Peloponnesus. Likewise, the policy supported by the war faction in 432 would involve actions outside the Peloponnesus and seemed likely to produce a long war in far-off places. Pericles must have known that his response would help the friends of peace in Sparta, and he therefore seems to have come out ahead in the first diplomatic skirmish.

Despite the rebuff, the Spartans continued to send ambassadors to Athens. These envoys told the Athenians to withdraw from Potidaea and restore autonomy to Aegina.[2] "And especially they proclaimed publicly in the clearest of language that there would be no war if [Athens] withdrew the Megarian Decree." (Thucydides 1.139.1) No doubt the Spartan offer was sincere. The Athenians might still choose to withdraw the decree, as the debate in Athens shows, and if they had, the Spartan war faction could hardly have carried the day against their doubtful, hesitant, and divided allies. Even without any Athenian concession, the Spartans were uncomfortable about the oaths they had taken in 445, conceding later that they were the ones who had broken the treaty. It would have been more difficult to get everyone to fight after the Athenians had accepted their condition.

The political climate in Sparta had clearly changed since the first embassy. This second embassy plainly represented a compromise. Archidamus "tried to settle the complaints of the allies peacefully and to soften their anger" (Plutarch, *Pericles* 29.5), but neither he nor his opponents were firmly in command. If Archidamus had been in control, we would have expected him to submit the disputes to arbitration. If the war faction had had a clear majority, they would have ended negotiations after the first embassy. Apparently Archidamus was strong enough to insist on continuing negotiations, although the war party was in a position to demand concessions on all points. Still, Archidamus was able to get a compromise that made rescinding the decree the only condition for peace.

Megara, a member of the Spartan alliance, was under economic attack. The Spartans interpreted that as a violation of the spirit if not the letter of the Thirty Years' Peace, which provided that neither side should interfere in the alliance of the other. Sparta could not allow economic aggression against Megara any more than the Athenians could permit the Corinthians to stir up rebellion at Potidaea. The lifting of the Megarian Decree, therefore, seemed to the Spartans an absolute necessity for a peaceful solution. The other conflicts, however, did not affect Sparta and could be abandoned. The Spartan proposal thus amounted to a betrayal of Corinthian interests. If the Corinthians were dissatisfied and threatened secession, Archidamus and the majority of Spartans were prepared to let them try. Perhaps the time had come to show the Corinthians who was hegemon in the Spartan alliance.

In spite of Archidamus' remarkable success in softening the Spartan position, Pericles remained obdurate. But the second Spartan embassy's sincere effort at compromise caused him serious embarrassment in a way that the crude propaganda of the first had not. The Spartan proposal made it seem that Athens was going to war over the Megarian Decree, originally a mere tactical maneuver and certainly not worth fighting over. Pericles could not simply reject the Spartan demand; he had to justify his policy in an unusual manner.

The official charges that had ostensibly provoked the embargo were now embodied in a formal decree, sent by herald to Megara and Sparta, defending the Athenian action. "This decree was proposed by Pericles and contained a reasonable and humane justification of this policy," says Plutarch (*Pericles* 30.3), and he relates a story that indicates how much pressure Pericles felt. In answer to repeated Spartan requests, Pericles defended his refusal to rescind the decree by pointing to some obscure Athenian law that prevented him from taking down the tablet on which the decree was inscribed. The Spartan answered: "Then don't take it down, turn the tablet around, for there is no law against that." (*Pericles* 30.1) Whether it is true or not, the story shows that Pericles was hard pressed to defend his stubborn refusal.

At last the Spartans sent a final embassy with this curt, laconic message: "The Spartans want peace, and there will be peace if you give the Greeks their autonomy." (Thucydides 1.139.3) It was an ultimatum. No longer would the Spartans try to keep negotiations open. The Athenian refusal to rescind the decree had undone Archidamus and his faction, permitting the hawks to withdraw the peace offer. There was no more room for negotiation; the Athenians must decide whether to yield or fight.

Although Pericles was still in control, the opposition was now strong enough to shape the debate in the assembly in its own way. He would have preferred to focus discussion on whether or not to accept the Spartan ultimatum; instead, it was decided "to give an answer after having considered everything once and for all." (Thucydides 1.139.3) This permitted his opponents to bring up the Megarian Decree, the one topic Pericles did not want discussed. Many spoke on each side of the question. No doubt among those who argued that "war was necessary" was Cleon, and among those who urged that "the Decree not be an impediment to peace but should be withdrawn" was Thucydides, son of Melesias.

Thucydides the historian reports only the speech made by Pericles, whom he describes as "at that time the foremost man among the Athenians and the most powerful in speech and action." (Thucydides 1.139.4) The tone of his speech makes it clear that Pericles still felt himself in control and did not expect his policy to be rejected. That tone was defiantly unbending and not likely to sway an undecided electorate, as the opening words make clear: "I am of the same opinion as always, O men of Athens, that we should not yield to the Spartans. . . . Even before this it was clear that the Spartans were plotting against us, and now it is plainer than ever." (Thucydides 1.140.1–2)

Pericles' defense of his policy rested mainly on what might seem a legal technicality. The Spartans have consistently refused to submit to arbitration as the treaty required. Instead, they hope to win their point by threats or force. "They want to resolve their complaints by war instead of by discussion, and now they are here, no longer requesting but already demanding. . . . Only a flat and clear refusal of these demands will make it plain to them that they must treat you as equals." (Thucydides 1.140.2,5)

Pericles was not unwilling to yield on any specific point. If the Spartans had accepted the offer of arbitration, he would certainly have abided by the result. What he could not accept was the precedent of Spartan interference in the Athenian Empire at Potidaea and Aegina or with Athenian commercial and imperial policy as represented by the Megarian Decree. That would make Athenian hegemony in the Aegean, and therefore Athenian security, dependent on the sufferance of Sparta and would place it at the mercy of domestic Spartan politics. If the Athenians gave way when threatened now, they would abandon their claim to equality and oppose themselves to future blackmail. Pericles made all this clear in his refusal to withdraw the decree.

> Let none of you think that you are going to war over a trifle if we do not rescind the Megarian Decree, whose withdrawal they hold out especially as a way of avoiding war, and do not reproach yourself with second thoughts that you have gone to war for a small thing. For this "trifle" contains the affirmation and the test of your resolution. If you yield to them you will immediately be required to make another concession which will be greater, since you will have made the first concession out of fear. (Thucydides 1.140.5)

It must have been as difficult for many on both sides to understand why the Athenians were ready to fight for this trifle of a decree as it was for the Germans and even some British in 1914 to understand why Great Britain was willing to fight for "the scrap of paper" that guaranteed Belgian neutrality. But in both cases the apparently trivial source of contention masked the important political and strategic considerations. Pericles' statement is a classic rejection of appeasement (remarkably similar to the arguments made by Churchill against the appeasers of the 1930s), and it is admirable in its courage and resolution. But was Pericles' policy justified?

If we confine ourselves to the immediate crisis, it is tempting to give a negative answer. The grievances at hand were not intrinsically important, and Sparta's single nonnegotiable demand involved nothing of material or strategic importance. If the Athenians had withdrawn the Megarian Decree, the crisis would probably have blown over. That danger averted, who can say what the future might have brought? Sparta's betrayal of Corinth would surely have led to a coolness between the two states, possibly a rift that would distract the Spartans from any thought of quarreling with Athens. Other troubles might arise within the Peloponnesian League, as they had in the past. For one thing, Sparta's treaty with Argos would expire in ten years, and there was no guarantee it would be renewed. The Spartans would certainly not start any trouble with Athens while the danger from Argos threatened, and meanwhile another decade of peace might reconcile all parties to the status quo. While all of that is speculation, it suggests there was nothing inevitable about a coming war if the crisis of 433–431 could be averted.

On the other hand, Pericles was right about the persistence of an implacably hostile faction in Sparta. An Athenian concession might have calmed the fears of the Spartan majority for a time, yielding on this point might also have led to a harder Spartan line in future conflicts. Pericles thus faced a very difficult decision, and with the advantage of hindsight we may conclude that he made the wrong choice. Perhaps he should have given in and thereby saved the Archidamian faction. The Spartans, after all, were not led by a demonic figure with a fixed purpose, in firm control of the state and driven by his own malignant needs to destroy his opponents, as Hitler was. The risks of withdrawing the decree were real, but they seem smaller than the risk of going to war. This may have been one of those rare occasions when circumstances justify compromising even so important a principle as not yielding under a threat.

Why then did Pericles hold rigidly and vehemently to his position? Part of the answer lies in the strategy he had conceived for fighting the war. Political leaders rely on their strategic plans to achieve diplomatic and political goals, and they rarely launch a war unless they have a good chance of winning. But sometimes their military strategy can determine their political and diplomatic choices. Germany, for instance, had only one strategy in 1914, the Schlieffen Plan, which required the Germans to invade Belgium in order to knock France out of the war quickly. But this violation of Belgian neutrality made certain that Britain would join the war against Germany, a diplomatic and military misfortune of the highest order. At the same time, strategic considerations persuaded the Germans that their chances of success were greater in 1914 than they would be a few years later. There was thus no German plot to bring on a major European war in August 1914. Rather the selection of a military strategy that seemed to promise victory created the expectations that made them willing to risk war.

In the same way, the Spartan decision was powerfully encouraged by a strategy that the war faction imagined would bring swift and sure victory. They did not believe that the war would be long, costly, difficult, and of doubtful outcome—as both Archidamus and the Athenians claimed. The Spartans assumed the Athenians would be unwilling to stand behind their walls and quietly watch their crops and houses destroyed. Instead, they believed the Athenians would come out to fight, as in 446/5; this time, however, there would be no cowardly truce. There would be a decisive battle, the Spartans would win, and the Athenian menace would be ended once and for all. Events would prove them wrong, but belief in their strategy made them deaf to talk of compromise, while the hope that they might be right helped convince other, more hesitant, Spartans.

Pericles, too, believed he had found the single strategy that would bring success, although he knew that he alone could make the Athenians adopt and hold to it. In his absence, the more aggressive groups would gain control and insist on a military confrontation, which he believed would be a profound mistake. Pericles was the only man who could manage his strategy—that was his strength and his strategy's weakness. Knowing how difficult the impending war would be, Pericles tried to avoid it as long as he could. After the Spartan vote for war, however, his strategy dictated that it should come as soon as possible, for he was already in his seventh decade, and he could not be certain how much longer he would live.

Still another consideration must have stiffened his intransigence in the final months. Every war depends on the morale of the population that supports it, but this was especially true for the kind of war Pericles planned. The balance between arousing the determination needed to prevent defeatism and exercising enough restraint to avoid a battle against the odds is very hard to maintain. Pericles might rely on his political and personal authority to achieve restraint; his main task would be to inspire the needed determination. The Spartans' second embassy, which was conciliatory in tone, had embarrassed Pericles and encouraged those in Athens who favored accommodation. But the harshness of the Spartans' ultimatum now relieved him of the need to defend his policy any further. Few Athenians were willing to abandon their empire and none would admit it if they were. The Athenians had only to think of the haughty words of the Spartans in order to be inflamed with martial spirit.

Another time the Spartans might not be so helpful to Pericles. They might offer apparent concessions without yielding on the essential question: the equality and independence of the Athenian Empire. Negotiations might stretch out for years. Each year the Athenian will to fight might grow weaker and Pericles would certainly grow older. Meanwhile, the enormous Athenian advantage in money and ships would be reduced as the Spartans carried out the prudent plan of Archidamus. It must have been clear to Pericles that if Athens must fight—and it now appeared inevitable—her chances of victory would be better sooner rather than later. So, in still another way, the Periclean strategy itself advanced the war.

Pericles' speech and policy carried the day. The Athenians adopted his very language in their answer to the Spartan ultimatum: "They would do nothing under dictation, but they were prepared to resolve the complaints by arbitration according to the treaty on the basis of reciprocal equality." (Thucydides 1.145.1) The Spartans took the answer home with them, and no more embassies came. But even then, they did not move. The war, begun in March of 431 as the result of a Theban attack on Plataea, was either a preemptive strike on the assumption that war was imminent or a stroke meant to prevent the Spartans from backing out.

The Theban attack was an unambiguous breach of the treaty and the first act of war. The Spartans did not dare hold back any longer and launched their invasion of Attica in May. Even at the last moment, Archidamus, who commanded the invading army, tried to avoid battle. He sent an envoy to Athens in the hope that the Athenians might yield when they saw the Spartan army really on the march. But the envoy was not allowed to enter the city, much less speak to the assembly, for Pericles himself had introduced a law forbidding the reception of Spartan embassies while an army was in the field. The terse words of Thucydides have the ring of an accurate report of the Athenian state of mind.

> They sent him away without listening to him and ordered him to be outside their boundaries on the same day. In the future the Spartans must withdraw to their own territory if they wanted to send an embassy. And they sent an escort with [the envoy] Melesippus so that he might approach no one. And when he arrived at the frontier and was about to depart, he went off speaking these words: "This day will be the beginning of great evils for the Greeks." (2.12.1–4)

When Melesippus reported the Athenian answer, Archidamus could delay no longer. He gave the order to march into Athenian territory. Thus the Spartans and Athenians embarked on a war that, as Archidamus had predicted, they would leave to their sons.

Pericles had not wanted war, and his policy had been aimed at avoiding it—until Spartan actions seemed to make it inevitable. But the war came, so his management of the crisis must be judged a failure in its own terms. The problems he faced were serious, of course, and the choices available terribly hard. His diplomacy was inventive, often original, and uniformly well-intended. It plainly rested on a careful calculation of dangers and opportunities, and constantly sought the middle way between unattractive extremes. It was, in short, an intellectual policy, depending not only on careful and precise execution, but no less on a cool and intelligent understanding of its intentions by the enemy. If Archidamus and his associates had been the only players on the other side it would have succeeded, as it almost did, in any case. But international relations and war are not chess. They often provoke strong emotions that overcome reason and cast intelligence aside. At crucial points, Pericles appears to have lost sight of that reality and put undue faith in the universality of reason. Actions meant to be moderate were taken to be aggressive and threatening and helped to undermine the prudent counterparts on whom success depended. When things went wrong, Pericles, motivated in part by the war strategy he had chosen, abandoned his inventive diplomacy and clung stubbornly to the path leading to war.

# 12

# STRATEGIST

**P**ericles' military strategy aptly illustrates Carl von Clausewitz' dictum that war is the continuation of politics by different means, for it carried forward the same goal aimed at by his diplomacy. Pericles was convinced that Sparta's belligerence was a temporary aberration that would change when the true military situation became clear and reason prevailed over passion. He accordingly adopted a strategy meant to persuade the Spartans of their mistake and to restore peace on the basis of the status quo ante—a world in which both powers, realizing they had no way of imposing their will, would respect one another's integrity.

A successful strategy should rest on a clear understanding of the aims for which a war is undertaken and an accurate assessment of the resources on both sides. It seeks to employ one's own strength against the weakness of the enemy, or at least to have superior strength at the crucial times and places. It makes use of, but is not bound by, the experience of the past. It adjusts to changes in conditions, both material and psychological. It anticipates that its first expectations may be disappointed and has an alternate plan ready. The Greeks, of course, had no Clausewitz nor, in Pericles' time, any developed theory of war. Few states or statesmen, however, embarking on a war at any time in history, have been well enough prepared strategically.

Sparta's declared aim in breaking the Thirty Years' Peace was "to liberate Greece"—that is, to restore autonomy to the Greek states subject to Athens, thereby destroying the Athens Empire. Although the Spartans were always slow to go to war, Athens' use of her power against Sparta's allies made the situation unendurable, and Thucydides tells us that "the Spartans decided they must try with all their might to destroy that power if they could and launch this war." (Thucydides 1.118) But whether the Spartans made war to free the Greeks, to defend their allies against Athens and thus continue to enjoy the security provided by the Spartan alliance, or to restore the uncontested supremacy that Sparta had enjoyed during the Persian War—or for all of these reasons—makes no difference. Each of these goals required the destruction of Athenian power—that is, destruction of the walls that made Athens secure against assault by land, of the fleet that gave her command of the seas, and of the empire that supported her navy. A strategy aiming at a peace that left these intact was of no value. Sparta's war aims required that she take the offensive.

Pericles' strategy did not aim at defeating the Spartans in battle but rather was meant to convince them that war was futile. It was really a form of persuasion or education in which Athenian actions sought to affect Sparta's desire rather than its capacity for fighting the war. Pericles' strategic goals, therefore, were entirely defensive. He told the Athenians that if they "would remain quiet, take care of their fleet, refrain from trying to extend their empire in wartime and thus putting their city in danger, they would prevail." (Thucydides 2.65.7)

Accordingly, the Athenians were to reject battle on land, abandon their fields and homes in the country to Spartan devastation, and retreat behind their walls, forcing the Spartans to adopt a mode of siege warfare in which they had little skill. Meanwhile, the Athenian navy would launch a series of commando raids on the coast of the Peloponnesus. This strategy would continue until the frustrated enemy was prepared to make peace. The naval raids and landings were not meant to do serious harm but to annoy the enemy and to suggest how much damage the Athenians could do if they chose. The strategy was to exhaust the Peloponnesians psychologically, not physically or materially. Pericles meant to convince the Spartans, the chief enemy, that they could not win a war against Athens and must, therefore, make peace.*

No such strategy had ever been attempted in Greek history, for no state before the coming of the Athenian imperial democracy ever had the means to try it. The Athenians were in a position to use it in the latter part of the First Peloponnesian War but had not done so, perhaps because Pericles was not yet able to persuade them. To do so was not easy, for this unprecedented strategy ran directly against the grain of the heroic tradition, which placed bravery in warfare at the peak of Greek virtues. Most Athenians, furthermore, were farmers whose lands and homes were outside the walls. The Periclean strategy required them to look on idly while their houses, crops, vines, and olive trees were damaged or destroyed.

In the face of these facts, it is hard to understand, even in retrospect, how Pericles could have convinced the Athenians to adopt his unorthodox strategy. He was probably the only man who could have conceived a plan so contrary to the deepest attachments and prejudices of his people and certainly the only one with the influence and ability to put it into effect. For doing so an outstanding modern military historian awards him a place "among the greatest generals in world history." His greatness lay not only in conceiving the plan and implementing it decisively by yielding all of Attica instead of taking half measures, but, most of all, in being able to put the plan through a democratic assembly by the force of his personality and to see that it was carried out. "The fulfillment of this decision is an act of generalship that may be placed on a level with any victory."[2]

Pericles' first victory, in other words, was won against the natural resistance of his own people. Historically, democracies have been relatively easy to rouse to war when the cause seems good and there is an opportunity for a quick decision in battle. This was the case with the French, British, and American democracies in World War I and

---

* A modern scholar has put it well: "[Pericles] must first prove that the existence of Athens and the Athenian Empire could not be destroyed and then that Athens, too, could harm her enemies. . . . It was a reasonable calculation that the nerve and will-power of her opponents might well be exhausted before the treasures of the Acropolis, and that they might admit that the power and determination of Athens were invincible."[1]

with the British and Americans in World War II. When a war drags on beyond calculation, there is generally discontent; the people continue to support the fighting only so long as the goal is a decisive victory. Most difficult of all is to maintain the support of a democratic people in a war that defines victory as a stalemate, where instead of using all available resources to bring the battle to the enemy and defeat him, the leader seeks a negotiated settlement by wearing the enemy down. Such was the strategy employed by Harry Truman in Korea and by Kennedy, Johnson, and Nixon in Vietnam. It helped destroy Truman's popularity, drove Johnson from office, and contributed to the destruction of Nixon's presidency. Yet Pericles' strategy made even greater demands. The Athenians were required to exercise restraint and patience beyond anyone's experience, and his ability to persuade them to adopt such a course may be his greatest triumph as an educator.

For all its difficulty, Pericles had reason to think that his was the best available strategy and that Athenian resources were adequate to make it succeed. At the beginning of the war, the Athenians had an army of thirteen thousand infantrymen of an age and condition to fight and another sixteen thousand able to man the border forts and city walls surrounding Athens and Piraeus. Plutarch tells us that the Peloponnesians invaded Attica in 431 with an army of sixty thousand. That number must be inflated, but Pericles himself admitted just before the war that in a single battle the Spartans and their allies were a match for all the other Greeks put together. Recent history, moreover, had shown that intelligent Athenians were aware of the relative weakness of their army. During the First Peloponnesian War, in 457, they had fought bravely at the Battle of Tanagra despite superior numbers, suffering heavy casualties. When the Peloponnesian army invaded Attica in 446, the Athenians had made a truce and abandoned their land empire rather than fight. That memory must have helped the anti-Athenian party in Sparta convince their fellow-citizens to go to war again. Either the Athenians would yield without a battle as before, or they would fight and be destroyed. In either case, the war would be short and victory certain.

It was precisely to prove the Spartan "hawks" wrong that Pericles went to war. He made this purpose quite clear to the Athenians: "If I thought I could persuade you I would urge you to go out and devastate your own property to show the Peloponnesians that you will not take orders from them to save it." (Thucydides 1.143.5) Once the Spartans saw that the Athenians were prepared to make the necessary sacrifices, they would see that war was futile and negotiate a peace. The resulting agreement, although no different in substance from the Thirty Years' Peace, would be secure and lasting, because the Spartans would have recognized Athenian invincibility.

To carry out his strategy, Pericles had resources that dwarfed those of his opponents and were unmatched in Greek history. The power and hopes of Athens rested on her magnificent navy, consisting of at least three hundred seaworthy warships, as well as some others that could be repaired and used in case of need. Apart from the subject states of their empire, which supplied money payments and rowers for the fleet, their free allies—Lesbos, Chios, and Corcyra—could also provide ships, perhaps more than a hundred. Against this armada the Peloponnesians could only send about one hundred ships. Furthermore, the skill and experience of their crews were no match for the Athenians, as the first decade of the war would prove again and again.

Pericles knew that the key to naval warfare, and therefore to his strategy, was money to maintain the ships and pay their crews. Here, too, Athens had a great advantage. In 431, the annual income of Athens was 1,000 talents, of which 400 came from internal revenue and 600 from tribute and other imperial sources. Although about 600 talents were available for the war each year, that would not be enough to support the Periclean plan. As Pericles pointed out, "accumulated surpluses, not compulsory taxation sustains wars." (Thucydides 1.141.5) Athens would therefore need to dip into her capital, where she was also uniquely well provided. At the beginning of the war, the Athenians had 6,000 talents of coined silver in the treasury, another 500 talents in uncoined gold and silver, and 40 talents' worth of gold plates on the statue of Athena in the Parthenon that could be removed and melted down in an emergency. Against this extraordinary wealth, on the other hand, the Peloponnesians were no match. Archidamus spoke for most of them when he said, "We have no money in the public treasury nor can we easily raise money by taxation." The Corinthians were better off than the others, but they had no reserve fund, and Pericles was justified in telling the Athenians that "the Peloponnesians have no money, either public or private." (Thucydides 1.80.4, 1.141.3)

Archidamus led the first Peloponnesian invasion into Attica in a deliberately leisurely manner. The quickest road to the heart of Attica turned east and south past Megara, to Eleusis and into the fertile plain of Athens; but that is not the road Archidamus took. Instead, he turned north to besiege the town of Oenoe, an Athenian fort on the

Boeotian border. It presented no threat to the invading army, and there was no military reason for attacking it at that time. But Archidamus' thinking was more political than military. At the Spartan assembly the previous summer he had argued that the Spartans should be very slow to ravage the land of Attica. "Do not think of their land as anything but a hostage for us, and the better it is cultivated the better hostage it will be." (Thucydides 1.82)

When the Athenians did not respond, Archidamus was forced to abandon the siege and begin ravaging the land around Eleusis. Still the Athenians took no action, so the Spartans moved eastward and began devastating Acharnae, a large deme with many citizens, "inexorable, tough as oak," as Aristophanes called them (*Acharnians* 180). They, surely, would not look on quietly but would be outraged and press their fellow-citizens behind the walls to come out and fight. Even now Archidamus had not given up hope that the Athenians would see reason; as long as possible he wanted "to hold as a hostage" the most prized fields of Attica.

When the Athenians heard that the Spartans were marching toward Attica, they followed Pericles' plan and began to move in from the countryside. Wives and children were sent to the city, sheep and oxen to the island of Euboea. Most Athenians lived in the country, and few were alive who had seen it devastated by the Persian army almost half a century earlier. "They were dejected and angered at having to abandon their homes and the temples which had always been theirs, ancestral relics of the ancient polity, at facing a change in their way of life, at nothing less than each man having to abandon his own polis." (Thucydides 2.16.2) At first they were all crowded within the city walls; every vacant space was occupied, even sanctuaries of the gods. The Pelargikon at the foot of the Acropolis was occupied in spite of an oracular curse from the Pythian Apollo, a state of affairs that scandalized the pious. The very towers of the city walls were used by squatters. Later, the displaced were spread to Piraeus and to the territory between the Long Walls; but for the moment the discomfort was extreme.

When the enemy appeared at Acharnae, however, and began to lay waste its land less than seven miles from the Acropolis, the mood in Athens changed from disgruntled dejection to fury. Here was the first serious test of Pericles' restraining influence. The Athenians directed their anger not only at the Spartans but also at Pericles, whom they held no less responsible for their predicament. It did not matter that he had predicted these events or that the suffering was a necessary part of the strategy they had accepted. In the heat of the moment, his careful explanations of why Athens had to avoid great battles on land were forgotten, and his critics accused him of cowardice because he would not lead them out against the enemy.

The foremost of these bellicose opponents was Cleon, the man who would emerge as the leader of the Athenian "hawks" after the death of Pericles. The comic poet Hermippus, perhaps a member of Cleon's faction, gives us an idea of the tone of these attacks in a play performed in the spring of 430, abusing Pericles as follows: "King of the Satyrs, why won't you ever lift a spear but instead use only dreadful words to wage the war, assuming the character of the cowardly Teles. But if a little knife is sharpened on a whetstone you roar as though bitten by the fierce Cleon." (Plutarch, *Pericles* 23.7). Even some of his friends urged Pericles to go out and fight. But he held fast to his policy in spite of the pressure, and it took all his skill and influence to prevent the Athenians from abandoning his strategy at once.

The modern distinction between civilian and military authority did not exist in Athens. This sometimes had disadvantages, but the two-sided character of the office of general was a great help to Pericles in keeping the Athenians in line despite their instinctive reaction against his chosen strategy. Thucydides describes the scene:

> Pericles saw that they were very angry at the situation in which they found themselves and that their thinking was not at its best. He was confident that his decision not to go out and fight was correct, so he prevented the calling of an assembly or any other meeting, fearing that if the people came together they would make a mistake by acting out of anger instead of using their judgment. He watched over the city and kept it peaceful, so far as was possible. (2.22.1)

In wars and other serious crises democratic leaders sometimes feel the need to abridge legal rights and normal constitutional practices. Lincoln suspended habeas corpus during the American Civil War, and Grant did the same to deal with the Ku Klux Klan during Reconstruction. Likewise, during a brief but critical period in Athens, normal political debate and discussion were suspended. No law was passed, no emergency powers were granted to Pericles or to the board of generals as a whole. Ordinarily, the assembly had regular meetings that did not depend on the actions of the ten generals, of whom Pericles was one. How was he able to put politics aside long enough to protect his strategy?

Athens was under siege, and the necessities of war gave the generals more power than usual. The citizens were under arms, guarding the walls. If they were called to assembly the city would be undefended; if they stayed at their posts the assembly would be less than representative. These were good reasons for canceling regular meetings, and no doubt Pericles prevailed on the other generals, some of whom were his political associates, to see the matter his way. Against there combined recommendation no official would have dared call the citizens to assembly. In Roman terms, Pericles achieved his purpose not by *imperium* but by *auctoritas*.

Pericles had chosen a strategy, had the political means to hold the people to it, and seemed to have the resources to carry it out. Even so exacting a judge as the historian Thucydides was certain that it deserved to succeed:

> Pericles lived two years and six months after the beginning of the fighting, and after he died his foresight in regard to the war was acknowledged even more. He said that if the Athenians would remain quiet, take care of their fleet, refrain from trying to extend their empire in wartime and thus putting their city in danger, they would prevail. . . . Pericles had more than sufficient reason at that time for his personal forecast that Athens would win quite easily in the war against the Peloponnesians. . . . (2.65.6–7; 13)

Thucydides attributed the ultimate failure of the Periclean strategy to its abandonment by his successors, who "did everything contrary to his plan in every way." (2.65.7) But Pericles' strategy remained intact for two years after his death, into the fifth year of the war, without achieving success. Even more to the point, in retrospect, we can see that it was already a failure while he was alive.

It is tempting, but inadequate, to point to an unforeseen and unforeseeable disaster. In the second year of the war a terrible plague fell upon Athens. The plague did great harm to the Periclean strategy by weakening the will of the Athenians and encouraging the Peloponnesians. But after negotiations failed, the Athenians' will to fight was revived, and there is no reason to believe that the Spartans' determination would have weakened even if there had been no plague. The reasons for the strategy's failure must be sought elsewhere.

To evaluate his plan we need to know how long Pericles expected the Spartans to hold out before they saw reason. The question is not generally asked by those who regard the outcome of the Archidamian War (431–421) as justification for his strategy,[3] but their assumption is that a war of ten years was not outside his calculations. This conclusion rests, in part, on the content of Pericles' speech to the Athenians on the eve of the war. The Peloponnesians, he said, "have had no experience with wars overseas or extended in time; they only wage brief wars against each other because of their poverty." (Thucydides 1.142.3) The great majority of the Peloponnesian soldiers—all but the Spartans themselves—farm their own lands; they cannot stay too long away from their farms and must bear the costs of an expedition from their own funds. Such men will rather risk their lives than their property, "for they are not sure that they won't use up their funds first, especially if the war lasts longer than they expected, which is quite likely." (Thucydides 1.141.5–6)

Pericles rightly argued that the Peloponnesians lacked the resources to launch the kind of campaign that would have endangered the Athenian Empire, although nothing prevented them from continuing to invade and devastate Attica every year. These invasions needed to last no longer than a month, and their only cost was in provisioning the soldiers. Thus the important question was really how long the Athenian treasury could hold out at the annual rate of expenditure required to sustain the Periclean strategy.

We can get some idea of the war's average annual cost by examining the first year, when Pericles was firmly in control. When the Peloponnesians invaded Attica in 431, the Athenians sent a hundred ships round the Peloponnesus. A squadron of thirty ships was sent to protect the crucial island of Euboea. Another seventy were already blockading Potidaea, making a total of two hundred in service for the year. It cost one talent to keep a ship at sea for a month, and eight months was the usual tour of duty (although the blockade probably required the ships at Potidaea to stay year-round). These estimates would result in an outlay of 1,600 talents for naval expenses. To this must be added the military costs, of which the greatest portion was spent at Potidaea. There were never fewer than three thousand infantry in the siege there, and sometimes more; a conservative average would be thirty-five hundred. The soldiers were paid a drachma a day and another to pay a retainer, so that the daily cost of the army was at least 7,000 drachmas, or one talent and a sixth. If we multiply this figure by 360, a round number for a year, we arrive at 420 talents. There were certainly other military costs that need not be detailed here; but even if we included only the naval expenses and the cost of troops at Potidaea, we arrive at a sum of over 2,000 talents. Two other calculations, based on different kinds of data, yield a similar figure.[4]

Pericles must have expected to spend at least 2,000 talents a year to carry on the war. Three years of such a war would cost 6,000 talents. In the second year of the war, the Athenians voted to set aside 1,000 talents from their reserves to be used only "if the enemy should make a naval attack against the city and they should have to defend it" (Thucydides 2.24.1), assigning the death penalty to anyone who proposed to use if for any other purpose. This left a usable reserve fund of 5,000 talents; if we add three years of imperial revenue, 1,800, we get 6,800 talents. Pericles, therefore, could maintain his strategy for only three years. He could calculate all this as well as we can, so we must not imagine that he expected a war of ten years, much less the twenty-seven it ultimately lasted.

Pericles' goal was to bring about a change of opinion in Sparta, the true decision-maker in the Peloponnesian League. That hope was not unreasonable when we remember how difficult it was to get the Spartans to go to war in the first place: the long interval between their vote for war and their first action, their attempt to negotiate a peace in the interim, and the great and continuing reluctance of Sparta's king to begin hostilities. To persuade the Spartans to consider making peace required winning over only three of the five ephors. To get them and the Spartan assembly to accept a settlement, the Athenians needed merely to help restore the natural majority that kept Sparta at peace and inside the Peloponnesus most of the time.

In light of these facts, Pericles' plan seemed to make excellent sense. Archidamus had warned his people that their expectations about the character of the coming war were mistaken. The Athenians would not fight a land battle, and the Spartans had no other strategy. They did not believe him, but Pericles' plan aimed at proving to the Spartans that their king had been right. The offensive naval actions were deliberately unimpressive, for they were intended only as evidence that an extended war would be damaging to the Peloponnesians. To engage in more aggressive and effective actions would conflict with the plan, for they could not bring victory, but they might outrage the enemy and prevent the reasonable view of Archidamus from winning the upper hand.

A policy of restraint at home and abroad would sooner or later bring the friends of peace to power in Sparta. Pericles might have expected such a change in Spartan opinion to come quickly, possibly after only one campaigning season. Perhaps it would take two years of similar actions; but surely not more than three, for it would be wildly unreasonable for Sparta to continue to beat its fist without effect against the stone wall of the Athenian defensive strategy. Yet for all its intelligence, the plan did not work. The very first year brought signs of trouble. The Athenians stayed behind their walls and refused to fight a land battle. Meanwhile their ships sailed around the Peloponnesus devastating coastal regions of several enemy states, defeating small armies that came against them, and capturing several strategic ports. After the Spartans withdrew from Attica, Pericles himself led a large Athenian army against Megara and thoroughly ravaged its land. Despite all this, the end of the war was nowhere in sight.

As one scholar has observed, "In a war of attrition the side that does all the damage must win in the end," and the Spartans had done most of the damage. In addition to paying the psychological price of watching their crops cut down, their vines and olive trees destroyed, their houses torn or burned down, the Athenians had lost their vital grain supply. This could be replaced by imported supplies but at a cost. The exports used to maintain a balance of trade were the olive oil and wine whose source had been destroyed. Payment for the imported foodstuffs, whether private or public, reduced their financial resources and therefore the amount of time they could hold out. By comparison, the attacks on the Peloponnesus, apart from extra-Peloponnesian Megara, were mere pinpricks, irritating but not really damaging. Sparta herself was untouched; in all her territory of Laconia and Messenia, only one coastal town had been annoyed. Some allies had suffered a bit of damage but nothing serious. The Megarians, to be sure, suffered badly, but not enough to make them seek peace even after ten years.

Things were not going well for the Athenians. Their victories had little strategic significance. They were also disappointed when the resistance of the Potidaeans, and the accompanying Chalcidic rebellion, continued. The Athenians had spent considerable time and money with little to show for their expenditure. They had already been compelled to borrow 1,300–1,400 talents from the reserve fund in the sacred treasuries, more than a fourth of their disposable war chest. The Peloponnesians showed no sign of discouragement, returning with spirit the next spring to destroy the large portion of Attica they had left untouched. There is no evidence of dissension within the Peloponnesian League or of a growing influence for the Spartan peace party. Cleon's complaints about the inefficacy of the Periclean strategy might still be a subject for comic poets, but they were only the tip of an iceberg of dissent that was bound to emerge more fully as the suffering continued. The "hawks" would grow in numbers and influence and insist on a more aggressive prosecution of the war. As the first year of the war came to an end the pressure on Pericles and his strategy increased.

Pericles could not ignore the discontent. He evidently needed to head off the growing power of the hawks. So, "because he wanted to cure these ills and also because he wanted to do some harm to the enemy" (Plutarch, *Pericles* 35.1), he himself led an expedition against the Peloponnesus in May of 430 with a fleet of 150 warships as well as transports carrying 4,000 infantry and 300 cavalry. This was a very large force, and its mission was to do more damage than had been inflicted the previous year. "When they arrived at Epidaurus in the Peloponnesus they ravaged most of the land. And when they made an attack on the city they arrived at the hope of taking it, but they were not successful. Leaving Epidaurus, they ravaged most of the land of Troezen, Halieis and Hermione, which are all on the coast of the Peloponnesus. From there they sailed to Prasiae, a coastal town of Laconia; they ravaged its land, took the town, and sacked it. When they had done this they returned home." (Thucydides 2.56.4–6) This campaign was not a change in strategy but was rather intended to speed up the "education" of the Peloponnesians. Nevertheless, Pericles was compelled to this new level of aggression because his strategy was not working.

Even before the expedition left Athens, Archidamus led the Peloponnesian army back into Attica to continue the devastation begun the previous year. This time he was merciless, sparing no part of Attica. He despoiled the great plain before the city of Athens, then moved on to the coastal regions, both east and west. By now he knew there was no point in holding the land of Attica hostage. His hopes for a quick and painless settlement had also faded. The army remained in Attica for forty days, their longest stay of the war, pillaging the whole country and leaving only when their supplies ran out. Instead of becoming more ready to make peace as their strategic expectations were refuted, both sides became more bitter and determined and increased their warlike efforts.

Then disaster struck the Athenians. A plague broke out and raged with unprecedented ferocity during the years 430 and 429 and, after a hiatus, broke out again in 427. Before it had run its course it had killed 4,400 infantrymen, 300 cavalry, and an untold number of men from the lower classes, wiping out perhaps one-third of the population. Nothing like it had ever been seen or heard of; modern scholars and medical experts continue to debate its identity. It has been called everything from bubonic and pneumonic plague to measles and, most recently, toxic shock syndrome. Whatever it was, with the entire population of Attica crowded into the walled area it was especially deadly. The plague had a crushing effect on Athenian morale, and it severely undermined Pericles' position, popular confidence in his strategy, and the continuation of a war that was blamed on his policy.

The Greeks had always thought of plagues as divine punishments for human actions that angered the gods. Such was the plague sent by Apollo to avenge Agamemnon's insult to his priest at the beginning of Homer's *Iliad*. These punishments were often connected with the failure to heed divine oracles and with acts of religious pollution. With the onset of the plague at Athens, the older men recalled an oracle from the past that said, "A Dorian war will come and a plague with it." (Thucydides 2.54.3) That implicitly cast blame on Pericles, the firmest advocate of war against the Dorian Peloponnesians and a man known for associating with religious skeptics. Many others recalled the answer of the oracle at Delphi when the Spartans had asked whether they should embark on the war against the Athenians. The god replied that "if they made war with all their might they would win, and he himself would help them." (2.54.4) Pericles had ignored the implications of that divine message, and believers now connected his manifest impiety with the Athenian suffering, pointing out that the plague had not entered the Peloponnesus. No doubt many Athenians also remembered the Spartan demand that they drive out the curse, and blamed their misery on the Alcmaeonids connected to their leader.

Political opponents, probably from both sides, lost no time in blaming Pericles for causing the war and for imposing a strategy that had intensified the effects of the plague. They argued that the plague was caused by crowding the people together in unsalubrious conditions in the heat of summer, without work to keep them busy or exercise to keep them healthy. He allowed them to be penned like cattle to fill each other up with corruption, providing no change or rest. (Plutarch, *Pericles* 34.3–4)

At last, the Athenians turned sharply against him and his policies. The withdrawal of the Spartan army ended the immediate military emergency, and, with his popularity eroded, Pericles could no longer prevent the meeting of an assembly. Contrary to his wishes, the Athenian assembly sent ambassadors to ask for peace. The plague appears to have sapped the power of all those who favored the war, Cleon's "hawks" as well as Pericles. The antiwar faction had come to power and at once tried to negotiate an end to the conflict.

We are not told what terms were discussed, but evidently even those who wanted peace thought them too harsh, for the assembly rejected them and continued the war. The Spartans probably insisted on the terms of their original ultimatum: that Athens should free the Greeks—that is, abandon its empire. Sparta's rebuff struck a blow from which the peace faction at Athens did not recover for almost a decade. Their attempt to negotiate at a time of weakness proved that Pericles had been right in his main point: The Athenians could achieve no satisfactory peace until they had convinced the Spartans that Athens would not yield and could not be defeated. Some appear not to have given up hope of renewing negotiations, but the influence and eloquence of Pericles stood in their way. Frustrated by the failure of their policy, they launched a personal attack on Pericles, and he rose to defend himself in his last reported speech.

At no time since his rise to leadership had his popularity and influence been at a lower ebb; but his problem was simplified by the character of his leadership. He had always told the people the truth, even while pursuing disputed and unpopular policies. No one could claim that he had not presented the issues clearly or honestly or that they had not been fully and freely debated. He may have underrated the fierceness of Sparta's anger and determination, but the people had had the opportunity to dispute his estimate when they voted on his policies. "If you were persuaded by me to go to war because you thought I had the qualities necessary for leadership at least moderately more than other men," he said to them, "it is not right that I should now be blamed for doing wrong." (Thucydides 2.60.7)

Aided by Spartan intransigence and the harshness of their terms, Pericles won the debate over policy. The Athenians sent no more embassies and took up the war with renewed vigor. But the advocates of peace had not given up. They still saw Pericles as the chief barrier to peace, and they were determined to remove him. Indeed it seems likely that the two extreme factions in Athens, the supporters of peace and those favoring a more aggressive war, joined forces to remove the moderate leader who stood in the way of both.

Having failed to win in the political arena, they turned to the law courts. The method of attacking unwanted policies by charging their political sponsors with corruption was well known. Pericles had begun his public career with such an attack on Cimon; Ephialtes had cleared the way for his reform of the Areopagus by bringing charges against individual Areopagites; and in 438, Pericles' enemies had used the same device against his friends and himself. Now, in September of 430, Pericles was deposed from his office as general to stand trial on a charge of embezzlement.

Amid the misery caused by the plague, the evident inadequacy of Pericles' strategy, and with no prospect of either victory or an acceptable peace, it is not surprising that he was convicted and punished with a heavy fine. The jury must not have been fully convinced of his guilt, for the crime of peculation could carry the death penalty. Still, the conviction and fine appear to have included disfranchisement, which means that the verdict temporarily removed him from public life. No doubt Pericles soon paid the fine; but he was out of office and away from the conduct of affairs from September of 430. The next spring, however, he was reelected general.

Thucydides offers an explanation for this new reversal of public opinion: "Not much later, as the mob loves to do, they elected him general again and turned everything over to him, for their individual feelings were less keen over their private misfortunes, whereas for the needs of the state as a whole they judged him to be the ablest." (2.65.4) This explanation says more about Thucydides' view of Athenian democracy than about the cause of the change. The passage of time had accustomed the Athenians to their sufferings and had shown that the removal of Pericles had no useful consequences. Further, the unnatural coalition that had brought about his downfall could not last, and the great moderate bloc that Pericles had formed and consolidated over the years gradually reasserted itself.

Nevertheless, Pericles' return to public life did not restore the steady and vigorous execution of policy that had always characterized his guidance of Athenian affairs. By midsummer 429, when he resumed office, he was mortally ill and had only a few months to live. The disease that killed him, probably the plague, did not attack him suddenly but lingered, "using up his body slowly and undermining the loftiness of his spirit." (Plutarch, *Pericles* 38.1) By the fall of the same year he was dead.

At the time of his death, Pericles' strategy was a manifest failure. His expectations about Sparta had been proven wrong, which rendered his estimate of the adequacy of Athenian resources incorrect. By 428, the reserve fund was all but exhausted, and his successors were compelled to resort to a direct tax, perhaps the first in Athenian history, and an increase in the tribute—neither measure planned for by Pericles nor mentioned by him at the beginning of the war. The direct tax was always unpopular with the propertied classes and might have shaken Pericles' control of Athens had he tried to institute it. The great increase of the tribute was something he could never have counted on, and in normal times, it would have provoked rebellion. But in 425, Cleon and Demosthenes departed from Pericles' policy and won a great victory that destroyed Sparta's prestige. No ally dared rebel at that moment, and the tribute could safely be raised. This was the result of a strategy employed by Pericles' more aggressive successors. A distinguished Italian scholar concludes that "If the plan of war did not change, if the Athenians did not try those bold strokes which Pericles wanted to avoid at all costs, it does not appear in any way that the conflict could have been concluded victoriously . . . ; both, after a few years, would have emerged from the conflict drained and impoverished by means of a compromise peace which would not at all have the effect of strengthening Athenian dominion over her empire, as Pericles had promised." Whatever security Athens gained by the Peace of Nicias in 421 was "owed above all to the abandonment of the plan of war that Pericles had advised."[5]

Thucydides, on the contrary, attributes the failure of Pericles' strategy to its abandonment by his successors. But the strategy remained intact for two years after Pericles' death without showing any promise of success, and its failure was already demonstrated while he was alive. The chief proof is the embassy that was sent to Sparta against Pericles' advice in the second year of the war. Although they chose not to, the Spartans could have offered acceptable terms while still falling far short of what Pericles sought. Had this occurred, the war would have been lost by Pericles' definition. The very rejection of Pericles' counsel, moreover, shows that his strategy was thought a failure by his fellow-citizens, and his persistence in it cost him his position of leadership.

Pericles' strategy may be seen as a continuation of the course he pursued in the crisis leading to war, a combination of diplomatic and military actions meant to steer between the dangerous extremes of yielding on vital questions and acting to provoke a war. The goal was to limit risk while holding fast to essential points and principles. During the crisis the emphasis was on the diplomatic front and the aim was to deter war. After war broke out the emphasis shifted more to military action and was aimed at bringing a satisfactory peace by teaching the enemy that victory was impossible and causing him just enough pain to encourage concessions without provoking greater violence. In both cases, Pericles trusted to the intelligence and reason that shaped his own policy and that he hoped would come to the fore in the enemy camp.

His hopes were disappointed, but his error, though serious, is very common. He expected the enemy to learn a rational lesson from their experience and understand the futility of further fighting. In our own time, the failure of strategies based on aerial bombardment, superior firepower, and naval supremacy has shown that the enemy need not suffer psychological collapse but often becomes more determined as punishment increases. This is particularly true when policymakers are not remote aristocratic or professional diplomats but citizens of a state where public opinion is a powerful force and where passion and hatred of the enemy often obliterate more rational considerations. The twentieth century has seen very small states hold out against vastly superior enemies; in the war between Athens and Sparta, when the two sides were roughly equal, stubborn resistance and sacrifice were even more likely.

The Peloponnesian War was a classic confrontation between a great land power and a great naval power. Each entered the war hoping and expecting to keep to its own element and to win a swift victory at relatively low cost. Within a few years events showed that victory would not be possible on those terms for either side. Each side would have to learn how to fight in the other's element. To win a true victory rather than a Periclean standoff, the Athenians would have had to beat the Spartans on land or at least undertake more aggressive seaborne ventures that might lure them into a fatal error.

The Periclean strategy could not win even the limited victory that he sought, much less one that would deprive the enemy of the capacity and will to fight. For that, the Athenians would have had to take the offensive; but Pericles and his immediate successors shrank from such an undertaking—an understandable reaction for a state that had come to think of itself as an invulnerable island. Athens had developed a way of fighting that avoided much of the danger and unpleasantness of ordinary warfare. It allowed the Athenians to concentrate their forces quickly and attack the enemy before they were prepared; it also permitted them to strike without danger to their own city and population. Success in this style of fighting made it seem the only one necessary, and defeats with great losses on land made the Athenians reluctant to risk other land battles.

Pericles carried this attractive strategy to its extreme by refusing to use the army even in defense of Athenian soil. This left him with no hope of disabling the enemy but only of punishing the Spartans and their allies to a greater or lesser degree. The nature of the enemy rendered this plan inadequate, and Pericles' rational strategy became a kind of wishful thinking. Yet Pericles remained resolute in holding to his position. When his calculations went awry during the prewar crisis, and the Megarian Decree became a fighting issue, he held firmly, even stubbornly, to his original policy in the face of mounting criticism. During the war, when the Athenians challenged his strategy and sought peace with the Spartans, he was no less obdurate. To his dying day, he passionately clung to the path that his reason had laid out for him.

# 13

# HERO

In the last two years of his life Pericles suffered a series of disasters—both political and personal—so great as to bring to mind that reversal of fortune which Aristotle, a century later, connected with the tragic heroes portrayed in the theater of Dionysus. In his last reported speech, he had declared himself inferior to no one in his ability to determine the best policy and to persuade others of its soundness, in his patriotism, and in his incorruptibility. Yet his policy was for a time rejected; he was removed from office, prosecuted, and convicted for taking bribes. The man who had been foremost among the Athenians, "the most powerful in speech and action," had lost his influence and lived in disgrace, blamed for all his city's misfortunes. His brief return to office only months before his death did not affect this fundamental situation.

His private and personal anguish was no less dreadful. Even before the war he had experienced the pain of estrangement from his oldest son, Xanthippus, and the embarrassment of being publicly defamed by him. While the two sons from his first marriage lived, he could still enjoy the prospect of legitimate heirs; but both sons, along with his sister and several of his relatives and friends, died in the plague. He tried to maintain his usual calm demeanor in the face of these calamities, but he gave way as he laid a wreath on the grave of his younger son and "broke out into wailing and shed many tears, something he had never done in all the rest of his life." (Plutarch, *Pericles* 36.5) In that same year, the proud and lofty leader was reduced to asking the Athenian people for an exception to the citizenship law he himself had proposed more than twenty years earlier, in order to permit the enfranchisement of young Pericles, his illegitimate son by Aspasia. Plutarch tells us that the Athenians regarded the misfortunes that had struck the house of Pericles "as a kind of penalty for his haughtiness and arrogance." (*Pericles* 37.5) Thinking he had suffered enough, they allowed the exception and enrolled the boy as a citizen.

Perhaps the worst reversal for Pericles was in the condition of the city to which he had devoted his life. The prosperous, powerful, growing, and confident city, which he had led so long and successfully that they became extensions of one another, had been pitifully reduced by war and disease. Its wealth was rapidly evaporating, the number of its citizens fell sharply, their power and confidence diminished to the point where they asked the enemy for terms of peace. The reputation of the Athenian alliance had also been badly tarnished. A decade earlier, when his political opponents had accused the Athenians of behaving like tyrants to their allies, Pericles had vigorously defended them. But in the last years of his life he was forced to admit that Athens held its empire "as a tyranny, which it may have been wrong to acquire but is too dangerous to let go." (Thucydides 2.63.2) So great was the general dislike of the Athenian Empire that the Spartans, who both before and after the war showed themselves unable to treat Greeks under their leadership with decency, could make their slogan "freedom for the Greeks."

The war and plague had also made a mockery of the lofty vision of a great imperial democracy that Pericles projected in his Funeral Oration. Then, he had boasted of the Athenians' devotion to law: "We do not break the law chiefly because of our respect for it. We obey those who hold office and the laws themselves, especially those enacted for the protection of the oppressed and those which, although unwritten, it is acknowledged shame to violate." He had urged the fathers of the fallen warriors to take comfort in the honor won by their sons: "For the love of honor alone is ageless, and when you come to the time of life of physical incapacity, it is not gain that brings you greater joy, as some men say, but honor." (2.44.4)

But the plague tore away the veneer of civilization in Athens and destroyed all respect for tradition and virtue.

> No one was eager to deny himself for the sake of what was thought to be honorable, . . . but immediate pleasure and all that contributed to it were established as both honorable and expedient. Fear of the gods or the laws of mankind restrained nobody: on the one hand they saw that all alike were dying and judged that it was the same whether they were pious or not; on the other, no one expected to live long enough to be brought to trial and pay the penalty for his crimes. . . . (2.53.3–4)

This spectacle of lawlessness and nihilism must have been particularly painful to behold. The ravages of war and disease demoralized and diminished the Athenians in still another way. Even before the war, Pericles had seen the beginnings of a rejection of the enlightened ideas and outlook he valued so highly. He had been forced to endure attacks on his intellectual associates and to see some of them driven into exile. In his Funeral Oration he had praised the Athenians' intelligence, character, education, institutions, and customs without once mentioning the gods. Yet the student of Anaxagoras and Protagoras lived to see his people turn away from advice based on intelligence and reason to give greater heed to prophets and soothsayers.

Our last glimpse of Pericles shows that this tragic reversal weighed on his mind to the end. Plutarch describes the scene at his deathbed. The best men of Athens and his personal friends were gathered in his room discussing the greatness of his virtues and the power he had held. Thinking he was asleep, they counted up the nine victories he had won as a general. In fact, he was awake and expressed astonishment that they should be praising victories that were as much the result of good fortune as of his own talents and what many others had accomplished. Instead, he said, they should be praising the finest and most important of his claims to greatness: "No Athenian now alive has put on mourning clothes because of me." (*Pericles* 38.4)

That assertion, the last words of Pericles reported to us, must have astounded his hearers, as they would have surprised any other Athenian. Even his friends would have had to admit that his policy had contributed at least something to the coming of war and that his strategy had something to do with the intensity of the plague. His final words show how deeply he felt the wounds caused by the ungrateful accusations hurled against him.

In the spring of 425, Sophocles presented his greatest tragedy, *Oedipus Tyrannus*.[1] A careful reading of that play suggests that the Athenian spectators sitting in the theater on the south slope of the Acropolis were likely to have seen their own city and its leader reflected in the story of Thebes and its unfortunate king.[2]

As the play opens the city is suffering from a terrible plague. A priest laments, "The fever-god swoops down on us, hateful plague, he hounds the city and empties the houses of Thebes. The black god of death is made rich with wailing and funeral laments." (27–30)[3] The legend of Oedipus had never included any reference to a plague; it was a Sophoclean innovation. The cause of the plague, moreover, is not Apollo, but Ares, the war-god. The plague, therefore, appears to be the product of a war. The Athenian audience would not have missed these innovations in the story. Nor would it have taken long for them to recognize in Oedipus an image of the man who had been the leader of their own city during the first appearance of the plague. The priest calls Oedipus "first of men" (*andron de proton*) (1.33), as Thucydides called Pericles the "first man" (*protos aner*).

Soon Creon arrives with an answer from the oracle of Delphi to the question: What must be done to rid the city of the plague? "He ordered us in clear terms to drive out [*elaunein*] the thing that defiles this land. . . ." "What is the nature of our misfortune?" asks Oedipus. "How are we to rid ourselves of it—by what rites?" "Banishment," Creon answers, "or repaying blood for blood. We must atone for a murder which brings this plague-storm on the city." (11. 95-99) The audience knew well that Oedipus himself is the source of the pollution, and that it is he who must be exiled. Pericles, too, was commonly considered heir to a curse which was said to have brought pollution on the city as the result of an unexpiated murder. The Spartans had offered to avoid war if the Athenians would "drive out [*elaunein*] the curse" (Thucydides 1.126.3) in the person of Pericles. But the Athenians had refused; Pericles, like Oedipus, remained leader of his city, and the war-god had brought a plague upon Athens.

Still another attribute of Oedipus should have made the Athenian audience think of Pericles. The title *tyrannos* is applied to the ruler of Thebes and *tyrannis* to his monarchical power and kingdom some fourteen times in the play. These words had an ambiguous meaning in fifth-century Athens and were sometimes used in a neutral sense to mean simply "king" and "kingdom." They are so used most of the time in Sophocles' play, sometimes by Oedipus himself. There are rulers in Sophocles' other plays, some more deserving of this negative description than Oedipus; yet the designation is rare compared to its frequency in *Oedipus Tyrannus*. Sophocles plainly intended to emphasize the special character of Oedipus' authority. A *tyrannos*, in fact, was a special kind of monarch. Unlike a legitimate king, called *basileus*, he came to the throne in some unorthodox way, not by the normal and constitutional route of legitimate inheritance. Usually, the *tyrannos* was a usurper who came to power by means of violence—for example, murder, coup d'état, or popular revolution. The usurpers themselves were often good rulers and liked by their subjects; but the *tyrannis* generally deteriorated in the second or third generation into a harsh and despotic regime that fits the modern sense of the word "tyranny."

Oedipus is a classic *tyrannos* of the first generation, for he has come to power by extraordinary means—applying his remarkable intelligence to the riddle of the sphinx, thus saving Thebes from an earlier plague. Since then he has been an exemplary and beloved monarch, so neither he nor his people are reluctant to call him *tyrannos* in a neutral and even respectful sense. The tragic irony is that unknown to himself and the Thebans, but well known to the audience, he is also a *tyrannos* in the most negative sense: He has come to the throne by an act of the worst kind of violence. Many years before, he killed a stranger in a roadside quarrel, not knowing that his victim was both the king of Thebes and his own father. Later, he came to Thebes, solved the riddle, and acquired the throne. The play's central choral ode sings of the dark side of tyranny;

> *The despot* [tyrannos] *is the child of violent*
> *pride* [hubris],
> *Pride that vainly stuffs itself*
> *With food unseasonable, unfit,*
> *Climbs to the highest rim*
> *And then plunges sheer down into defeat*
> *Where its feet are of no use. . . .*

*The man who goes his way*
*Overbearing in word and deed,*
*Who fears no justice,*
*Honors no temple of the gods—*
*May an evil destiny seize him*
*And punish his ill-starred pride. (11.873–81,*
   *883–88)*

Pericles was no tyrant in any sense of the word. But his enemies had often asserted that he was, and even his admirers suggested that his place in the Athenian state was uniquely lofty. Thousands of Athenians had heard the comic poet Cratinus call him "the greatest *tyrannos*" in the theater. Political opponents for years had compared him with Peisistratus, who had established a tyranny in Athens during the previous century, and accused him of trying to establish his own. In the great debate before the ostracism of 443, his critics had blamed him for turning the Delian League into an Athenian tyranny. Even so friendly a judge as the historian Thucydides called Athens under Pericles "in name a democracy, but really a government by the first citizen." (2.65.9) The Sophoclean Oedipus, especially in the first part of the play, resembles such a leader rather than an arrogant, violent despot. He is unarmed and unguarded, law-abiding; he rejects secrecy for open discussion, and listens to the advice of others. As Bernard Knox puts it, "Thebes under Oedipus may be a *tyrannis*, but what it most resembles is a democracy ruled by its first citizen."[4] The Athenian audience is not likely to have missed the resemblance.

This is not to say that the comparison is exact. Knox is certainly right to say that the "similarities are only incidental details of a basic pattern," and he is persuasive when he further says that this pattern suggests a comparison of Oedipus" not to any individual Athenian but to Athens itself."[5] Here is his description of Oedipus' character:

> He is a great man, a man of experience and swift courageous action, who yet acts only after careful deliberation, illuminated by an analytic and demanding intelligence. His action by its consistent success generates a great self-confidence,but it is always directed to the common good. His is an absolute ruler who loves and is loved by his people, but is conscious of the jealousy his success arouses and suspicious of conspiracy in high places. He is capable of terrible, apparently ungovernable anger, but only under great provocation, and he can, though grudgingly and with difficulty, subdue his anger when he sees himself isolated from his people.[6]

This description of Oedipus, with a few modifications, may be applied to the Athenian people as well. Nothing in the ancient record indicates that Pericles himself was subject to jealousy, suspicion, or unrestrained anger. On the contrary, he was noted for his calm, dignified, and elevated deportment; for his restraint and refusal to give way to public displays of emotion. But the rest of this description may be applied to Pericles with perfect accuracy. The Athenian audience, no doubt, noticed and remarked on the many similarities between the protagonist of the play and their recently departed leader.

For us, the startling resemblance allows us to see Pericles and his remarkable career from an unusual perspective and in a way that may permit a deeper understanding. Instead of limiting ourselves to a direct comparison between Pericles and Oedipus, we may measure his life and character against the general pattern of the tragic heroes portrayed by Sophocles in all his extant works. Once again, Bernard Knox is our best guide to the nature of the Sophoclean hero. He is "one who, unsupported by the gods and in the face of human opposition, makes a decision which springs from the deepest layer of his individual nature, his *physis*, and then blindly, ferociously, heroically maintains that decision even to the point of self-destruction."[7]

Knox delineates the features that define the hero in the tragic world of Sophocles. "In six of the extant plays . . . the hero is faced with a choice between possible (or certain) disaster and a compromise which if accepted would betray the hero's own conception of himself, his rights, his duties; the hero decides against compromise, and that decision is then assailed, by friendly advice, by threats, by actual force. But he refuses to yield; he remains true to himself. . . ."[8]

This is the character that we see in Pericles from the onset of the prewar crisis until his death. The series of moderate actions he took were compromises between extreme possibilities; but they were merely a part of his own calculations as the best way to achieve his goal. With his critics, and in dealings with the enemy, there was no compromise. To the Corinthians, who offered peace and friendship if the Athenians would stand aloof from Corcyra he insisted on Athens' right under the Thirty Years' Peace to make a treaty with a neutral. When the Spartans offered compromises that might avoid the war, Pericles demanded that they obey the letter of the peace and submit all disputes to arbitration. In both cases there were extenuating circumstances that might have argued for a less rigid interpretation; but Pericles would not compromise.

The Sophoclean hero holds firmly to his decision, and Knox compares him with the aged hero of the *Oedipus at Colonus*, who is like "some sea cape in the North, with the storm waves beating against it from every quarter." Pericles' speeches repeatedly reveal this same obdurate character. In his speech in favor of war he says: "I *must give you* the same advice as in the past, and *I demand* that those of you were are persuaded shall support the common decisions. . . . (Thucydides 1.140.1) *"None of you must think* that we are going to war over a trifle . . . and *let there be no blame left* in your mind that you went to war over a trifle." (1.140.4–5) *"You must know* that it is necessary to go to war." Our fathers did great things, and *"we must not fall short* of their example, but *we must defend ourselves* against the enemy in every way, and *we must try* to hand over an undiminished power to future generations." (1.144.4)

The same tone dominates his defiant last speech in 430. Challenging his political opponents and the mass of Athenians at the same time, he says: *"Do not be led astray* by such citizens as these, and *do not hold* to your anger against me. . . ." *"You must bear* the afflictions that have no human source with an understanding that they are unavoidable, and those that come from the enemy with courage." (2.64.1–2) *"Achieve* both things [honor in the future and the avoidance of shame in the present], and *send no negotiators* to the Spartans. . . ." (2.64.6) [author's emphasis]

In the tragedies of Sophocles, the hero's resolve is always challenged and tested by appeals and arguments. Attempts are made to persuade the hero and make him change his mind. He is asked to accept the wisdom of others and be taught by them. These appeals to emotion and reason, as Knox points out, "the advice to reflect and be persuaded," amount to the demand that the hero yield (*eikein*). But the true heroic temper refuses even to hear these demands. So it was with Pericles on the eve of the war and during its course. After the Spartan ultimatum in 432, those Athenians who wanted peace forced a debate in the assembly focusing on the Megarian Decree, the withdrawal of which they thought might still avoid war. Only Pericles' part of the debate is recorded, but his critics certainly must have asked him to think again, to be persuaded, to change his mind—in short, to yield. His response was heroically defiant: "Men of Athens, I hold to the same judgment as always, that *we must not yield* [*me eikein*] to the Spartans." Like Sophocles' heroes, he scornfully separates himself from those who have weaker minds and wills: "I know that people who do not act in the same temper when they are actually engaged in war as when they were persuaded to undertake it, changing their minds with changing events. And now I also see that I must give you the same advice as in the past, and I demand that those of you who are persuaded shall support the common decisions even if, somehow, we may fail, or to make no claim of intelligence if we succeed." (1.140.1)

In the first year of the war he was assailed by the aggressive faction in Athens who wanted him to abandon his strategy and lead them out into battle against the Peloponnesian army. He did not want to hear their words for fear they would persuade others, so he prevented meetings of the assembly. There was, of course, no chance that he himself would yield to their arguments. In 430, in the midst of the plague, it was once again the peace faction that clamored against his determination to continue the war. He gave much the same answer as before; he would not yield: "As for me, I am the same, and I do not give way; it is you who have changed." (2.61.2) Notably, Pericles ascribed this same heroic posture to the city that was plainly an extension of himself. He tells the Athenians to "know that Athens has the greatest name among all mankind because it has *never yielded* [*me eikein*] to misfortunes" (2.64.3), just as in the Funeral Oration he praised the men who "thought it better to fight off the enemy and suffer death than to save themselves *by giving in*." (2.42.4)

Pericles never wavered from "that fierce sense of independence of the thorny individual" that is the mark of tragic heroes. "They will not be ruled, no one shall have power over them or treat them as a slave, they are free."[9] That characterization plainly fits Pericles himself in the last years of his life. But it is striking that he uses precisely the language of freedom and slavery in urging the Athenians to sustain the Megarian Decree:

> Make up your minds here and now to submit before any harm comes to you or, if we intend to go to war, as I think is better, do not yield on any pretext, great or small, and do not hold what we have in fear. For it means slavery just the same when equals impose either the greatest or the smallest demands upon their neighbors, instead of seeking a legal settlement. (1.141.1)

"There is no dealing with these incorrigible natures."[10] Time alone, the others hope, can make the hero see the error of his stubbornness. It may seem odd to find this quality in Pericles, the careful statesman who usually counseled restraint and caution. This was the man who urged Tolmides not to invade Boeotia in 457, uttering in the assembly one of his most memorable remarks: "If you will not be persuaded by Pericles, wait for the wisest of all advisers, time." (Plutarch, *Pericles* 18.2) After the battle of Sybota in 433, however, Pericles was not the same man. He firmly believed that he must act swiftly and vigorously to deter an expansion of the quarrel with Corinth and the outbreak of a major war. When the Spartans voted for war in 432, he became certain that it could no longer be avoided, and time became an even more dangerous enemy. In 457, he had still been a young man; but at the outbreak of the war he was past sixty, and time was against him. He believed that only one strategy could bring victory, and only he could impose and direct it. Every year that passed was a threat to Athens' capacity to confront the Spartans, convince them of the futility of using force, and establish the basis of a lasting peace that would preserve the city and its empire. There can be no doubt that many Athenians urged him to wait, to delay the dangerous actions he took; then they asked him to withdraw the Megarian Decree to avoid immediate war in the expectation that time might make it unnecessary. But Pericles held firmly to the conviction that the war must come while he still guided Athens' destiny. So the war came, and with it the destruction of what he had tried to protect.

But heroes do not wait, and times does not change them. By the end of *Oedipus Tyrannus*, the hero is "the same imperious figure as he was at the beginning, issuing requests to Creon that are phrased like commands, rejecting persuasion, insisting on his own way; he even has to be reminded, in the last line of the play, that he is no longer *tyrannos* in Thebes."[11] On his deathbed, Pericles showed the same character. His friends praised his military achievements, but he chided and instructed them as to what they should praise instead. His insistence, moreover, that "No Athenian now alive has put on mourning clothes because of me," certainly seems the statement of a man whom time had not persuaded of his errors. Many Athenians had lately died fighting in a war that he had insisted should not be delayed. All about him thousands were dying because of the plague that was, at the very least, intensified by the strategy he had insisted upon. Thousands more would die in a recurrence of the plague and in the many battles still to come before the war was over. As he lay dying, everywhere in Athens people blamed him bitterly for what they believed to be the failure of his statesmanship and strategy. But Pericles conceded no error and accepted no blame.

In still another way Pericles rejected the power of time in the heroic manner. "Remember," Pericles says to the Athenians,

> that Athens has the greatest name among all mankind because it has never given way to misfortune but has expended more lives and effort in warfare than any other polis, gaining the greatest power that has ever existed down to our time. The memory of this power, even if now we should some day give way (for all things that have grown must also decay) will be passed on forever to those who come after us.

This is the language of Sophoclean tragedy. Here, as Knox points out, we can also discern the tragic qualities of Athens itself. "It was, like a Sophoclean hero, in love with the impossible."[12] But it was Pericles who spoke the words and whose mind, spirit, and character lay behind them. If we substitute his name for that of Athens, the statement is equally exact and true. Pericles, no less than his city, was like a tragic hero.

Both Athens and Pericles are undone by the dark side of their own admirable qualities, for the very enterprise and determination that brought them to greatness plunged them into disaster. Pericles' strength and uniqueness lay in his extraordinary confidence in reason and intelligence, especially his own. This confidence served him well, as it did Oedipus, raising him and his city to unprecedented heights. In the last years of Pericles' life, however, his stubborn adherence to reason brought him down. His notorious commitment to natural philosophy provoked a popular opposition that deprived him of friends and associates and caused him great political embarrassment. The same forces worked against him when the war broke out, especially with the coming of the plague. Charges of the neglect of oracles and of irreligious attitudes helped stir up the passions that led to his removal from office. Ordinary Athenians did not share his confidence in the power of human intelligence. They were always uncomfortable with reason alone and needed comfort and assurance from nonrational sources, supernatural elements that Pericles scorned and neglected.

His confidence in reason also failed him in another way: His careful diplomacy aimed at deterrence missed the mark when his measured moves provoked a passionate response in Sparta. In the enemy camp, fear and honor proved more powerful than rational calculation. His strategy, intended as a moderate device for persuading the enemy to make peace, was too weak to bring victory but strong enough to cause anger and intensify determination.

All this showed that in diplomacy, and especially in war, passion and the will to victory usually play a larger role than intellectual calculation anticipates; in ignoring them, Pericles badly miscalculated. But even perfect reasoning without error is not impeccable. There are always elements beyond the compass of control of the human mind, even at its best. Pericles learned this fact to his sorrow; yet before the outbreak of war he brushed it aside with bold confidence: "We are accustomed to blame chance for what turns out contrary to our calculations." (Thucydides 1.141.2) And when the plague broke out he conceded the limits of his foresight only grudgingly: "Do not be led astray and do not hold your anger against me . . . because the enemy has invaded and done precisely what he was certain to do when you refused to obey his orders, even though this plague has come upon us—the only thing that has happened outside our expectations." (2.64.1) But several very important things had happened outside Pericles' calculations even before the coming of the plague, and like any tragic hero, he could not admit them.

Pericles' heroic quality, for good and ill, was to persevere not only against the appeals of weaker minds and wills, but also in the face of the hard, inescapable fact that some of his calculations had been mistaken and that unforeseen things had occurred. It is easy to find fault with the errors of leaders who were forced to make difficult decisions quickly without knowing all the relevant facts. Even so, Pericles' calculations were never very far from correct. He had understood the political situation in Sparta well, and his diplomacy nearly succeeded. Even his flawed military strategy might have been successful had the plague not broken out. The same inflexibility might have been the keys to success had events gone slightly otherwise.

The difference between perseverance and disastrous inflexibility can be terribly thin, as the experience of a heroic figure of our own time can attest. Winston Churchill was no less stubborn and unyielding in his determination to resist the enemy than Pericles. Taking office at a low point in the fortunes of his country, he breathed defiance in a speech of Periclean eloquence:

I have, myself, full confidence that if all do their duty, if nothing is neglected, and if the best arrangements are made, as they are being made, we shall prove ourselves once again able to defend our island home, to ride out the storm of war, and to outlive the menace of tyranny, if necessary for years, if necessary alone. . . . We shall go on to the end, we shall fight in France, we shall fight on the seas and the

oceans, we shall fight with growing confidence and growing strength
in the air, we shall defend our island, whatever the cost may be, we
shall fight on the beaches, we shall fight on the landing grounds, we
shall fight in the fields, and in the streets, we shall fight in the hills;
we shall never surrender.[13]

Yet England came within a hair's breadth of losing the war and suffering the horrors of invasion and occupation by Nazi Germany. Had
Hitler and Goering continued bombing the RAF's landing fields and
ground facilities instead of using their planes to bomb cities, Germany might have won the battle of Britain, and control of the air
would have made their success inevitable. In that case, Churchill's
bulldog determination—his refusal to accept a relatively generous
peace offer after the fall of France—would seem in retrospect the
magnificent, if wrong-headed, defiance of a tragic figure who brought
his people low by is his own heroic intransigence.

That is the judgment our study requires us to make of Pericles.
His confidence in the power of his intellect and in the capacity of
reason to shape a better world went beyond what is possible for
human beings. That superhuman confidence is part of the heroic
temper, and it explains what makes the tragic hero terrible as well as
great. Pericles' greatness, however, goes beyond his heroic character.
He was right to claim immortality for Athens, although what made it
so was not its power, as he thought; that power was soon surpassed
and overcome. Rather, the real source of his city's undying fame was
Pericles' unique and original vision of the good society and the good
citizen. It was a vision of a free people who would achieve their
highest goals and capabilities as members of a free community in
which the people took turns governing and being governed and made
the most important decisions in common. The Periclean vision valued
intelligence and talent and was not embarrassed to reward both with
public honor. It cherished the arts as a powerful force for public
education and as a delight in themselves. It reconciled the tension
between liberty and equality by rejecting the imposition of equality
by state control (as in Sparta), and insisting on freedom of opportunity
as the road to both equality and honor. It was a vision of a democracy
that sought not to reduce all aspects of life to the lowest common level
but aimed at excellence for the individual as well as for the state. It
demanded participation and sacrifice from its citizens while retaining
a wide space for private activities where the state had no claim. It
recognized the right of each citizen to pursue his own road to hap-

piness at the same time that it required him to respect the needs of his fellow-citizens and of the community as a whole. This is a vision of timeless value; and as long as there are human societies struggling with the problems posed by political freedom, that vision will continue to inspire and instruct.

# 14

# THE SHADOW
## OF PERICLES

t has been aptly said that "Great men have two lives; one which occurs while they work on this earth; a second which begins at the day of their death and continues as long as their ideas and conceptions remain powerful."[1] This was also true of Pericles. Like many great leaders he left a dangerous vacuum which no one could fill. Athenian politics quickly reverted to the antagonistic character of former times, as the leading men of Athens competed for the position Pericles had left vacant. Lacking his unique eminence, however, they competed in a manner more typical of democratic contests by seeking new ways to please and flatter the voters.

Thucydides judged these successors to be failures, and he blamed their deficient leadership for the loss of the war. Their private ambitions and personal greed not only led them to abandon the Periclean strategy but to choose policies that were bad for the Athenian cause. "When these policies succeeded they brought honor and benefit only to individuals, but when they failed they harmed the entire state as it fought the war." (Thucydides 2.65.7) That judgment is too harsh, for these successors inherited a desperate situation, and some—if not all—pursued policies that they believed best for Athens. None of them, however, combined the necessary qualities of leadership demanded by the moment. None possessed the virtues and experience that were required in order to become "first citizen" in more than name, as Pericles had been. Yet each in his own way seems consciously to have tried to emulate some Periclean qualities.

The most important politician in the years immediately following Pericles' death was Nicias. He had served as a general alongside Pericles and seemed to inherit his mantle, for he held firmly to the Periclean strategy. For this he earned the enmity of Cleon, who favored a more aggressive strategy and who attacked him as he had Pericles. Lacking the great man's stature and persuasive gifts, Nicias tried to emulate his style. He did whatever he could to call attention to the similarities, remaining aloof in his private life and avoiding conviviality, public events, and even conversation. Like Pericles, Nicias buried himself in official work whether he was serving as general or as a member of the Athenian council. He posted his friends at the doors of his house to ask the pardon of those who came, on the grounds that "at that very moment Nicias was occupied with important public business." (Plutarch, *Nicias* 5.2) He also employed what we would call a public relations expert. Plutarch calls him Nicias' "chief fellow-tragedian in these matters and his colleague in placing round him a cloak of dignity and reputation." This man, Hiero, was assigned to circulate stories about the hard life Nicias was leading in order to serve the city.

> Even when he is taking his bath and while eating dinner some kind of public business is engaging him. He neglects his private affairs by thinking always of the common good and barely begins to lie down to sleep until the first watch of the night. That is why he is not in good physical condition and is not gentle and kind to his friends, and he has lost friends, as well as money, while serving the city. Others gain friends and enrich themselves while taking pleasure in the public forum and toying with the public interest. (5.3.4)

This was, of course, a caricature of the lofty manner natural to Pericles, and Nicias soon showed that he lacked his predecessor's foresight and persuasiveness. But Nicias was unwaveringly patriotic and entirely above corruption. He retained great power in Athens for the sixteen years he survived Pericles, in no small measure because of his success in associating himself with his model.

Strangely, the shadow of Pericles influenced even Cleon, the man who had attacked him and his policies most sharply. In almost every way he was the opposite of Pericles. While Pericles acted with calm restraint, Cleon is described as "most violent." (Thucydides 3.36.6) Pericles favored moderation both in the treatment of allies and in the city's war aims; Cleon advocated exemplary cruelty toward rebellious allies, an aggressive strategy, and war aims that could only be achieved at great cost. Pericles invited free discussion of important questions, welcoming new ideas; Cleon denounced the Athenians' willingness to engage in prolonged debate, to listen to many opinions, and to change their minds when persuaded by a new argument.

Even so, Cleon, a notorious demagogue, liked to assume the role of Periclean statesmen, defying and even chastising the majority when he thought them wrong. On one occasion he began a speech by saying "I hold them to the same opinion as before," almost the same words Pericles had spoken in opposition to the majority on the eve of the war. In that same speech, Cleon blamed the Athenians themselves for their troubles, just as Pericles had done on many occasions. He was clever enough to use Pericles' manner and style while seeking very un-Periclean ends.

It is less surprising that Alcibiades, Pericles' ward, who grew up in the great leader's house, should also have been influenced by him. The boy's talents, temperament, and the greatness of his father would, in any case, have launched him into a political and military career. But the evidence suggests that his guardian's example influenced its pace and direction. He passed his boyhood during the height of Pericles' career, when he stood alone as the most influential man in Athens. Alcibiades' ambition and the encouragement of his friends led him to expect not merely a great career but one that challenged the achievements of his guardian.

His career got off to a brilliant start when, like Pericles, he was elected general in his early thirties. After Cleon's death, he became the leader of the faction that opposed Nicias and his policy of peaceful co-existence with the Spartans. He pursued the contrary plan of creating an alliance between Athens, Argos, and Sparta's other enemies in the Peloponnesus, following a strategy modeled closely on the one pursued by Pericles in the First Peloponnesian War. It came very close to knocking Sparta out of the war and bringing total victory to Athens, but it failed at the battle of Mantinea in 418.

It did so, at least in part, because neither Alcibiades, Nicias, or any other Athenian had the political support to carry through his policy in the face of even a single setback. Athens badly needed a Pericles to unite the people and guide them firmly and steadily in pursuit of one policy or another. Without wise and effective leadership, the democracy stumbled aimlessly into destructive brutality and self-destructive adventurism. Perhaps the worst example involves the islanders of Melos, who had heretofore stayed aloof from Athens and her alliance, and for more than sixty years the Athenians had allowed them to do so. No pressing need compelled the Athenians to change their policy, but in 416, their mounting frustration led them to order Melos to join the Athenian Empire. When the Melians refused, the Athenians laid siege to the island. When the Melians finally surrendered, the victorious Athenians killed all the men and sold the women and children into slavery. This was the most notorious atrocity the Athenians ever committed, and it has haunted them and stained their reputation throughout the ages. They had never perpetrated such an act in the time of Pericles, even when serious rebellions had threatened their power and survival.

In the next year, thrashing about for some way to gain the upper hand over Nicias, Alcibiades proposed an expedition to gain control of the distant but wealthy island of Sicily. This was the kind of adventure Pericles had consistently opposed. Nicias also opposed it, but his attempt to derail the scheme only produced an expeditionary force much larger than the one originally proposed. The result was to turn what might have been a minor mistake into a major disaster. Alcibiades was tried and condemned for treason in absentia; by 413, he was in exile in Sparta. Nicias was dead, and with him had fallen thousands of Athenian and allied soldiers; most of the Athenian fleet had sunk in Sicilian waters, and the treasury was almost empty. The Athenians seemed beaten. Their allies broke out in rebellion, the Spartans were confident of easy and imminent victory, and even neutrals planned to join in to share the spoils.

At this terrible moment, the Athenian people themselves showed that the memory and influence of Pericles was alive among them. Recognizing the need for prudent and trustworthy political leadership of the Periclean kind, they invented a new device to provide guidance and stability in the absence of an outstanding individual. They voted "to elect a board of older men to serve as *probouloi*, offering advice and proposing legislation, concerning current problems as the situation may require." (Thucydides 8.1.3) Some ancient writers and modern scholars have seen this device as a step away from democracy, because this council of forty elders had the ability to limit the powers of the democratic assembly and council. But that view is clearly mistaken. The assembly freely and without coercion chose to establish the council in response to an emergency, and its members were freely elected.

The names of only two of these forty are known, Hagnon and Sophocles, but both had been closely connected with Pericles in the public mind. Hagnon had served as general with Pericles at least three times, at Samos in 440, and in other theaters in 430 and 429. In 438, he had played a prominent part in defending Pericles from the attacks of his political enemies, and he served as founder of the important colony of Amphipolis in 437. The tragedian Sophocles carried out a delicate diplomatic mission for Pericles during the Samian War, and it was well known that he was close to Pericles.[2] Evidently the Athenians put as many old Pericleans as they could find on the new council of elders.

Thucydides was no admirer of post-Periclean Athens, and his praise of the Athenians' efforts in 413 is grudging: "In the terror of the moment as is the way of the *demos*, they were ready to do everything with discipline." (8.1.4) In fact, the behavior of the Athenian democracy in this crisis seems remarkably Periclean. When Pericles feared that passion would interfere with sound policy in the first year of the war, he had used his great personal authority to limit the democracy by preventing the meeting of assemblies. Now the Athenian assembly, acting in a thoroughly Periclean spirit—determined, practical, restrained, prudent, and economical—voluntarily placed a limit on itself by giving unprecedented powers to a board of respected and trusted moderates schooled in his tradition. They also demonstrated remarkable fiscal integrity. "They decided, so far as the situation permitted, not to give in but instead to prepare a fleet, obtaining timber and money wherever they could, to see to the security of their alliance . . . and to reduce public expenses." (8.1.3)

Under the *probouloi*, the Athenians made a stunning recovery. They came close to suppressing the rebellions in their alliance and almost drove the Peloponnesian fleet from the seas. The intervention of the Persians on the Spartan side, however, revived the enemy cause. It did not seem that Athens had a chance against a Peloponnesian alliance backed by the Great King. Meanwhile, Alcibiades had fled from Sparta under a sentence of death and was serving as personal adviser to Tissaphernes, the Persian satrap who had negotiated the new agreement with Sparta. Alcibiades was eager to return to Athens, but could not do so while the democracy continued, for serious criminal charges still stood against him. He negotiated with Athenians in the Aegean, promising to bring Tissaphernes and the Persians over to the Athenian side if the democracy were overthrown and he were restored to Athens. Even patriots and friends of democracy were prepared to accept his return under these conditions if it would bring Persian aid, victory, and salvation. The result was a successful coup in 411 and the establishment of the rule of the Four Hundred, the first interruption of democratic government in Athens in a century.

The dominant faction among the Four Hundred soon showed themselves to be true oligarchs and haters of democracy. They launched a reign of murder and intimidation against democrats and moderates and were on the point of betraying the city to the Spartans when the moderates took charge. Only four months after the coup, the Four Hundred were replaced by a broader government, and within the year the full democracy was restored. This restored democracy produced no great leaders, made mistakes, and, in the end, lost the Peloponnesian War. For all this it was reviled in antiquity and has had few defenders over the centuries. Yet its achievements were considerable, its courage and determination remarkable; and, in fact, it almost won. The assessment by Thucydides is its greatest tribute:

> Even after their defeat in Sicily, where they had lost most of their fleet as well as the rest of their forces, and faction had already broken out in Athens, they nevertheless held out for ten more years, not only against their previous enemies and the Sicilians who joined them and most of their allies, who rebelled against them, but also later against Cyrus, son of the Great King, who provided money to the Peloponnesian for a navy. Nor did they give in until they destroyed themselves by falling upon one another in private quarrels. (2.65.12–13)

Thucydides makes this point to support Pericles' prediction that the Athenians would easily win the war if they followed his original strategy. We need not agree with that view to share the great historian's admiration of the extraordinary tenacity and courage shown by the Athenian democracy even after the loss of their leader. Instead, we may be struck by their devotion to his vision of democracy, clinging to it through the darkest times. That devotion remained unshaken even after defeat had deprived the Athenians of their empire, their autonomy, and their democracy.

In 404, the Spartans imposed drastic terms of surrender upon the defeated and starving Athenians. The losers were required to abandon their alliance and their fleet; the city's defensive walls were breached; and the Athenians lost control of their own foreign policy as their city became a member of the Peloponnesian League, promising "to follow the Spartans wherever they should lead." The Spartans next installed a puppet government of oligarchs whose brutality earned them the name "The Thirty Tyrants." The new regime soon began another reign of terror consisting of widespread confiscations and judicial murder, turning first for political reasons against well-known leaders of the democracy, then against rich men for the sake of gain, and finally against moderates, even those among their own number, who complained of these atrocities. As hostility and resistance grew, the Thirty had to call in a Spartan garrison to protect them from their fellow-citizens.

Having taking control of the former Athenian Empire, the Spartans now dominated the Greek world. They seemed to be firmly entrenched, suppressing democracy everywhere and replacing it with oligarchic satellite governments. Athens itself was occupied territory where even suspicion of democratic sympathies could bring denunciation and death. The light of Pericles' democracy once again seemed thoroughly extinguished.

In these dark times, the Athenians found a leader in the Periclean mold. Thrasybulus, son of Lycus, had been one of the moderates who wanted to bring Alcibiades back as the way to save Athens and win the war. When the oligarchic conspirators of 411 tried to spread their coup to Samos, where Thrasybulus was a captain in the Athenian fleet, he led the democratic resistance to victory. Under the moderate regime that succeeded the Four Hundred and then under the fully restored democracy, he served brilliantly as a commander of Athenian fleets, winning the greatest naval victories of the war. He was a child of the Periclean democracy and a product of his civic education, schooled in the traditions of duty and dedication to the Athenian Empire, and he adhered to these ideals throughout his life.[3]

After the Spartan victory, Athenians faced choices similar to those confronting the French in 1940. Most Frenchmen accepted their defeat and occupation by the Germans as best they could and tried to continue their lives as normally as possible. Some chose to collaborate with the Germans either out of conviction, because it brought safety and opportunity, or in hope of helping their country-men by moderating the effects of the occupation. Other Frenchmen, a very small number, led by Charles de Gaulle decided at once to work for liberation, seeking a base and support in Great Britain.

Thrasybulus was the Athenian De Gaulle. He fled to Thebes, formerly hostile to Athens but now alienated from Sparta. There, escaped Athenian democrats and patriots rallied to him and formed a small army, which he established in a fort in the mountains on Ath-ens' northern frontier. When the forces of the Thirty could not de-stroy the rebels, more Athenians were encouraged to flee and join the resistance. Finally, Thrasybulus was strong enough to march out and capture the Piraeus and to fight a Spartan army to a standstill. The Spartans chose to abandon Athens, and in 403, Thrasybulus and his men restored the full democracy. Small wonder that the Athenians honored him at his death by burying him in the public cemetery, next to the tomb of Pericles.

Angered by the outrages committed by the Thirty, many citizens wanted to hunt down and punish the guilty men and those who had collaborated with them. That would have brought trials, executions, and banishments. Athens would have been torn by the factional strife and civil war that destroyed democracy in so many other Greek states. Instead, Thrasybulus joined with other moderates to impose an am-nesty that protected all but a few of the worst criminals. The newly restored democracy held firmly to a policy of moderation and re-straint, behavior that later won extraordinary praise from Aristotle: "The reaction of [the Athenian democrats] to their previous calami-ties, both privately and publicly, seems to have been the finest and most statesmanlike that any people has demonstrated." Not only did they declare and hold to the amnesty, they even raised public money to pay back to the Spartans the sum the Thirty had borrowed to fight the democrats. "For they thought that this was the way to begin the restoration of harmony. In other cities, when democrats came to power, there is no thought of expending their own money; on the contrary, they seize and redistribute the land of their opponents." (*Constitution of the Athenians* 40.2–3) The moderation of the dem-ocrats of 403 was rewarded by a successful reconciliation of the classes and factions that permitted the Athenian democracy to flourish with-out a civil war or coup d'état almost to the end of the fourth century.

Thus, the spirit of Pericles had triumphed. Half a century after the restoration of democracy, moderate Athenian democrats praised him and his achievements in the highest terms: He was one of those great men, along with Solon, Cleisthenes, and Themistocles, who had brought Athens democracy and greatness. He had been incorruptible, "a fine political leader, the best orator, and he had so adorned the city with monuments and all kinds of other ornaments that even today those who come to Athens believe it worthy to rule over not only the Greeks but the whole world." (Isocrates, *Antidosis* 234)

In the last decade of the twentieth century, it might seem that such enthusiastic endorsements of Pericles and Athenian democracy had carried the day. Professions of belief in the virtues of democracy are more widespread than at any time in history. Some even argue that the age-old debate between democracy and its opponents, which began in ancient Athens, has come to an end. A glance at the record, however, suggests a more sober conclusion.

For more than two thousand years, democracy has had many powerful enemies and few friends. Powerful thinkers in the century following the Periclean period condemned democracy and cited Athens as evidence of its fatal flaws. Most ancient writers portrayed its leaders as self-seeking demagogues, destroyers of the common good. They called democracy unstable, a scene of devastating struggles between factions and classes, where the poor majority trampled on the better-off minority, careless of the rights of the individual; its inherent instability inevitably led to civil war, and thence to anarchy and tyranny. Plato attacked Pericles directly and blamed the Athenians for praising democratic politicians:

> people say that they have made the city great, not seeing that it is swollen and rotten underneath because of these former leaders; for they have filled the city full of harbors and docks and walls and revenues and all that kind of nonsense, and have left no room for moderation and justice. And when the crisis of the disease comes, the people will blame the advisers of the moment, and applaud Themistocles and Cimon and Pericles, who are the real authors of their calamities. (*Gorgias* 518e–519a)

This hostile portrayal persisted unchallenged into the eighteenth century and dominated Western thought. Rulers and writers from the Renaissance through the Enlightenment embraced Plato's critique, for it was in their best interest to do so. Kings, nobles, and conservative supporters of hierarchy feared the consequences of giving power to "the mob." Artists and writers feared the debasement of culture under the rule of the common man; religious leaders foresaw the incompatibility between the authority of the church and popular government—all the powerful forces and institutions of royal and aristocratic Europe were hostile to the idea of democracy and readily accepted the view that Athens under Pericles had been a disastrous failure.

In the fierce debates that characterized the Age of Enlightenment and swirled about the French Revolution, the Greek experience was repeatedly used as a crushing argument against the advocates of democracy. So powerful and widespread was this opinion that even men who founded the world's most successful and stable democracy took it for granted in their debates over the American constitution. Alexander Hamilton used Pericles' career to illustrate the opportunity for the abuse of power by a popular leader in a pure democracy:

> Men of this class, whether the favorites of a king or of a people, have in too many instances abused the confidence they possessed; and assuming the pretext of some public motive, have not scrupled to sacrifice the national tranquility to personal advantage or personal gratification.
>
> The celebrated Pericles, in compliance with the resentment of a prostitute [Aspasia], at the expense of much of the blood and treasure of his countrymen, attacked, vanquished, and destroyed the city of the *Samnians* [sic]. The same man, stimulated by private pique . . . was the primitive author of that famous and fatal war, distinguished in the Grecian annals by the name of the *Peloponnesian* war; which . . . terminated in the ruin of the Athenian commonwealth.[4]

Even James Madison echoed Plato's judgment of ancient Athens: "such democracies have ever been spectacles of turbulence and contention; have ever been found incompatible with personal security or the rights of property; and have in general been as short in their lives as they have been violent in their deaths."[5]

The facts about Periclean Athens, as we have seen, were very different. Plato's assault on its character is a travesty. The Athenian people did not permit their leaders to usurp power. They were not slow to remove and punish even the most powerful men in their democracy, as Pericles learned to his sorrow, and they withstood external as well as internal threats to their democracy. Through the horrors of almost three decades of the Peloponnesian War, military defeat, foreign occupation, and an oligarchic coup d'état, the people of Athens showed that combination of commitment and restraint that is necessary for the survival of popular government and life in a decent society.

This restraint is all the more remarkable when we consider how simple it would have been for the Athenian majority to plunder the rich and take revenge upon their enemies. Plainly they had embraced the democratic vision, and their experience had proven its validity. They did not think of the customs and laws that governed Athens as a conspiracy by which the rich and propertied ruled over the exploited masses. Instead, they believed that respect for and obedience to the law were the fundamental safeguard of the weak and poor against the rich and powerful, and that popular government, which alone could give freedom, dignity, and self-respect to the ordinary man, depended on adherence to the law. Disrespect for the law, they thought, was the way of tyranny: "In a democracy it is the laws that guard the person of the citizen and the constitution of the state, whereas the tyrant and the oligarch find their protection in suspicion and armed guards." (Aeschines, *Against Timarchus* 4–5) Soon after the democratic restoration of 403, an orator beautifully expressed the Athenian devotion to law in a funeral oration reminiscent of the one Pericles had delivered a generation before. Earlier Athenians, he said, were the first to establish a democracy,

> believing the liberty of all to be the strongest source of harmony; by sharing with each other the hopes that arose from their shared dangers they had freedom of soul in their civic life. They used the law for honoring the good and punishing the evil. For they thought that it was the way of the wild beasts to be ruled by one another by force, but that men should decide justice by law, to convince by reason, and to serve these two in act by submitting to the sovereignty of law and the instruction of reason. (Lysias, *Funeral Oration* 17–19)

In the nineteenth century, when modern democracy had begun to take root in the United States and Great Britain, the attitude toward Athenian democracy became more favorable. British friends of democracy rediscovered and celebrated the constitution of Periclean Athens and its democratic way of life. The publication of George Grote's great twelve-volume *History of Greece* between 1846 and 1856 transformed the understanding of Periclean Athens. As Britain moved toward fuller democracy, the Athens of Pericles, as interpreted by Grote, seemed more and more to provide a source of inspiration. Educated English men and women were raised with knowledge of and admiration for the Athenians of the fifth century.

During World War I, London buses carried posters that displayed excerpts of Pericles' Funeral Oration. The people who chose them believed that the words of Pericles asking for the Athenians to stand fast against the Spartans had contemporary meaning for the citizens of a modern liberal, commercial democracy at war with a militaristic autocracy. They thought his call for each Athenian to make the necessary sacrifices for his community would ring true to the British people, and they expected the values of equality, obedience to law, free speech, political participation, and the love of goodness and beauty as well as power and glory, to appeal to the ordinary citizen.[6]

In 1915, a distinguished British classical scholar was in no way embarrassed to say that

> Greek ideas and Greek inspiration can help us today, not only in facing the duties of the moment, but in the work of deepening and extending the range and the meaning of Democracy and Citizenship, Liberty and Law, which would seem to be the chief political task before mankind in the new epoch of history on which we have suddenly entered.[7]

The reputation of democratic Athens has generally prospered since that time, but modern democracy itself has been severely threatened by armed aggression and ideological challenge. The Great Depression of the 1930s, followed by the rise of the Fascist and Nazi dictatorships, seemed to make a mockery of nineteenth-century expectations that democracy would triumph as the result of a natural progress toward rationality, prosperity, and self-government. For a time it seemed that popular government might disappear from most of the world, giving way to tyrannies made more savagely effective than ever before by the products of modern technology.

World War II destroyed one kind of despotism, but another fixed its grip on a vast portion of the earth. The Western democracies met the new challenge; but ironically, many Western intellectuals renewed the attack on democracy begun by Plato, although their criticisms came from a different angle. Plato, and the early modern monarchists and aristocrats who followed his lead, blamed Periclean democracy for its excessive commitment to equality. Twentieth-century critics, on the other hand, have largely complained of its inequalities, particularly the unequal distribution of wealth inevitable in a free society, demanding not equality of opportunity for all citizens but equality of result. Marxists, both in the Communist and non-Communist worlds, have derided "bourgeois democracy" as really a form of oppression and exploitation. Relativists have suggested that democracy might be a good thing for those countries where it had already taken root, but that it was really a Western phenomenon not suitable to other parts of the world. Right up until the revolutions that broke out in the Communist world in 1989, many Western intellectuals excused and even praised regimes that had abandoned political liberty and democracy in the name of economic equality.

Political equality was the cornerstone of Athenian democracy, but economic equality, as we have seen, was no part of the democratic program in the age of Pericles or after. Early in the sixth century, the Athenian peasantry had demanded a redistribution of land and *isomoiria* (equal portions) of the land of Attica, but the demand was not met; nor was it ever renewed. The experience of social revolutions in other states, where violations of the right to property had produced civil war, anarchy, tyranny, and poverty, showed that equality before the law, not equality of possession, was the only form of the principle compatible with prosperity, freedom, and security. For the Athenians, therefore, social justice did not mean economic leveling. The Athenian democrat demanded equality of opportunity, a "career open to talents." But he also believed that excellence and superior ability should be rewarded. Through disasters and temptations, through prosperity and poverty, the Athenians abided by these principles.

Ancient and modern critics of democracy have shared a basic attitude. Both have distrusted the ordinary person and overridden his autonomy in search of a higher goal: a utopian idea of justice. For Plato, that meant government by a small group of philosophers who would rule in the light of a divine, unchanging knowledge. For Marxian theory, it meant a utopia of equality and total liberty without exploitation or alienation. In its earthly manifestation that came to mean the rule of the "proletariat"—in fact, a small dictatorial "revolutionary vanguard" led by such men as Lenin, Mao, and Castro—governed such utopias as the Soviet Union, Communist China, and Cuba. Both critiques of democracy share the beliefs that individual freedom and self-government are secondary to the construction of a truly just society, and that there is a small class of people who alone know the right goals and how to achieve them.

Most defenders of democracy deny that there is an art or science of government, known or knowable only by some elite group. They believe that good government and the achievement of a good society require the participation of all citizens. The elements of democracy—individual liberty, equality before the law, equal opportunity, the right to vote, and the right to hold office—are not means to a higher end. Rather, the system of democratic self-government is an end in itself. Human dignity and flourishing require a reasonable level of economic well-being and the exercise of those human qualities that are needed for a life of freedom and autonomy. Politics, therefore, not economics, is primary. The evidence is strong that democracy and economic freedom are more likely to bring prosperity than any other system. No political system can guarantee prosperity, but a democratic system can at least provide a part of what is needed.

The story of the Athenians in the time of Pericles suggests that the creation and survival of democracy requires leadership of a high order. When tested, the Athenians behaved with the required devotion, wisdom, and moderation in large part because they had been inspired by the democratic vision and example that Pericles had so effectively communicated to them. It was a vision that exalted the individual *within* the political community; it limited the scope and power of the state, leaving enough space for individual freedom, privacy, and the human dignity of which they are a crucial part. It rejected the leveling principle pursued by both ancient Sparta and modern socialism, which requires the suppression of those rights. By rewarding merit, it encouraged the individual achievement and excellence that makes life sweet and raises the quality of life for everyone. Above all, Pericles convinced the Athenians that their private needs, both moral and material, required the kind of community Athens had become. Therefore, they were willing to run risks in its defense, make sacrifices on its behalf, and restrain their passions and desires to preserve it.

The new and emerging democracies of our time are very fragile, and they all face serious challenges. Few can rely upon strong democratic traditions, and all suffer economic conditions that range from bad to disastrous. Many are now confronting long-suppressed ethnic divisions that threaten to destroy the needed unity and harmony. The image and example of the prosperous, free nations of the world, conveyed to their people by modern technology, has meanwhile raised material expectations to unrealistic levels. If the newly free nations see democracy chiefly as a quick route to material well-being and equal distribution of wealth, they will be badly disappointed, and democracy will fail. To succeed, they need a vision of the future that is powerful enough to sustain them through bad times as well as good and to inspire the many difficult sacrifices that will be required of them. They must see that democracy alone of all regimes respects the dignity and autonomy of every individual, and understand that its survival requires that each individual sees his own well-being as inextricably connected to that of the whole community.

This new faith will be especially hard to instill in societies that have learned to be cynical about the use of political idealism. The new democracies will, therefore, need leaders in the Periclean mold, leaders who know that the aim and character of true democracy should be to elevate their citizens to the highest attainable level, and that cutting down the greatest to assuage the envy of the least is the way of tyranny. They need leaders who understand that individual freedom, self-government, and equality before the law are of the highest value in themselves. And they especially need leaders with the talents to persuade their impatient citizens that these political institutions are the necessary first foundation for a decent regime and a good life for all.

Such a vision and such leadership are not readily available in our era. The world has been astounded to see thin shoots of democracy trying to break through the hard surface of oppression. Those who wish to help them grow and flourish could do worse than to turn for inspiration and instruction to the story of Pericles of Athens and his city, where once, against all odds, democracy triumphed.

# NOTES

## INTRODUCTION

1. Voltaire, *The Age of XIV* (Berlin, 1751), Introduction, p. 1.

2. Robert Gilpin, *War and Change in World Politics* (Princeton, 1981).

3. The latest congress—called "Hegemonic Rivalry: Athens and Sparta, the United States and the Soviet Union" and organized by Ned Lebow and Barry S. Strauss of Cornell University—met in Italy in June 1988.

4. Quoted in Richard T. Bienvenu, *The Ninth of Thermidor: The Fall of Robespierre* (New York, 1968), p. 38.

5. They first appear in the epics of Homer, where they are part of the funeral games honoring the great chiefs and heroes. By the time of Pericles regular athletic contests had become the central feature of festivals at Olympia, Delphi, Nemea, and the Isthmus of Corinth honoring one or another of the Olympian gods. At Athens, the Panathenaic games celebrated the city's patron goddess, and the Dionysian festival included athletic contests as well as the famous competitions in tragedy and comedy.

## 2. POLITICIAN

1. One story says she had improper relations with the great painter Polygnotus, who rewarded her by using her face to depict a Trojan woman in a mural on the famous Painted Porch in the Agora. Another accused her of sleeping with Cimon

himself and even of the two living together openly as man and wife, but these stories can hardly be true.

2. J. K. Davies, *Athenian Propertied Families 600–300 B.C.* (Oxford, 1971), p. 305.

## 3. DEMOCRAT

1. The Athenians often lingered in the Agora on assembly days, either because of the love of conversation or a disinclination to attend the meeting. To get them to the assembly all exits were closed except the one leading to the Pnyx. Then, as an encouragement to the timely performance of public duty, a rope dripping with red dye was carried forward toward that exit, and anyone whose cloak was marked by the dye was fined.

2. The quotations and information come from Aristotle's *Constitution of the Athenians* 43.4–6. That work describes the democratic constitution as it functioned in the fourth century, but there is no reason to believe that the assembly's procedure and agenda was much different in the time of Pericles, a century earlier.

## 5. IMPERIALIST

1. This translation is based on a plausible and widely accepted, though necessarily imperfect, restoration of a fragmentary inscription, #47 in *Greek Historical Inscriptions*, edited by Russell Meiggs and David Lewis (Oxford, 1969), p. 121.

2. There are no more vigorously contested questions in ancient Greek history than those surrounding the Peace of Callias. Since antiquity, its reality has been denied, and the argument continues to this day; an article on the subject appears on the average of every two years. Ancient writers give slightly different versions of the details, but the differences are not important. Most modern scholars who deny the reality of an official peace treaty concede that a de facto cessation of hostilities took place. In recent years, some scholars have defended the authenticity of a peace treaty but placed it not long after the battle of the Eurymedon, in the 460s (see E. Badian, "The Peace of Callias," *Journal of Hellenic Studies* 107[1987]:1–39). For a defense of the position and date presented here, see Russell Meiggs, *The Athenian Empire* (Oxford, 1972), pp. 129–51.

3. Raphael Sealey, "The Entry of Pericles into History," *Hermes* 84(1956): 247.

4. Eduard Meyer, *Forschungen zur alten Geschichte*, vol. 2 (Halle, 1899), pp. 19–20.

5. Some scholars have doubted the authenticity of the Congress Decree, as it is called. For a good discussion see Meiggs, *The Athenian Empire*, pp. 151–52, 512–15. Plutarch does not give a date for the decree, but the sequence adopted here is the one chosen by those who accept its reality.

6. Ibid., p. 153.

7. The restoration of the Papyrus Decree is far from certain in its details, but H. T. Wade-Gery and Benjamin Meritt's description of their version seems fair: "We do not hold that we have recovered word for word the language which he [the ancient commentator who mentions the decree] used in making his summary, but . . . we may take our stand on the preserved portion of the papyrus with confidence in our interpretation, no matter what the precise restoration may be" (*Athenian Tribute Lists*, vol. 2, p. 188.)

8. *The American Heritage Dictionary of the English Language* (Boston, 1969).

## 6. PEACEMAKER

1. The Delphian priests favored Sparta because the Spartans had supported them against the Phocians, the allies of Athens. They proved their devotion at the beginning of the Peloponnesian War when the priests reported Delphic Apollo as saying to the Spartans that "if they fought with full vigor they would achieve victory, and he said that he himself would give his aid whether he was called upon or not." (Thucydides 1.118.3)

2. Plutarch (*Pericles* 26.3–4) speaks of the mutual branding of prisoners. He also reports stories of crucifixions and other atrocities committed by the Athenians as told by Duris of Samos (28.1–3), but he dismisses them as calumnies. And so they must have been, but they give some sense of the intensity of anger felt at the time.

## 8. EDUCATOR

1. Russell Meiggs, "The Political Implications of the Parthenon," in *Parthenos and Parthenon, Greece and Rome*, Supplement to vol. 10 (1963), p. 37.

2. Ibid., p. 39.

3. J.J. Pollitt, *Art and Experience in Classical Greece* (Cambridge, 1972), p. 78. My understanding and account of the architecture and sculpture on the Acropolis owes much to this stimulating analysis.

4. Ibid., p. 79.

5. Such is the concept suggested by Édouard Will in *Le Monde Grec et l'Orient, tome I, Le V$^e$ siecle* (510–403) (Paris, 1972), p. 558.

6. Pollitt, p. 79.

7. Ibid, p. 78.

8. C. J. Herington, *Athena Parthenos and Athena Polias* (Manchester, 1955), p. 62.

9. Pollitt, p. 87.

10. Ira S. Mark, "The Gods on the East Frieze of the Parthenon," *Hesperia* 53 (1984): 332.

11. Ibid., p. 336.

12. Cynthia Farrar, *The Origins of Democratic Thinking* (Cambridge, 1988), p. 77.

13. Herington, p. 56.

14. Will, p. 270.

## 9. PRIVATE MAN

1. Davies, *Athenian Propertied Families* (Oxford, 1971) pp. 329–30.

2. Gustav Glotz, *Histoire grecque*, vol. 2: *La grece au V$^e$ siecle* (Paris, 1938), p. 169.

3. The dates of the events in Pericles' private life cannot be determined with precision. In suggesting approximate dates for them I have followed the reasoning of Davies (pp. 457–58). Plutarch (Pericles 24.8) says that Pericles was his wife's second husband, but Davies makes a convincing case that she married Pericles first and Hipponicus second.

4. Davies, p. 18.

5. Plutarch (*Pericles* 31.5) says that Phidias went to prison, where he died, but

the account of Philochorus, a writer of Athenian local history who lived in the fourth and third centuries B.C. and seems to have better evidence, should be preferred.

6. Some scholars have been skeptical of Plutarch's account (*Pericles* 32.3) on this point, but his source, Aeschines the Socratic, lived no more than a generation after the event and was in a position to talk with eyewitnesses. His evidence should not be lightly discarded.

7. F. J. Frost, "Pericles, Thucydides son of Melesias, and Athenian Politics Before the War," *Historia* 13 (1964): 396.

8. F. J. Frost, "Pericles and Dracontides," *Journal of Hellenic Studies* 84(1964): 72.

9. Édouard Will, *Le Monde Grec et L'Orient, tome I, Le V^e siecle (510–403)* (Paris, 1972), p. 275.

## 11. CRISIS MANAGER

1. An attempt to deny that the Megarian Decree was intended as an economic embargo in the central thesis of a thick and detailed volume by G. E. M. de Ste. Croix, *The Origins of the Peloponnesian War* (Ithaca, 1972). As far as I know, the theory has won no other adherents.

2. Aegina had become a member of the Athenian Empire by force during the First Peloponnesian War. All such subjects lost their autonomy, and the nature of this special complaint is unclear, so it is hard to understand why the Spartans included this as a condition of peace.

## 12. STRATEGIST

1. F. E. Adcock, "The Archidamian War, 431–421 B.C.," *Cambridge Ancient History*, vol. 5 (Cambridge, 1940), p. 195.

2. Hans Delbruck, *Geschichte der Kriegskunst*, vol. 1, *Das Altertum* (Berlin, 1920, reprinted 1964), pp. 125–26.

3. This includes most students of the subject. For a brief review of some of the most distinguished examples, see D. Kagan, *The Archidamian War* (Ithaca, 1974), p. 345.

4. For these calculations and a fuller discussion of the cost of the war, see Kagan, *The Archidamian War*, pp. 35–40.

5. Gaetano de Sanctis, *Pericles* (Milan and Messina, 1944), pp. 253–54.

## 13. HERO

1. I have written this chapter on the assumption of the accuracy of this date, accepting the very persuasive arguments presented by B. M. W. Knox in "The Date of the *Oedipus Tyrannus* of Sophocles," *American Journal of Philology* 77 (1956): 133–47, as do most scholars, but the date of the play cannot be fixed with certainty. Nor can we be sure of the reactions of the audience whenever the play was produced or of Sophocles' intentions. The argument presented here, however, does not depend on the date. It rests, instead, on my opinion that the heroic similarity between Pericles and Oedipus emerges clearly from a study of life of Pericles and the text of *Oedipus Tyrannus*.

2. My understanding of Sophoclean tragedy and particularly of his *Oedipus Tyrannus* derive from two great works by B. M. W. Knox, *Oedipus at Thebes* (New Haven and London, 1957) and *The Heroic Temper* (Berkeley, Los Angeles, London, 1964). He recognizes many of the similarities between Oedipus and Pericles but rightly points out the significant differences. His very persuasive argument is that Oedipus represents the city of Athens, with both its positive and negative qualities. I accept his interpretation, but I take the similarities somewhat further. I also believe that, since Pericles had so shaped Athens and become a symbol for it, some of the portrait of Athens that Sophocles created in Oedipus also reflects on its greatest leader.

3. Throughout I use the crisp and perceptive translation of B. M. W. Knox, *Oedipus the King* (New York, 1972).

4. Knox, *Oedipus at Thebes, p. 60.*

5. Ibid., p. 77.

6. Ibid., p. 29.

7. Knox, *The Heroic Temper*, pp. 5 and 6.

8. Ibid., p. 8.

9. Ibid., p. 40.

10. Ibid., p. 25.

11. Ibid., p. 26.

12. Ibid., p. 60.

13. Winston S. Churchill, "A Speech to the House of Commons, June 4, 1940," in *The War Speeches of Winston S. Churchill* compiled by Charles Eade, vol. 1 (Boston, 1953), p. 195.

## 14. THE SHADOW OF PERICLES

1. These words were spoken by Adolph Berle about Franklin D. Roosevelt soon after the president's death. His speech appears in Adolph A. Berle, *Navigating the Rapids*, ed. Beatrice Bishop Berle and Travis Beal Jacobs (New York, 1973), p. 535. The passage is quoted by William E. Leuchtenburg in *In the Shadow of FDR* (Ithaca, 1983), pp. viii–ix.

2. See D. Kagan, *The Outbreak of the Peloponnesian War* (Ithaca, 1969, pp. 149–51, 175–177).

3. W. Schwann, "Thrasybulos," in *Kroll, Realenzyklopaedie der klassischen Altertumswissenschaft*, ed. A. Pauly, G. Wissowa, and W. Kroll, pp. 568–74.

4. *Federalist* Number 6, p. 109.

5. *Federalist* Number 10, p. 133.

6. This paragraph is a paraphrase of the observations of Frank M. Turner, *The Greek Heritage in Victorian Britain* (New Haven, 1981), p. 187.

7. Alfred E. Zimmern, *The Greek Commonwealth: Politics and Economics in Fifth-Century Athens* (Oxford, 1915), p. 5, cited by Turner, p. 188.

# INDEX

Printed in the United States
79511LV00005B/67-81